THE YEAR OF OUR LORD 1943

THE YEAR OF OUR LORD 1943

Christian Humanism in an Age of Crisis

Alan Jacobs

OXFORD
UNIVERSITY PRESS

OXFORD
UNIVERSITY PRESS

Oxford University Press is a department of the University of Oxford. It furthers
the University's objective of excellence in research, scholarship, and education
by publishing worldwide. Oxford is a registered trade mark of Oxford University
Press in the UK and certain other countries.

Published in the United States of America by Oxford University Press
198 Madison Avenue, New York, NY 10016, United States of America.

Library of Congress Cataloging-in-Publication Data

Names: Jacobs, Alan, 1958–author.
Title: The year of our Lord 1943 : Christian humanism in an age of crisis /
Alan Jacobs.
Description: New York : Oxford University Press, 2018. | Includes
bibliographical references and index.
Identifiers: LCCN 2018001911 (print) | LCCN 2018028421 (ebook) |
ISBN 9780190864668 (updf) | ISBN 9780190864675 (epub) |
ISBN 9780190864651 (hardcover)
Subjects: LCSH: Christian humanism. | Twentieth century. | Twenty-first
century.
Classification: LCC BR115.H8 (ebook) | LCC BR115.H8 J33 2018 (print) |
DDC 261.5/1—dc23
LC record available at https://lccn.loc.gov/2018001911

1 3 5 7 9 8 6 4 2

Printed by Sheridan Books, Inc., United States of America

I have suggested that the cultural health of Europe, including the cultural health of its component parts, is incompatible with extreme forms of both nationalism and internationalism. But the cause of that disease, which destroys the very soil in which culture has its roots, is not so much extreme ideas, and the fanaticism which they stimulate, as the relentless pressure of modern industrialism, setting the problems which the extreme ideas attempt to solve. Not least of the effects of industrialism is that we become mechanized in mind, and consequently attempt to provide solutions in terms of engineering, for problems which are essentially problems of life.

—T. S. Eliot, 1944

To all of us, I believe, in the middle of the twentieth century, the Roman Empire is like a mirror in which we see reflected the brutal, vulgar, powerful yet despairing image of our technological civilization, an imperium which now covers the entire globe, for all nations, capitalist, socialist, and communist, are united in their worship of mass, technique and temporal power. What fascinates and terrifies us about the Roman Empire is not that it finally went smash but that . . . it managed to last for four centuries without creativity, warmth or hope.

—W. H. Auden, 1952

CONTENTS

CONTENTS

PREFACE

The Casablanca Conference

On January 14, 1943, most of the leaders of the Allied nations met at Casablanca to determine a strategy for the remainder of the war. President Roosevelt and Prime Minister Churchill attended, along with leaders of the Free French, and many military officers. (Stalin, occupied with the presence of the Wehrmacht in his country and especially with the siege of Stalingrad, declined to participate.) When the parties arrived, they expected to plan a multifront invasion of the Continent that would drive the Germans back into their own country. After debate, they decided to postpone the vast project of sending armies across the English Channel—that would not happen for more than a year—but they agreed to a full-scale assault on Italy. Still more ominously, they began to plan the "strategic bombing" of Germany. And even before the conference had ended, the Combined Chiefs of Staff composed a directive to their generals that began with a blunt order: "Your primary object will be the progressive destruction and dislocation of the German military, industrial, and economic system, and the undermining of the morale of the German people to a point where their capacity for armed resistance is fatally weakened."[1]

Such a comprehensive program could only be articulated by leaders certain of their ultimate victory. The key underlying assumption of this memorandum, entitled "The Bomber Offensive from the United Kingdom," was that the Luftwaffe was incapable of offering serious resistance to the bombing campaign. (This did not prove to be true.) Of course, the congenitally optimistic Churchill had possessed such confidence since December 1941: when an aide came into his office to say that, after the attack on Pearl Harbor, Germany had declared war on the United States, Churchill blandly replied, "So, we have won after all." But now, more than a year later, all parties involved agreed that the tide had turned, that the era of the unstoppable Blitzkrieg was over, and that Germany would hereafter be on the defensive. The tone of the leaders' public pronouncements changed accordingly: whereas earlier in the conflict their emphasis had been on the need for fortitude and hard work, now Roosevelt, in reporting to the American people on Casablanca, spoke of "inevitable disaster" for the Axis powers, and not just for the Germans. "There are many roads which lead right to Tokyo," he said. "We shall neglect none of them." Most telling of all was Roosevelt's insistence that official statements from the Conference include the proclamation that the Allies demanded nothing less than the "unconditional surrender" of the Axis powers and would not end the war on any other terms.[2]

One result of this newly absolute confidence—the Allied leaders had of course long prophesied victory, but not in such uncompromising terms—was that, on the home front, thoughts began to turn to life after war. What kind of world would be left to us when the Axis powers had suffered that "inevitable disaster"? There would be much remaking and reshaping to do: who would do it, and what principles would govern them? Such thoughts were on the minds of many, and some of the more ambitious and provocative ideas emerged from a small group of Christian intellectuals. This was a time—it seems so long ago now, a very different age, and one that is unlikely to return—when prominent Christian thinkers in the West believed that they had a responsibility to set a direction not just for churches but for the whole of society. And, stranger still, in that time, many of their fellow citizens were willing to grant them that authority—or at least to listen when they asserted it.

Boswell tells us that Dr. Johnson once said, "Depend upon it, sir, when a man knows he is to be hanged in a fortnight, it concentrates his mind wonderfully."[3] Throughout the world, a similar concentrating of minds had been intensifying for some years—beginning no later than Hitler's rise to power in 1933—but it was in early 1943 that this intensification of focus produced some especially remarkable work.

In the months following the Casablanca Conference, *Christianity and Crisis*, the magazine founded in 1941 by Reinhold Niebuhr and his colleagues at Union Seminary, published a series of articles endorsing and explaining a document called "Six Pillars of Peace."[4] The document itself had been produced by an organization called the Federal Council of Churches' Commission on a Just and Durable Peace, chaired by John Foster Dulles, then the chief foreign policy adviser to Republican presidential candidate Thomas E. Dewey. The emphasis of this document, and of the responses to it in *Christianity and Crisis*, was on the creation of a body of international lawmaking to replace the failed League of Nations, autonomy for nations then under occupation, and a repudiation of the draconian and punitive measures taken a quarter-century earlier in the Treaty of Versailles.[5]

But the thoughts of certain other Christian thinkers followed a different course. On the very day that the Casablanca Conference began, Jacques Maritain gave the first of his four Terry Lectures at Yale University. His subject: "Education at the Crossroads." The next day, January 15, W. H. Auden delivered a lecture to the students of Swarthmore College called "Vocation and Society." His concern was to explore the power of liberal education to prepare young people to assume responsible and meaningful callings in a world that needed their skills. At the same time, across the Atlantic in the city of Newcastle, C. S. Lewis was preparing to give a set of lectures he would later call *The Abolition of Man: or, Reflections on Education with Special Reference to the Teaching of English in the Upper Forms of Schools.* This emphasis on education was shared by the French refugee Simone Weil, who had recently moved to London, where she devoted the last months of her life to an impassioned plea for the reconstitution of European culture. To this plea she gave the title *Enracinement*—"Rootedness," or, as it would later be called in English, *The Need for Roots.* And elsewhere in the great English metropolis, the American-born poet T. S. Eliot had just completed his poetic testament—in "Little Gidding," the last of his *Four Quartets*—and, having sought the spiritual peace that comes from the faith that "all shall be well, and all manner of thing shall be well," now turned his attention, in a series of essays published in that January and February, to what he called "the definition of culture."

In a time of unprecedented total war, these thinkers concerned themselves primarily with a renewal of Christian thought and practice, especially in the schools of the Western world. Collectively they developed a response to the war that could scarcely be more different from the political pragmatism of the "Seven Pillars of Peace." Their absorption in theological and pedagogical concerns, which reached its highest pitch just as the war pivoted toward an Allied victory, may seem inexplicably unworldly, at best quixotic.

But there is an underlying logic to such thoughts that is worth of serious exploration.

And they were not alone in their emphases. England in the war years was a highly pedagogical island. In *Human Voices*, the novel in which Penelope Fitzgerald describes a slightly fictionalized version of her experiences working for the BBC during the war, we meet a "Junior RPA" (Recorded Programmes Assistant) named Willie Sharpe, whose "notebook contained, besides the exact details of his shift duties, a new plan for the organisation of humanity." At one point, when the whole staff is being trained in first aid, Willie gets an unexpected opportunity to describe his plan to one of the higher-ups:

> We mustn't grudge the time we're spending on this Red Cross course, Mr Haggard. In fact, personally speaking, I'm very glad of the training because it contributes in a small way to one of my general aims for all humanity. I mean the maintenance of health both in mind and body. Education will be a very different thing in the world of tomorrow. It will start at birth, or even earlier. It won't be a petty matter of School Certificate, the tedious calculations of facts and figures which hold many a keen and hopeful spirit back to-day. It will begin as we're beginning now, Mr Haggard, you and I and all these others here this evening, with a knowledge of our own bodies and how they can be kept fighting trim—fighting, I mean, needless to say, for the things of the spirit. Yes, we shall learn to read our bodies and minds like a book and know how best to control them. Oh boy, will the teachers be in for a shock.[6]

There were very many like Willie in England in those days: indeed, the searcher through libraries and archives can easily come to the conclusion that people then thought about little other than "the organisation of humanity" and how one might "fight for the things of the spirit" in the postwar world to come. This is effectively the subject of Dorothy L. Sayers' *Begin Here: A War-Time Essay* (1940), and of F. R. Leavis's *Education and the University: A Sketch for an "English School"* (1943), and of Christopher Dawson's *The Judgment of the Nations* (1942), and of Lewis Mumford's *Faith for Living* (1940) and *Values for Survival* (1946), and of Walter Moberley's *The Crisis in the University* (1949), which arose from his wartime work and reflections, and of countless articles, essays, and newspaper editorials—including Dwight MacDonald's famous "A Theory of Popular Culture" (1944), which Eliot believed to be "the best alternative" to his own account that he had read.[7] These arguments had little in common with one another except a conviction that the world had gone astray because its people had been poorly educated, and if the total destruction of the human world were to be averted, new ways of educating had to be found. Even a treatise on political, economic, and social polity like Fredrich Hayek's later-to-be-famous libertarian manifesto *The Road to Serfdom* (1944) took the fact of such miseducation (and its influence on the unpopularity of his ideas) for granted, as did, from the other end of the political spectrum, Horkheimer and Adorno's *Dialectic of Enlightenment*, written in Los Angeles between 1942 and 1944.[8] Penelope Fitzgerald's Willie Sharpe was but one voice in a vast, vast chorus.

In Britain, with its tradition of national educational policy, this impulse was seen in what the social historian David Kynaston has called "a flurry of wartime action" featuring "three main elements": "The Norwood Report of 1943, which examined what should be emphasized in the curriculum at secondary schools . . . ; the Butler Act of 1944, which vastly expanded access to free secondary education; and, from the same year, the Fleming Report on the public schools."⁹ In America, individual colleges and universities took up similarly reflective tasks, though some got more attention than others: the most talked about was Harvard College's so-called Redbook of 1945, a report made by a faculty committee to the university's president, James Bryant Conant. Its proper title is *General Education in a Free Society*, and it set the tone for many schools' reconsideration of their core curricula. The unspoken question underlying all these explorations was the same: if the free societies of the West win this great world war, how might their young people be educated in a way that made them worthy of that victory—and that made another war on that scale at worst avoidable and at best unthinkable?

Perhaps, though, we might say that there was one other point on which most of these thoughtful observers were agreed: miseducation had left the ordinary citizens of the Western democracies in the helpless thrall to the propagandistic machinations of unscrupulous nationalist movements. In 1941, George Orwell had insisted, "One cannot see the modern world as it is unless one recognizes the overwhelming strength of patriotism, national loyalty . . . . Christianity and international Socialism are as weak as straw in comparison with it." Indeed, "Hitler and Mussolini rose to power in their own countries very largely because they could grasp this fact and their opponents could not."¹⁰ The thinkers whose ideas I will describe in this book agreed with Orwell on these points, but did not think he had described inevitable realities, but rather, contingent and to some degree reversible ones. They thought it possible—and necessary—to restore Christianity to a central, if not the dominant, role in the shaping of Western societies. Why they thought this was necessary, how they planned to achieve it, and what particular visions of Christianity moved them are the chief topics of this book.

During the war years, these figures were quite astonishingly prolific. The various challenges of wartime life seem to have acted as a profound stimulant on them all. In the last six months of her life, Weil wrote the equivalent of two substantial books—indeed, the intensity with which she pursued her ideas surely contributed to the pleurisy that killed her. Lewis gave several series of broadcast talks to the BBC, lectured to Christian groups throughout Britain, published books of Christian apologetics, theological fantasy, science fiction, and literary criticism—all while continuing his lectures and tutorials at Oxford and faithfully answering letters from readers and listeners. Auden wrote four exceptionally ambitious book-length poems and dozens of articles and reviews, while holding down a day job as a teacher. Maritain published fifteen books during the war years, while also working for the Free French. Eliot's output, as measured by page count, seems comparatively small, yet he wrote the most important poems of his career during the war, while keeping up a steady stream of lectures and periodical essays, attending countless meetings of various study groups, serving as an air-raid warden, and continuing his work as an editor at Faber and Faber.

A book that tried to give even a reasonably full accounting of such ceaseless and frenetic intellectual activity would need to be a thousand pages long—and still longer if it took into full account those Christian thinkers like Niebuhr who were more active in practical politics and stood nearer, or hoped to stand nearer, to the primary sites of governmental power. This book has a narrower set of concerns. The war raised for each of the thinkers I have named a pressing set of questions about the relationship between Christianity and the Western democratic social order, and especially about whether Christianity was uniquely suited to the moral underpinning of that order. These questions led in turn to others: How

might an increasingly secularized and religiously indifferent populace be educated and formed in Christian beliefs and practices? And
what role might people like them—poets, novelists, philosophers,
thinkers, but not professional theologians or pastors—play in the
education of their fellow citizens of the West? The circulation of
those questions among these five figures is the subject of this book.
All that they did and thought and suffered and wrote that does not
relate to the circulation of these questions will be set aside here,
though sometimes referred to parenthetically and in notes for the
benefit of those who may be curious.

A NOTE ON NARRATIVE METHOD

Touch of Evil, that Gothic masterpiece by Orson Welles, begins with
the most famous tracking shot in the history of cinema. In muted
light, we see a close-up of a kitchen timer attached to what appears
to be an explosive device, held in a man's hands. The camera pulls
back to show him darting towards a nearby automobile: he sets the
time—it looks like around three minutes—then furtively drops the
device in the car's trunk and scampers off. We are, we now see, in
a city at night. The camera remains focused on the car as an oldish
man and a young woman get into it and drive away. The camera
pulls back to the rooftops and tracks backwards ahead of the car,
which is soon stopped by some goats in the road. As various people
move in and out of the frame, the camera continues its retreat and
soon picks up a couple walking down the street. Eventually the car,
having overcome its obstacles, re-enters the frame; its driver and
the couple come simultaneously to a border crossing. Conversation
ensues with the border patrol. When the car is waved through, it
passes out of the frame; the camera stays with the couple as they

embrace. Then their kiss is interrupted by the blast and flash of an explosion.

I have imitated Welles in this book. A chapter or section begins with one figure, whose ideas and writings are explored. Then, at a point when those ideas intersect, thematically and (roughly) temporally, with those of another figure, the focus shifts. We remain with that thinker for a while, then link to a third. Eventually the one with which we began rejoins the scene. The lives of the people who populate this book only rarely meet, or even correspond; but their ideas circulate from one to another constantly. It is this circulation I have tried to capture by an eccentric means of narration. What might correspond to the explosive device of Welles's film I leave as an exercise for the reader.

The account that follows will be generally, though not meticulously, chronological. The development of the war, from its anxious beginnings to the confidence in Allied victory that became widespread by 1943, caused certain intellectual themes to emerge, or to become centrally important, at particular moments, and then to recede into the background. For instance, the question of whether intellectual and scholarly pursuits are legitimate in time of war arises primarily in 1939 and 1940, after which most of the people concerned deemed that they had settled that issue to their own satisfaction, or at any rate had handled it as well as they could. I have tried to track the major themes in the order of their emergence; but when some text from a different moment provides particular insight into the character of an idea, I have not hesitated to cite it, even at the cost of violating chronology.

The first two chapters provide the intellectual background to what follows by describing both the debates that raged—and "raged" is often just the right term—in the years leading up to the war and the elements of the history of Christian thought that my protagonists believed particularly germane to the challenges of their moment. The third chapter describes the attempts by these figures to adapt to the exigencies of thinking, and exhorting people to think, in the midst of worldwide war. The fourth and fifth chapters outline their diagnosis of and responses to the "principalities and powers" that, as the war extended its reach and grew more obviously horrific, they came to believe were dominating their historical moment. After a brief interlude that serves to remind us that other modes of Christian thought and practice—some chosen, some imposed—were possible valid responses to a world at war, the sixth chapter describes the ideas that consolidated themselves in the climactic year 1943. That chapter is therefore the pinnacle of the narrative, and the one that follows describes the diminished urgency, the abating of intellectual intensity, the shifting into a more meditative and less hortatory mode, that characterized all these thinkers—those who survived—in the last year of the war. And finally, the afterword looks at a certain younger figure who took up the torch my protagonists had laid down—or, perhaps it would be better to say, declined to take up that torch, preferring instead one with the power to illuminate a very different segment of the cultural spectrum.

DRAMATIS PERSONAE

September 1, 1939

Jacques Maritain, age fifty-six, philosopher and theologian, is in Paris, embroiled in a heated dispute with his fellow Catholic Paul Claudel over Maritain's support for the leftist rebels in the Spanish Civil War. In Claudel's thinking, Maritain's position is nothing less than a betrayal of the Church: he refers to Maritain in a letter to a friend as "cet imbécile."[1] But for both men the issues go far beyond Spain and embrace the most fundamental questions about the role of the Church in a disintegrating society. Earlier in the year, Maritain had published a book called *The Twilight of Civilization*—a title whose implicit judgment the dyspeptic Claudel would have warmly endorsed.

Thomas Stearns Eliot, age fifty, poet and editor, is in London. He continues his work for the publisher Faber & Faber; he signs up to serve as an air-raid warden in Kensington, where he has a flat; to the book he had recently completed, *The Idea of a Christian Society*, he writes a postscript:

> September 6th, 1939. The whole of this book, with Preface and Notes, was completed before it was known that we should be at

war. But the possibility of war, which has now been realised, was always present to my mind, and the only additional observations which I feel called upon to make are these: first, that the alignment of forces which has now revealed itself should bring more clearly to our consciousness the alternative of Christianity or paganism; and, second, that we cannot afford to defer our constructive thinking to the conclusion of hostilities—a moment when, as we should know from experience, good counsel is liable to be obscured.[2]

A few weeks earlier, the poet George Barker had visited Eliot at his Faber office. The poet had stared out the window for a time, and then said in a quiet voice, "We have so little time."[3]

CLIVE STAPLES LEWIS, age forty, Fellow of Magadlen College, Oxford, is in Stratford-upon-Avon to give two lectures on Shakespeare, though the second is canceled after the news comes that Germany has invaded Poland. "I had a pretty ghastly time," he writes to his brother, a retired Army officer who had suddenly been called back to service: "—a smart, nearly empty hotel in a strange town with a wireless blaring away all the time and hours and hours to get through without work compose perhaps the worst possible background to a crisis." The "ghastly time" presumably involves, among other things, Lewis's memories of World War I, in which he had fought and been seriously wounded. In the spring of 1938, just after the Austrian Anschluss, he had written to a friend, "I have been in considerable trouble over the present danger of war. Twice in one life—and then to find how little I have grown in fortitude despite my conversion." And then to that friend again, some months later: "I was terrified to find how terrified I was by the crisis. Pray for me."[4]

WYSTAN HUGH AUDEN, age thirty-two, poet, having left his native England for New York earlier in the year, is in a trashy dive bar, Dizzy's Club, in Manhattan. Only the day before he and his lover, Chester Kallman, had returned—via cross-country bus—from a voyage to the West Coast. Kallman wants to go with his friend Harold Norse to Dizzy's, which Norse later describes as "the sex addict's quick fix, packed to the rafters with college boys and working-class youths."[5] Auden eventually comes along, and once there, finding himself out of place among people a decade or so younger, heads for a corner and—Norse would later say, drawing on a memory that is perhaps too convenient in what it supplies—starts writing in a notebook. The poem that Auden would ultimately associate with that evening begins by setting his scene: "I sit in one of the dives / On Fifty-second Street / Uncertain and afraid." But quickly he moves to a somber reflection on historical cause and effect:

> Accurate scholarship can
> Unearth the whole offence
> From Luther until now
> That has driven a culture mad,
> Find what occurred at Linz,
> What huge imago made
> A psychopathic god:
> I and the public know
> What all schoolchildren learn,
> Those to whom evil is done
> Do evil in return.[6]

SIMONE WEIL, age thirty, thinker, is ill with pleurisy—she is often ill—and taking a kind of rest cure, with her parents, in the mountains near Nice. Immediately after the outbreak of war, they return to their apartment in Paris, where she tells her friend Simone Pétrement that, while she supports the war against Hitler, she worries that this will be hard to do without the benefit of a clean conscience—and a nation with colonies can scarcely have a clean conscience. Around this time she writes, "We should not think that because we are less brutal, less violent, less inhuman than those we are confronting, we will prevail. Brutality, violence, and inhumanity have immense prestige"—*un prestige immense,* a compelling power to draw people to them, to provoke not just obedience but worship. "The contrary virtues, so as to have an equivalent prestige, must be exercised in a constant and effective manner. Whoever is only incapable of being as brutal, violent, and inhuman as the adversary, yet without exercising the opposite virtues, is inferior to this adversary in both inner strength and prestige; and he will not hold his own against him."[7]

Chapter 1

"Prosper, O Lord, Our Righteous Cause"

In November 1939, six weeks after the beginning of World War II and ten months after his arrival in New York, the English poet W. H. Auden went to the movies. The theater was in Yorkville, on the Upper East Side of Manhattan, which was then largely populated by people of German descent. (Thomas Merton, then teaching at Columbia University while contemplating entering the religious life, mentions in his journal that one could hear German spoken in the streets there as often as English.[1]) Perhaps unsurprisingly, especially since the United States had not yet entered the war, the moviegoers were generally sympathetic to the Nazi cause: since many of them had come to the United States during the economic crises that debilitated Germany in the 1920s, they knew what Hitler had done to restore German pride and economic and cultural stability.

But Auden was not prepared for the viewers' reactions to this film. Whenever the Poles appeared on the screen—always as prisoners of the Wehrmacht—the audience would shout, "Kill them! Kill them!" Auden was utterly taken aback. "There was no hypocrisy," he recalled many years later: these people were unashamed of their feelings and attempted to put no "civilized" face upon them.

"I wondered, then, why I reacted as I did against this denial of every humanistic value." On what grounds did he have a right to demand, or even a reason to expect, a more "humanistic" response? His inability to answer this question, he explained, led him by a circuitous yet sure route back to the Christian faith in which he had been raised.

The return to faith began with this inquiry into the foundations of value. There had to be some standard by which Hitler's wrongness—and that of his fanatical supporters in the American movie-house—could be established. Auden soon began to look skeptically on the intellectual network that had nourished and admired him throughout his career; he told Golo Mann (son of the novelist Thomas) that "the English intellectuals who now cry to Heaven against the evil incarnated in Hitler have no Heaven to cry to; they have nothing to offer and their prospects echo in empty space." And around the same time he gave a commencement address at Smith College in which he said, "Jung hardly went far enough when he said, 'Hitler is the unconscious of every German'; he comes uncomfortably near being the unconscious of most of us."[2]

By what laws are we governed? In another poem written in September 1939, Auden raised the question wryly but incisively. "Law, say the gardeners, is the sun"; but "Law is the wisdom of the old, / The impotent grandfathers feebly scold"; by contrast, the priest says, "Law is my pulpit and my steeple," and the judge says, "Law is The Law."

> Others say, Law is our Fate;
> Others say, Law is our State;
> Others say, others say,
> Law is no more,
> Law has gone away.

After all this (and more), what does the poem's speaker dare to conclude? "Like love I say."

> Like love we don't know where or why,
> Like love we can't compel or fly,
> Like love we often weep,
> Like love we seldom keep.[3]

Auden was by no means the only one, in this time of war, inquiring into those foundations of value, those world-governing laws. The tenor of the whole period might best be seen by looking ahead just a few years, to a moment just after war's end. In an autobiographical essay called "Trotsky and the Wild Orchids," the philosopher Richard Rorty described his arrival at the University of Chicago as a freshman in the fall of 1946. The postwar world was being envisioned, prepared for, even created there—or so the institution's leaders, especially its president, Robert Maynard Hutchins, believed. "When I got to Chicago," Rorty wrote, "I found that Hutchins, together with his friends Mortimer Adler and Richard McKeon . . . , had enveloped much of the University of Chicago in a neo-Aristotelian mystique." This brain trust had come to believe that the pragmatism of John Dewey, who had been the dominant intellectual force at Chicago in previous generations, "was vulgar, 'relativistic,' and self-refuting. As they pointed out over and over again, Dewey had no absolutes." This lack made him useless: "Only an appeal to something eternal, absolute, and good—like the God of St Thomas, or the 'nature of human beings' described by Aristotle—would permit one to answer the Nazis, to justify one's choice of social democracy over fascism."

Even the powerful and enigmatic political philosopher Leo Strauss, no Thomist, agreed that "something deeper and weightier than Dewey was needed if one was to explain why it would be better to be dead than to be a Nazi." And another figure, one located far from Chicago, loomed equally large in Rorty's young mind:

> Like many of my classmates at Chicago, I knew lots of T. S. Eliot by heart. I was attracted by Eliot's suggestions that only committed Christians (and perhaps only Anglo-Catholics) could overcome their unhealthy preoccupation with their private obsessions, and so serve their fellow humans with proper humility. But a prideful inability to believe what I was saying when I recited the General Confession gradually led me to give up on my awkward attempts to get religion. So I fell back on absolutist philosophy.[4]

That is, Rorty "fell back on absolutist philosophy" for a time, before ultimately becoming the late twentieth century's strongest advocate for the Deweyan pragmatism that his teachers at Chicago had so forcibly rejected as inadequate to the moral challenge of Nazism.

The claim that the young Richard Rorty considered and eventually dismissed—that the threat of National Socialism could only be properly resisted by an equally universal but substantively opposite ethic—is the claim in the light of which each of the figures I study in this book begins his or her hopes for the renewal of Christian thought. That claim in no way entails Christianity in any of its many forms, or religious belief of any kind. There were many leaders (political and intellectual) along the Allies who tried to make democracy itself the substantive alternative to Nazism, in much the way that Richard Rorty would later articulate a model of democracy as something close to first philosophy. But given a cultural emplacement of an at least residual Christendom, it was inevitable that some thinkers would see Christianity as integral to a resistance to Nazism.

In the first book of Milton's *Paradise Lost*, Satan, reflecting on the great angelic War that led to his exile from Heaven, speaks of the Almighty as one "Whom reason hath equalled, force hath made supreme / Above his equals." The idea becomes a constant theme of Satanic rhetoric: it is simply victory itself, strength of arms, by which the winner deems himself God and his cause righteous. As World War II progressed and the balance of power began to tilt more and more strongly toward the Allies, supporters of the Allied cause came more and more to fret about the likelihood of this charge being made against them. After all, it had already been made in the aftermath of the Great War, and not only by Germans. Especially famous in this regard is the response of John Maynard Keynes to the manifest injustices of the Treaty of Versailles: "The glory of the nation you love is a desirable end,—but generally to be obtained at your neighbor's expense. The politics of power are inevitable," and this war was simply the most recent in a long series. "Prudence required some measure of lip service to the 'ideals' of foolish Americans and hypocritical Englishmen," but those who understood the rules of the game knew that what politicians called "the principle of self-determination" was simply "an ingenious formula for rearranging the balance of power in one's own interests."[5]

And Keynes was no cynical bystander, but an active participant in the British negotiations as a delegate for the Treasury. His view that the Allies had at Versailles imposed a "Carthaginian peace" became influential in the years following that war and became the object of renewed attention as another war approached. (It was perhaps on T. S. Eliot's mind when, just before the outbreak of that second war, he wrote, "Certainly there is a sense in which Britain and America are more democratic than Germany; but on the other hand, defenders of the totalitarian system can make out a plausible case for maintaining that what we have is not democracy, but financial oligarchy."[6]) There

the evil of Hitler, can we be sure that our ways are necessarily superior?

Lewis continued his protest in later conversations with his vicar and recommended to him, as an alternative to such "audacity," a prayer that Thomas Cranmer had composed when England was at war with Scotland in 1548:

> Most merciful God, the Granter of all peace and quietness, the Giver of all good gifts, the Defender of all nations, who hast willed all men to be accounted as our neighbours, and commanded us to love them as ourself, and not to hate our enemies, but rather to wish them, yea and also to do them good if we can: . . . Give to all us desire of peace, unity, and quietness, and a speedy wearisomeness of all war, hostility, and enmity to all them that be our enemies; that we and they may, in one heart and charitable agreement, praise thy most holy name, and reform our lives to thy godly commandments.

A rather different tone than that embodied in "Prosper, O Lord, our righteous cause," in that the petitioner is in as much need of divine grace as any enemy whose cause might be less "righteous." Lewis concluded this section of his letter by saying flatly, "I see no hope for the Church of England if it allows itself to become just an echo for the press"—or the government. The Church must bear witness to the Christian Gospel in complete independence of any patriotic imperatives.[9]

Whether the cause for which England had begun to fight was indeed righteous was one that Lewis felt that he could not decide for himself in the way typically favored by Christian intellectuals, which was by invocation of "just war theory." In May 1939, he had written a letter to the editors of the journal *Theology* that argued that "the rules for determining what wars are just were originally rules for the guidance of princes, not subjects," and that therefore, he concludes "with some reluctance," "the ultimate decision is one which must be delegated" to the elected leader of the nation. However, he insisted, this does not mean that one's conscience can be offloaded to leaders: "A man is much more certain that he ought not to murder prisoners or bomb civilians than he can ever be about the justice of a war."[10] Threaded through everything Lewis wrote in those early days of the war—and indeed, later—is a complex weave of skepticism about the state's motives, fear that even righteous causes can be prosecuted unjustly, and sheer dread. Again to his brother, just a few lines after his fears for the moral integrity of the Church of England, he writes, "One of the worst features of this war is the spectral feeling of all having happened before. . . . If one could only hibernate. More and more sleep seems to me the best thing—short of waking up and finding yourself safely dead and not quite damned."

Lewis's deepest anxieties were confided only to his brother, and his controversy with his vicar was conducted mostly in private. Perhaps by October 22 he had resolved some of his doubts, or perhaps he decided that before an audience of students he should be properly patriotic, but in any case, in a sermon he preached at the University Church, he said, "I believe our cause to be, as human causes go, very righteous."[11]

*   *   *

How righteous is our cause? And if it is righteous, what makes it so? Many intellectuals on both sides of the Atlantic tried to articulate answers to those telling questions, but were soon to discover that agreement was hard to come by. Some particularly noteworthy episodes in this debate arose from the dynamic work of Louis Finkelstein, a rabbi and Talmud scholar at the Jewish Theological

Seminary (JTS) in New York. Finkelstein convinced a number of other American religious thinkers that they needed to describe the role of the intellectual in time of war, and spearheaded the creation of the awkwardly named Conference on Science, Philosophy, and Religion and Their Relation to the Democratic Way of Life, which met for the first time on September 9–11, 1940, at the JTS. Finkelstein managed to recruit some major figures right from the beginning: listed among the founders of the Conference were, among many others, Mortimer Adler, Van Wyck Brooks, Enrico Fermi, Sidney Hook, and Paul Tillich. The preliminary announcement for the Conference expressed the hope that it would "serve as the first step toward a more general project, looking to the integration of Science, Philosophy, and Religion," but Finkelstein repeatedly emphasized that the chief impetus for the Conference's creation was the need to provide an intellectual answer to totalitarianism, and a number of the papers delivered in the early meetings of the Conference directly addressed this problem.[12]

During that first meeting, it was Adler who set the intellectual cat among the professorial pigeons with this claim: "Democracy has much more to fear from the mentality of its teachers [especially its university professors] than from the nihilism of Hitler." And the danger posed by the American professoriate, in Adler's view, stemmed from the dominance of "positivists" in that profession. "Positivism" was a dirty word for Adler in almost exactly the same way that "relativism" would be for later conservative critics of the academy: positivists were people without firm moral commitments and therefore without any means of resisting the dogmatic certainties of communism and fascism.

In the autobiographical reflection I cited earlier, Richard Rorty noted that Adler was among the chief warriors on behalf of President Robert Maynard Hutchins at the University of Chicago. When

Hutchins had been named to the presidency in 1929, at the age of thirty, his thinking about education was mainstream and uncontroversial. But almost immediately he came to question the values and commitments underlying undergraduate education, and when he hired Adler from Columbia University a year later, they began to rethink their university's mission, and eventually sought to restructure its curriculum according to a model that drew on Aristotelian and Thomist modes of thinking: they conceived of knowledge as hierarchical and susceptible of detailed categorical organization, grounded in unchanging human nature, and pursued via dialectical means, primarily in seminars. They thought of their emerging model as providing the only real alternative to a philosophy of education that they associated with the pragmatism of John Dewey, who had been the leading intellectual light of the University of Chicago in a previous generation. From the vantage point of today, it may seem that pragmatism and positivism are highly unlikely bedfellows, but for Hutchins and Adler they both grew in the same soil, the soil of skepticism about morals: it was disbelief in the universality of moral truth, and the failure to see that human beings are by nature capable of gaining access to moral truth, that created the intellectual perversions of pragmatism and positivism alike.[13]

On these matters Adler and Hutchins spoke with something like a single voice. Just three months before Adler's speech claiming that professors were more dangerous to America than Hitler, Hutchins had given a Convocation address at the University of Chicago under the title "What Shall We Defend?" The United States had not yet entered the war, and would not for another year and a half, but Hutchins sees America as already allied in a contest of values with the European democracies against fascism and communism—and does not like democracy's chances. "With our vague feeling that democracy is just a way of life, a way of living pleasantly in comparative peace with the world and one another, we may soon begin to wonder whether it can stand the strain of modern times, which, as our prophets never tire of telling us, are much more complicated than any other times whatever."

The key questions for Hutchins are these: "Is democracy a good form of government? Is it worth dying for? Is the United States a democracy? If we are to prepare to defend democracy we must be able to answer these questions." And "our ability to answer them is much more important than the quantity or quality of aeroplanes, bombs, tanks, flame-throwers, and miscellaneous munitions that we can hurl at the enemy."[14]

Already here we see a theme that will grow more prominent in the cultural discourse of the Allied world as the war progresses: a determination to understand the war primarily in moral, rather than military or technological, terms. When Hutchins wrote these words, the general fear was that the Western democracies could not match what he calls the "technical and organizing ability" of centrally controlled governments; by 1943 the fear had reversed its polarities, and intellectuals publicly worried that the victory of the Allies, wholly inevitable, would be a consequence of superior technology, engineering, and manufacture, a case of might once more making right, as perhaps it had at Versailles.

But whether the fear is of losing or of winning wrongly, it has, for Hutchins and Adler, the same foundation: their belief that the Western democracies do not understand what democracy is or why it is valuable, and are therefore in danger of being deprived of it. Hutchins continues his questioning: "What is the basis of these principles of law, equality, and justice? In the first place, in order to believe in these principles at all we must believe that there is such a thing as truth and that in these matters we can discover it." The idea that there can be scientific truth seems, to Hutchins, not especially controversial: "But there can be no experimental verification of the proposition that law, equality, and justice are the essentials of a good state . . . . Valuable as the truths are that may be found in it, truths about the ends of life and the aims of society are not susceptible of laboratory investigation." So he needs a model of truth-seeking and truth-finding that rejects the narrow positivist model of what counts as true. It is in the ability to seek and find truth in the moral sphere, Hutchins argues, that true human flourishing occurs.

But "are we prepared to defend these principles? Of course not. For forty years and more our intellectual leaders have been telling us they are not true. They have been telling us in fact that nothing is true which cannot be subjected to experimental verification." Hutchins perceives that the moral world is endangered by a kind of intellectual pincer movement: positivism in the sciences (where all legitimate questions must be subject to "experimental verification") and pragmatism in the great world beyond the "laboratory." And it is worth noting that, on this account, positivism produces pragmatism; pragmatism is what is left over once positivism claims its territory. But neither positivism nor pragmatism can explain why democracy is superior to totalitarianism.

In fact, Hutchins continues, by splitting the human lifeworld in the way they do, positivism and pragmatism leave us with "a colossal confusion of means and ends. Wealth and power become the ends of life," because the realm of value is the realm of opinion, in which I seek nothing more than easy justifications for my desires. "Men become merely means. Justice is the interest of the stronger." This corrupted and simplistic approach to decision-making, in which we have no higher ends than the satisfaction of our immediate desires, happens when "moral and intellectual and artistic and spiritual development . . . receive the fag ends of our attention and our superfluous funds. We no longer attempt to justify education by its contribution to moral, intellectual, artistic, and spiritual growth."

"Thus"—and here Hutchins becomes as provocative as Adler would be three months later—"we come much closer to Hitler than we may care to admit. If everything is a matter of opinion, and if everybody is entitled to his own opinion, force becomes the only way of settling differences of opinion. And of course if success is the test of rightness, right is on the side of the heavier battalions." And an educational system that does not have as its central concern "moral and intellectual and artistic and spiritual development" is ipso facto bequeathing to its young charges a decadent, impoverished ideal of "democracy" that cannot resist the greater coherence and articulateness of totalitarian movements. Before becoming president of the University of Chicago and rebuilding his whole intellectual equipment, Hutchins had been a law professor and an advocate of "legal realism"; it is in this context that he says, in words that offer a curious echoing counterpoint to Auden's poem "Law Like Love," "In law school I learned that law was not concerned with reason or justice. Law was what the courts would do. Law, says Hitler, is what I do. There is little to choose between the doctrine I learned in an American law school and that which Hitler proclaims."

So the message jointly delivered by Adler and Hutchins may be summarized: Americans have more to fear from their professors than from Hitler, because their professors make us all more likely, over the long run, to become Hitler. Only a clearly articulated and rationally defended account of true justice can resist totalitarianism. "In the great struggle that may lie ahead, truth, justice, and freedom will conquer only if we know what they are and pay them the homage they deserve." The third term of Hutchins's trinity is especially important, for he knows that the war was already being portrayed as a war for freedom. But, he had argued earlier in his address, "The moral and intellectual development of free men takes the form of bringing them through the family, through law, and through education to good moral and intellectual habits. This is true freedom; there is no other." Thus the centrality of education to democracy; thus the centrality of moral formation to education; and thus, as Hutchins and Adler understood it, the centrality of an Aristotelian-Thomist philosophy to moral formation.

When in 1936 Hutchins had published *The Higher Learning in America*, a book articulating his proposals for educational reform, it was reviewed scathingly by none other than John Dewey. Dewey saw in Hutchins's model of education an attempt to end dialogue and impose, by authoritarian administrative *diktat*, a single understanding of the world:

> There are indications that Mr. Hutchins would not take kindly to labelling the other phase of this remedial plan "authoritarian." But any scheme based on the existence of ultimate first principles, with their dependent hierarchy of subsidiary principles, does not escape authoritarianism by calling the principles "truths." I would not intimate that the author has any sympathy with fascism. But basically his idea as to the proper course to be taken is akin to the distrust of freedom and the consequent appeal to some fixed authority that is now overrunning the world . . . . Doubtless much may be said for selecting Aristotle and St. Thomas as competent promulgators of first truths. But it took the authority of a powerful ecclesiastic organization to secure their wide recognition.[15]

Dewey's implication, it seems, is twofold: first, that Hutchins's behavior is reminiscent of the Catholic Church, almost as though he thinks of himself and Adler as a kind of Magisterium establishing true doctrine; but second, that he probably lacks the true magisterial power to implement his vision. (And indeed by the late 1930s Hutchins and Adler and their supporters were deeply discouraged by their lack of progress in transforming their university.)

For Dewey, Hutchins is longing for, and trying to re-create, a premodern, predemocratic world in which truth is established and then disseminated *de haut en bas*. This charge made Hutchins uncomfortable. Though the son of a Presbyterian minister, he seems always to have avoided religiously specific language and may have had no Christian belief at all. It was Adler who—though Jewish by birth and not yet a Christian (he would convert only decades later)—spoke more openly and directly about the place of religion in education. For instance, in the same year he spoke to the Conference on Science, Philosophy, and Religion, he published a book in which he described the hierarchy of the disciplines of knowledge as ascending on this vector: from "history to science, from science to philosophy, from philosophy to theology, to mystical wisdom, and ultimately to the vision of God." And as James Gilbert has written in his invaluable book *Redeeming Culture: American Religion in an Age of Science*, Adler told Louis Finkelstein that this hierarchy should be the very foundation of the Conference:

> Adler sent a deliberately provocative "contract" to Finkelstein for agreement by other planners of the conference. This he titled "On the Fundamental Position" of the conference. For truth to prevail, he declared, hierarchy must rule. The conference should unanimously "repudiate the scientism or positivism which dominates every aspect of modern culture." This intellectual oath pledged intolerance for error. Most important, it declared that "religious knowledge, because supernaturally generated,

must be superior to philosophy and science as merely natural knowledge."

Finkelstein replied, "I agree with you absolutely, and unreservedly, in your strictures about the fundamental problems of American education." Only "a vivid, philosophical, and profound faith in God, which must permeate our whole field of thought," would be adequate to address the social crisis brought about, or rather revealed, by wars of the twentieth century. But he did not think that people with different views should be excluded from the Conference. He upheld this position of openness with some difficulty, since it was resisted not just by Adler but by other prominent figures he had brought into the initial conversations about the founding of the Conference. For instance, Jacques Maritain had told him that too many American intellectuals were "imbued with positivistic prejudices, misinterpreting philosophy and theology and making of experimental science the supreme standard of thought." Maritain did not think that any such persons should be invited to participate, no matter how passionately they loved democracy and hated totalitarianism.[16]

It was Finkelstein's determination to bring together such a diverse range of intellectuals that led to the fireworks at the first public meeting. Among those listening to Adler's denunciation of "the professors" was Sidney Hook, a former student and lifelong disciple of John Dewey. Hook was a pragmatist, an agnostic, and a former Communist who had been profoundly and lastingly alienated from the Soviet Union by the show trials in 1936–38. Finkelstein brought him in because of his passionate hatred of totalitarianism, though he was otherwise exactly the sort of person that Adler and Maritain wanted to exclude.[17] Unsurprisingly, Hook found Adler's speech to be wholly misbegotten. "We have just been told that American democracy is in greater danger from its professors than from Hitlerism. Such a statement is not merely false but irresponsible, and at the present time doubly so." Moreover, Adler's insistence on a hierarchy of the disciplines, with theology governing philosophy and the Beatific Vision hovering over all, seemed to Hook a recipe for "religious intolerance" and a move toward theocracy. He reports in his memoirs that he responded so angrily to Adler's paper that Finkelstein, sitting next to him, stomped on his foot to try to shut him up.[18]

We can see, then, that one of the questions raised by Finkelstein's Conference is this: Is a general and vigorous commitment to democracy sufficient to resist the encroachments of totalitarianism? In other words, is democracy philosophically self-sustaining— at least, sufficiently so to be getting on with, in time of war? For Adler and Maritain, the answer was no, and that negative had to be insisted upon even more strongly in time of war, and most strongly of all when the opponents are totalitarian regimes, with their comprehensive structures of belief and commitment. Adler's public vociferousness on this point led Sidney Hook to suspect that serious religious belief was not only unnecessary to democracy but probably inimical to it—as long as it sought enshrinement in the institutions of the public order, which it was always tempted to do. In a 1943 essay for *Partisan Review*, Hook laid out this argument in uncompromising terms:

> We are told that our children cannot be properly educated unless they are inoculated with "proper" religious beliefs; that theology and metaphysics must be given a dominant place in the curriculum of our universities; that churchmen should cultivate sacred theology before applying the social gospel; the business needs an inspired church that speaks authoritatively about

absolutes—this by the editors of *Fortune*; that what is basically at stake in this war is Christian civilization despite our gallant Chinese, Moslem, and Russian allies that the stability of the state depends on an unquestioned acceptance of a unifying dogma, sometimes identified with the hierarchical authoritarianism of Catholicism, sometimes with democracy; that none of the arts and no form of literature can achieve imaginative distinction without "postulating a transcendental reality."

For Hook all this was a sign that—and these are his italics— *Fundamentalism is no longer beyond the pale; it has donned a top hat and gone high church.*[19]

Hook contends all of these developments proceed from one central assumption: that "modern democracy has been derived from, and can only be justified by, the theological dogmas of Hebraic-Christianity according to which all men are created by God and equal before Him." Hook complains that Finkelstein had made this immovable first principle "the rallying point of the much publicized Conference on Science, Philosophy, and Religion and Their Relation to the Democratic Way of Life, whose pronouncements indicate that it has officially accepted Maritain's Catholic conception of a pluralistic, hierarchically organized culture, crowned by religion, as 'the cornerstone on which human civilization must be erected in our day.'"

Science, Hook says, "has no place" in this system. Rational thought is, if not wholly rejected, then utterly subjected to divine revelation. This mode of thought is for Hook worrying enough in itself, but he is still more concerned that its proponents seem to want to install it in the institutions, especially the governmental and educational institutions, of Western society. "Religious institutions based on supernatural dogmas tend towards theocracy," so the intrusion of those forces into the rest of society may well portend the theocratic transformation of the West, which would be anything but democratic. Thus Hook responds to the fears of intellectuals like Hutchins that the West could become like Hitler by agreeing—but assigning the blame very differently: "Out of [these antirational movements] will grow a disillusion in the possibility of intelligent human effort so profound that even if Hitler is defeated, the blight of Hitlerism may rot the culture of his enemies." This is very similar, and not coincidentally so, to the language Dewey used when complaining that Hutchins's views are "akin to the distrust of freedom and the consequent appeal to some fixed authority that is now overrunning the world."

Hook finds it particularly ironic that these religiously minded thinkers link the rise of totalitarianism with an overreliance on science, since fascism (he does not mention communism in this context) arose in "such strongly religious and metaphysical countries as Italy and Germany and not in such scandalously heretical and positivistic countries as England and America." For Hook, it was the absolutist habits of mind spawned by strong religious traditions that made Germany and Italy vulnerable to fascism; whereas in England and especially America, where pragmatism and positivism had recently grown strong, hope remained for democracy—but only if the urge toward theocracy is resisted and people continue to work toward a truly democratic socialism. "Until then it is necessary to prevent intellectual hysteria from infecting those who still cling to the principles of rational experiment and analysis."

* * *

Eventually, and in response to heated responses like those of Hook and Dewey, Louis Finkelstein would make his Conference private.

But privacy was always the watchword of a similar endeavor to think through the role of religion in public life, this one convened in England by a man named J. H. Oldham. He called his gathering the Moot; others called it Oldham's Moot. It began as an attempt to articulate a coherent Christian response to the coming war; it was needed, Oldham felt, because the Christian presence in English public life was sadly indistinct.

In one sense, the concerns of the Moot resembled not only those of Finkelstein but also those of Frank Buchman, an American missionary in England, who had been the driving force behind the Oxford Group—a Christian parachurch organization devoted to spiritual renewal, largely through a series of private meetings and discussions—and then of what he called "Moral Re-Armament." Buchman launched his campaign in May 1938, with a speech in which he claimed that the coming crisis in Europe is "fundamentally a moral one. The nations must re-arm morally. Moral recovery is essentially the forerunner of economic recovery. Moral recovery creates not crisis but confidence and unity in every phase of life."[20]

Oldham had convened the first meeting of the Moot a month earlier, but his emphasis was quite different. Like Buchman, Oldham had been a missionary, indeed the child of missionaries to India, and served in that country for some years before returning to the United Kingdom, where he became the perfect embodiment of a distinctive twentieth-century type: the religious bureaucrat. For many years he served as secretary of the International Missionary Council, an organization he helped to establish; after World War II he helped to create the World Council of Churches. He traveled all over the world building organizational relationships, convening meetings, and commissioning white papers; but the Moot represented his uneasy sense that none of this activity would do much good if Christianity could not reach the *minds* of the people of the Western democracies, especially their leaders. Oldham's sense that Christian thinkers had not offered a compelling intellectual alternative to other accounts of the world was the impetus for his convening of the Moot.

The Moot met several times a year from 1938 to 1947; its cast of characters varied, but among the most regular attenders were T. S. Eliot, the German sociologist-in-exile Karl Mannheim, the theologian Alec Vidler, the historian Christopher Dawson, the philosopher of education Walter Moberly, and the critic and editor John Middleton Murry. (It perhaps goes without saying that neither the Moot's members nor the Conference's were concerned to have women participate in their deliberations.) Sometimes visitors to England were asked to sit in—Reinhold Niebuhr did this on two occasions—and those who did not join the group but were deemed sympathetic to its concerns, like C. S. Lewis, were occasionally asked to write papers that the group could discuss.

Oldham assigned a secretary to record the substance of each conversation, and those records have been collected and published by Keith Clements as *The Moot Papers: Faith, Freedom and Society 1938-1944*. Read in order, the accounts tell a curious story. When the Moot began, just after the German annexation of Austria, war in Europe was very likely but not inevitable. The coming of war, the early Nazi successes, the gradual turning of the tide, and the ultimate victory all affected the character of the conversation, its tone, as well as its substance. Always hovering over the meetings was the question that had been raised so assertively by Adler and Maritain: the breadth of views that should be represented in the Moot.

In many respects, the odd man out in the Moot was, or should have been, Mannheim. A Hungarian Jew of no defined religious convictions, he nevertheless shared the other Moot participants' interest in the renewal of British society. (He became a British subject in 1940, and his friends often commented on his enthusiasm for

British ways of life.) He contributed more papers than anyone else in the group, and he often set the tone for the discussions. Alec Vidler commented many years later that "in some respects Mannheim was the central figure in the Moot. His conception of 'planning for freedom' as the proper alternative to totalitarianism, on the one hand, and to British laissez faire or muddling through, on the other, was one that commended itself to us." Indeed, Vidler commented that the Moot as a whole could be described as "exploring [the] philosophical, ethical, sociological, political, theological, and indeed all other aspects" of Mannheim's key ideas. "The centrality of Mannheim's role is shown by the fact that when he died suddenly in 1947, we spontaneously stopped meeting; at any rate Oldham never called us together again."[21]

After Mannheim's death, his widow wrote a touching letter to the regular members thanking them for accepting her husband so warmly, even though he was in so many ways different from the others.[22] But perhaps those differences made his presence so valuable. In the midst of the Battle of Britain, the question of what the Moot should be doing, and who should participate in it, returned to the forefront; there was, after all, a need to reconsider the shape of a project that had begun before war commenced. Mannheim, characteristically, wrote a whole paper on this subject, and in response to this paper, Eliot said,

> I can express what I mean best my mentioning one reason why I have found the Moot most profitable to myself: which is that I find in it, not merely agreement achieved or hoped for, but also significant disagreement. I mean that one can waste a great deal of time, in the present world, by disagreeing with people whose thought is really irrelevant to one's own thinking—however important it may be or may have been from some other point of view. What is valuable

is the formulation of differences within a certain field of identity—
though the identity may be very difficult, if not impossible, wholly
to formulate; what is valuable is the association with people who
may hold very different views from one's own, but are in general
at the same stage of development and detachment—these are the
people worth disagreeing with, so to speak. This I think we have in
the Moot, and this we ought to keep.[23]

Clearly Eliot was thinking primarily of Mannheim's own
contributions here—especially given that in the preface to his
postwar book, *Notes towards the Definition of Culture*, written exactly
a year after Mannheim's death, he singles out the sociologist for particular thanks, "since my debt to [him] is much greater than appears
from the one context in which I discuss his theory."[24]

Though charity seems generally to have reigned at the Moot—
largely, it would seem, because of Oldham's ability to generate positive yet meaningful conversations—and the kind of acrimony that
drove Finkelstein to make his Conference private seems never to
have emerged, not everyone was happy with the Moot. Middleton
Murry, who in the very first meeting had responded to a paper by
the Catholic historian Christopher Dawson by stating that what
the world in general and England in particular needed was "the
Renaissance of the Christian imagination," became increasingly dis-
satisfied with the meetings, at least in part because of the emerging
centrality of Mannheim. In January 1943 he announced, "My
feeling is that the Moot is no longer engaged in a corporate quest. It
flits from one idea to another of a multitude of things, but on none
drives its inquiry passionately home . . . . I no longer feel the ur-
gent and passionate search for truth which I once felt in the Moot."[25]
On these grounds he resigned from the Moot and went on to other
things.

By this stage, nearly five years into the conversation, it was possible to describe the participants' general orientation to the problems of the day, though they differed considerably on some details. The first agreed-upon point was that the disastrous wars of the twentieth century were the natural consequence of a loss of European religious focus and unity that had occurred over a very long period through gradual erosion. On this matter Christopher Dawson's role in the first meeting would have helped to set the tone, since Dawson had written several books arguing that Catholic Christianity during the Middle Ages had created a unified Europe whose loss had been catastrophic. In that meeting, Eliot had responded to Dawson by commenting that it might be better not to think of the current crisis as a product of recent causes—for example, the Treaty of Versailles and the subsequent rise of National Socialism and fascism, or the collapse of the Russian monarchy and its replacement by a Leninist regime—and more as a set of events whose roots ran centuries deep and might take centuries to resolve.[26]

(In response to this belief that the collapse of church authority had led to war, one might reasonably point out that in ages of far greater ecclesial power there had been a good many wars, some of them quite bloody. But in general, it seems, and this is noteworthy, for conservative-leaning intellectuals in the first half of the twentieth century, the more distant past was simply blotted out by the French Revolution and the Napoleonic Wars—as though nothing of general significance, especially for Christendom, had happened before that. The *laïcité* that the Revolutionaries made a permanent part of the French national identity was for them one of the key defining events of history. Perhaps the Moot to some extend borrowed this attitude from French thinkers such as Maritain, Paul Claudel, Leon Bloy, and others.)

The second point of agreement was that the churches of the European countries had allowed this erosion to occur, usually by inaction but sometimes by active collaboration with forces of secularism. The rise of the Deutsche Christen in Germany (a church wholly subservient to the demands of the state), or the demands by French bishops and Jesuit leaders that laypeople and theologians alike should cooperate with the Vichy regime, were merely dramatic and extreme examples of something that had occurred all over Europe. There was perhaps no need to create an alternative church to resist the corrupt one, as pastors in Germany and Switzerland, led by Karl Barth and Martin Niemöller, had created the Bekennende Kirche (Confessing Church); but it was useful to think of a "Church within the Church," a network of like-minded pastors, theologians, and laypeople who were capable or resisting the forces of social conformity. For, as can be seen from C. S. Lewis's comment on the prayer for the Lord to "prosper our righteous cause," the subordination of religion to patriotism was not just a problem in Germany.

For many of the same reasons, it was important to imagine a "University within the University." The Moot's thinking about this matter was intensified and focused by the appearance in 1943 of a book by Amy Buller called *Darkness over Germany*, with a preface by A. D. Lindsay, the Master of Balliol College, Oxford, and a regular Moot participant. Buller certainly believed that the moral abdication of the German church was tragic: in her prologue she writes, "I record these stories [of conversations with young Germans] to emphasize the need for youth and those who plan the training of youth to consider carefully the full significance of the tragedy of a whole generation of German youth who, having no faith, made Nazism their religion." But Buller insists that even this wholesale ecclesiastical collapse would not have been sufficient to ruin almost the whole of German youth if the universities had not been equally complicit in the Nazification of the country. (Like Eliot and Dawson, she understood the coming of the war as the culmination of a movement centuries in the making, and in focusing on the immediate circumstances in Germany "we may fail to realize the significance of the spiritual bankruptcy and real destitution underlying it all, for that is something which is evident in the whole of Western civilization, though in more insidious forms and subtle dress.") In her epilogue, she records interviews with English young people who have, she says, been "taught to believe in the League of Nations since they were in their cradles" and have been told by their parents, who experienced the Great War, that war accomplishes nothing.[27] They could see no reason to fight Hitler. Their attitude marked, Buller believed, a failure of political and moral education, and the blame for that failure goes to the schools as well as or even more than the churches. (This argument rhymes with the statements of Mortimer Adler to which Sidney Hook so vociferously objected.) So the need for a spiritual and moral renewal of the British educational system was the third point on which the Moot agreed.

The fourth point of agreement involved a distrust of the methods employed by Frank Buchman in his Moral Re-Armament program. Buchman is rarely mentioned in the Moot, but his public activism and evangelistic cheerleading were clearly not to the taste of the Moot's members, nor did their gifts run that way. As early as April 1939, they had already talked in some detail about the creation of a kind of secret society, an order of men—almost certainly they would all be men—devoted to influencing the major institutions of British society: the government, the Church of England, and the universities. (This idea was probably the first cause of serious uneasiness for Middleton Murry.) The proposed order resembled a cross between the Freemasons and the Fabian Society. The Fabians had been created at the end of the nineteenth century by Beatrice and

Sidney Webb, among others, and enthusiastically joined by such eminences as George Bernard Shaw and H. G. Wells, in order to bring about socialism not by revolution from below but by ameliorative actions from above—thus the long-standing joke that the best thing about being a Fabian was that your socialist commitments required you to attend cocktail parties with the rich and powerful.

The idea seems to have originated with Mannheim, who said, "Halfway between the freelance existence and the organised one stands what we call the 'order.' Its task is to revitalise the social body and to spread the spirit." It is by intention a mediating sort of body, situated "between the huge organised bodies which can only adapt themselves very slowly to changing conditions and the individual who is simply acting for himself and does not have to take a broader responsibility." Members of this order will certainly "get in touch with the people, find out what is going on in the nooks and corners of society," but also, and more importantly, "persuade organised bodies like the Churches and the Civil Service to accept the new ideas and the practical proposals which are necessary in an age of democratic change." Mannheim sees this order as an organ disseminated throughout the body politic, "an integral part of the social organism like its nervous system, coordinating its activities and spiritualising its aims."[28]

The Moot members' proposed order would probably have focused more on committee meetings than cocktail parties, but nevertheless betrayed a similar mistrust of purely democratic methods, of serious social change generated by ordinary people—even if they at least nominally wished to "get in touch with the people." And for those who shared Amy Buller's sense of what had gone wrong in Germany, and Christopher Dawson's of what had gone wrong throughout Europe, such mistrust was inevitable. A people whose moral formation had been ignored (at best) by churches and universities alike were scarcely in a position to understand the need for the complete transformation of churches and universities. In a 1942 meeting, Mannheim asks—this is the secretary's summary— "Is there a chance for a rebirth of a popular religion within the churches or will they in their rigidity expel from their ranks those who are able to cope with the new realities of the world, inner and outer?"[29] There is no record of a direct answer, but the sentiment of the Moot was clearly on the side of the latter alternative. A spiritual renewal of the working classes was clearly vital—Eliot at one point, again in response to one of Dawson's laments for a lost medieval unity, pleads for "more carnality, more materiality, and more super-stition"—but none of the members of the Moot were placed to offer much help in that regard. Thus the proposed order, which would support and implement Mannheim's "planning for freedom": that is, it would help to generate social and political structures that would in turn teach the citizens of democracies how to exercise freedom responsibly. Presumably, when people became fully and truly free, these structures would wither away, as in Marxist theory the dicta-torship of the proletariat was supposed to.[30]

Though conversations about the formation of this order, its governance, and its ideal size were frequent and extensive, it is not clear that anyone in the Moot had any idea how to go about creating it. Moreover, the members increasingly felt their own isolation, not just from the rest of British society but from like-minded people elsewhere in the world. After Reinhold Niebuhr's second visit to the group—in which he "suggested that a Christian civilisation was a civilisation which always knew itself to be ethically un-Christian"— Mannheim commented that the Moot suffered from not being in dialogue with partners in the United States and on the Continent.[31] Most of the participants continued to enjoy their meetings, and to learn from one another, but as the war went on, the energy seems gradually to have drained from the meetings. Great plans for social transformation gave way to friendly chat. It is no wonder that when Mannheim died there was no one remaining with the drive and energy to sustain the meetings.

* * *

Twenty years ago, the French philosopher Pierre Manent, in *The City of Man*, developed a sweeping argument about the rise of modernity. Manent contends that the Western world long struggled to resolve a twofold inheritance: a classical understanding of Man, the "party of nature," committed to a belief in humanity's inherent greatness and keyed to the virtue of magnanimity, versus a Christian understanding, the "party of grace," committed to an acknowledgement of our brokenness and emphasizing therefore the virtue of humility. But this contest proved interminable and fruitless, and was given up. What replaced it was a kind of non-understanding, an agnosticism about "human nature," an awareness that such speculations were not only irresolvable but unnecessary. We did not need to answer the ancient question *Quid sit homo?* We did not decide the grounds on which Man could be said to have rights; we needed only to define Man as the creature that has rights, and to see freedom as the goal toward which those rights tend. "Modern man is concerned only with the instruments of his emancipation project or with the obstacles to it. Nothing substantial, be it law, good, cause, or purpose, either holds his attention or holds back his advance any longer. He has become a runner and will go on running until the end of the world."[32]

The debates and disputes I have been recording in this chapter bear witness to a widespread concern—concern at times rising to the status of panic—that liberal instrumentalism, that willingness to defer ultimate questions as the price to be paid for getting along with one another, had left the democratic West unable to generate the energetic commitment necessary to resist the military and moral drive of societies that had clear answers to *Quid sit homo?* Suddenly, intellectuals throughout the democratic Western countries felt impelled to improvise an ethics and a metaphysics to suit the moment, in much the same way that their nations' militaries were scrambling to create new weapons and hasten the production and distribution of existing ones.

We have caught just a glimpse here of the variety of those answers. The full range could only be explored in a very large book indeed, or perhaps a series of them—though a good start on such a project has recently been made by Mark Greif in his book *The Age of the Crisis of Man.* The focus of these pages is on those who came to believe, in the harsh light of worldwide political crisis, that the decision to bracket, within the public sphere, fundamental questions about human nature had proved a disastrous one and needed to be rethought—and quickly. For these thinkers, vexed questions of human nature had to be raised once again, and raised in such a way that a Christian answer to them was made compelling.[33]

In the BBC radio talks that C. S. Lewis gave in 1941—talks that eventually became part of his book *Mere Christianity*—he said,

> First, as to putting the clock back. Would you think I was joking if I said that you can put a clock back, and that if the clock is wrong it is often a very sensible thing to do? But I would rather get away from the whole idea of clocks. We all want progress. But progress means getting nearer to the place where you want to be. And if you have taken a wrong turning, then to go forward does not get you any nearer. If you are on the wrong road, progress means doing an about-turn and walking back to the right road;

and in that case the man who turns back soonest is the most progressive man . . . . And I think if you look at the present state of
the world, it is pretty plain that humanity has been making some
big mistakes. We are on the wrong road. And if that is so, we must
go back. Going back is the quickest way on.[34]

For Lewis and the other thinkers we will explore here, that "going
back" could only happen in two distinct stages. First, there were the
immediate exhortations to be given to a war-weary and confused
populace. Lewis's radio talks were meant to meet that need, as were
the ideas generated by Finkelstein's Conference.

But the second stage was, in the minds of the thinkers we will
explore in this book, even more important. It involved, whether
the current war was won or lost, educating a new generation so that
the bracketing or suspension of ultimate questions that Manent
describes would no longer seem either natural or desirable. This
stage would involve not immediate improvisations but long-term
planning—of just the sort that was ever being discussed in Oldham's
Moot. As Dietrich Bonhoeffer put it in a summary of the Hitler
years that he wrote at the end of 1942,

> The ultimate question for a responsible man to ask is not how
> he is to extricate himself heroically from the affair, but how the
> coming generation is to live. It is only from this question, with
> its responsibility towards history, that fruitful solutions can come,
> even if for the time being they are very humiliating. In short, it
> is much easier to see a thing through from the point of view of
> abstract principle than from that of concrete responsibility. The
> rising generation will always instinctively discern which of these
> we make the basis of our actions, for it is their own future that is
> at stake.[35]

And the question of "how the coming generation is to live" cannot be extricated from another one: how should the coming generation be educated? What is perhaps most distinctive and remarkable about the figures we will be studying in this book is that their answer, generally speaking, involved not just theological and philosophical reflection but also literary experience. By striving to integrate literature into a specifically Christian model of education, they were, whether they knew it or not, reclaiming a tradition of Christian humanism that had its roots in the early Renaissance.

Chapter 2

The Humanist Inheritance

HUMANITIES: grammar, rhetoric, and poetry, for teaching of
which there are professors in the universities of Scotland, called
humanists.

—*Encyclopedia Britannica* (1768)

"Humanism" is a much-vexed, highly contested word whose
meaning has zigged and zagged in strange ways over the centuries,
and has equally often been used to praise and to damn. Its history is intrinsically fascinating, and moreover essential to any
attempt to make sense of the arguments about cultural renewal
that emerged among Christians during the Second World War.
Each of the figures we study here works within a nexus of ideas
first generated in the early modern period, and then reconfigured
in the nineteenth century. And this is equally true for those who
embrace that reconfigured humanist inheritance and those who
neglect or refuse it. It is the intersection of this tradition with
the inquiries into the basis of value we explored in the previous
chapter that generates much of the intellectual energy of these
wartime Christian thinkers.

Cicero, in his *Pro Archia*, refers to the *studia humanitatis ac
litteratum*: humane and literary studies. This phrase caught the eye
of some early Renaissance scholars, especially the Tuscan Coluccio

Salutati, correspondent of Petrarch, and his student Leonardo Bruni; it encapsulated their understanding of what education at its highest level should be. In the Italian universities of the fifteenth century, one who advocated for this model and taught according to it was known as an *umanista*—an inevitable coinage, since a teacher of jurisprudence had long been known as a *jurista*, a teacher of canon law as a *canonista*, and so on. So the term "humanist," from which "humanism" in turn derives, was originally the product of student slang.[1]

As Paul Oskar Kristeller explained long ago in what remains a useful treatment of the history, in the early modern period and especially in Italy, "the *studia humanitatis* came to stand for a clearly defined cycle of scholarly disciplines, namely grammar, rhetoric, history, poetry, and moral philosophy," primarily pursued through reading the greatest Latin writers, though eventually including in a secondary way the major Greek figures. Other philosophical subdisciplines, such as logic and metaphysics, played no part in the humanists' project. The *studia humanitatis* therefore were "concerned neither with the classics [as such] nor with philosophy [as such]"; their focus "might roughly be described as literature. It was to this peculiar literary preoccupation that the very intensive and extensive study which the humanists devoted to the Greek and especially to the Latin classics owed its peculiar character, which differentiates it from that of modern classical scholars since the second half of the eighteenth century."[2]

Kristeller's use of the word "peculiar" twice in that last-quoted sentence is a stylistic infelicity, but a telling one. The *umanistas* were doing something unprecedented in keying the search for wisdom—including specifically Christian wisdom—to the study of literature. This was, to put the point mildly, not in keeping with the dialectical approach of the medieval scholastic tradition, which they scorned.

Such rejection of scholastic procedures would have a major impact not only on the development of humanistic study in the early modern era, but also on the way that the history of humanism has been narrated. For in the last two hundred years it has been commonplace to read the history of humanism not merely as a rejection of scholastic *method* but also as a rejection of scholastic *interests*—especially theological interests.

Certainly the theology of the humanists—with its emphasis on literature over philosophy, and on the wisdom to be gained from pagan classical writers and thinkers—is dramatically different from that of the schoolmen, but it is not on that account less theological, or less Christian. But such was the story—a secularizing story—that came to be told, by admirers of the humanist enterprise and its detractors alike. Thinkers of the Enlightenment saw the humanists as their predecessors, those who had pried open a locked door and let the light of nonbiblical knowledge in; and (largely Catholic) defenders of the scholastic enterprise saw the humanists as enthusiastic participants in the dismantling of the beautiful edifice of medieval thought. It is the latter group with whom we are especially concerned here—but their story can only be discussed in relation to the secularizing narrative of humanism, which Christian celebrants of the high Middle Ages rightly perceived to be both simplistic and dominant.

What I will call the neo-Thomist interpretation of early modern history may be said to have its origins in a Dogmatic Constitution produced in 1870 by the First Vatican Council: *Dei Filius* asserted the complete compatibility of faith and reason, and affirmed the legitimacy of the disciplines of the arts and sciences.[3] Then, a few years later, in 1879, Pope Leo XIII issued the encyclical *Aeterni Patris*, "On the Restoration of Christian Philosophy," which affirmed the normative status of the thought of St. Thomas Aquinas.[4] These documents would bear ripe intellectual fruit some decades later in the thought of Jacques Maritain and Etienne Gilson, who would articulate a historical account that may be roughly summarized thus:

> *The scholastic culture of the Middle Ages built an increasingly complex but also harmonious and orderly intellectual edifice that reached its greatest amplitude in the thought of Thomas Aquinas—the philosophical and theological equivalent of the great cathedrals of the period, especially Chartres. In Thomas, biblical and pagan wisdom found their unity and were set in right relation to each other. But this great achievement was soon undermined, first by the inferior and destructive philosophy of the nominalists (Duns Scotus, William of Ockham), which paved the way for both a revival of un-Christian paganism and for the anti-intellectual and egocentric enthusiasms of the Reformation.*

This story began to take serious hold about a hundred years ago: its first great embodiment may be Maritain's 1920 book *Art and Scholasticism*, in which he described "the powerfully social structure of medieval civilization," in which the artist, to his great good fortune, "had only the rank of artisan, and every kind of anarchical development was forbidden his individualism, because a natural social discipline imposed on him from the outside certain limiting conditions." These limits and constraints, which were for Maritain intellectual as well as social, created a kind of paradise of theologically informed art: "Matchless epoch, in which an ingenuous people was formed in beauty without even realizing it, just as the perfect religious ought to pray without knowing that he is praying; in which Doctors and image-makers lovingly taught the poor, and the poor delighted in their teaching, because they were all of the same royal race, born of water and the Spirit!" In short, "Man created more beautiful things in those days, and he adored himself less. The blessed humility in which the artist was placed exalted his strength and his freedom. The Renaissance was to drive the artist mad, and to make of him the most miserable of men"—and to do so by preaching to him constantly of his own absolute freedom.[5]

Maritain repeatedly pursued this theme and helped to make it foundational to the neo-Thomist account of modernity. That account was developed concurrently by Gilson, whose introduction to Thomism (*Le thomisme*, 1922) was published two years after *Art and Scholasticism* and who would, in book after book, portray Thomas as the thinker who had achieved a perfect intellectual balance. (The emphasis on "balance" as a major intellectual virtue derives both from Aristotelian thought and from the continual comparison of Thomas's thought to Gothic architecture.) For instance, in *Reason and Revelation in the Middle Ages*, a small book based on lectures he had given in New York in 1937, Gilson presents Thomas as the Goldilocks of philosophical theology: whereas Augustine had been overreliant on revelation, and Averroes overreliant on reason, Thomas had perfectly united the two in a synthesis that could never be bettered. For Maritain and Gilson alike, Thomistic method could only be altered for the worse, never for the better.[6] The neo-Thomist account of modernity is therefore *necessarily* a declinist narrative. It provided the intellectual underpinnings of the Hutchins-Adler project at the University of Chicago and thus Adler's denunciation of all arguments against Hitler that were grounded in postmedieval thought. It captivated a young Southerner named Richard Weaver when he came to teach at Chicago in 1945 and led to his first (and still most famous) book, *Ideas Have Consequences*. It continues to govern some histories of ideas even today, most notably in Brad Gregory's *The Unintended Reformation* and Thomas Pfau's *Minding the Modern*. It is not, in my judgment, a very good historical thesis, but it has been almost the only one to offer significant resistance to the emancipatory narrative of the Enlightenment that casts the schoolmen as dull, benighted, superstitious logic-choppers.

One of Maritain's most distinctive contributions to this neo-Thomist account is the attention he gives to humanism. Where other thinkers were content to dismiss humanism as a perversion of true (Catholic, Christian) thought, indeed to accept the verdict of the Enlightenment that humanism and religion are irreconcilable, Maritain perceived the term as standing on contested ground—ground eminently worth fighting for. What was called for, in his view, was not a rejection of humanism but a reclamation of it. As early as 1933 he wrote, "The quarrel is not between humanism and Christianity. It is between two conceptions of humanism."[7] Thomism therefore was not something that preceded humanism and was replaced by it, but was rather its ideal form. "The great defect of classical humanism," he wrote, "the brand of humanism which, since the Renaissance, has occupied the last three centuries ... lies not so much in that which is affirmed in this sort of humanism, as in that which consists of negation, denial, and separation; it lies in what one might call an *anthropocentric* concept of man and culture." The core problem is its picture of "human nature as closed in upon itself or absolutely self-sufficient."[8] Maritain believed that the humanism of the Renaissance, and still more the later interpretation of that movement by the key figures of the Enlightenment, celebrated and affirmed a truncated humanity, a sad parody, almost, of what humans ought to be and can be. What is needed, he insists, is the restoration of something lost since Thomas: a *full* humanism, an *integral* humanism.

Maritain published his fullest statement of this view, *Integral Humanism*, in 1936. His argument for the restoration of a true humanism begins with the assertion that the "dissolution of the

Middle Ages" was a "catastrophe" that "opens the epoch of modern humanism," which embodies itself as "the cult of humanity, of sheer man." But "sheer man" is not Man at all, for Maritain: "The misfortune of classical humanism is to have been anthropocentric, and not to have been humanism" at all. That this was indeed a misfortune Maritain concludes by reading the history of late modernity, within which "the rationalist [i.e., anti-supernaturalist] idea of the human person has received a mortal blow."[9] That blow has been administered dually by Darwinian and Freudian ideas, which, in Maritain's understanding, leave the Christian understanding of humanity untouched but inflict damage on anthropocentric humanism from which it cannot recover. (Since in these contexts Maritain tends to mention Nietzsche also, we can discern in his argument an anticipation of Paul Ricoeur's famous identification of the three great "masters of suspicion."[10]) The seemingly irresistible rise of Soviet Communism and National Socialism, to which—again this familiar point, made by so many in those dark days—the "cult of humanity" has no answer, proves that anthropocentric humanism is dead. What remains, he believes, is a choice between "two *pure positions*: the *pure atheist* position, and the *pure Christian* position."[11]

Later in the book, though, Maritain has to acknowledge that, at least from the Christian side, matters are a little more complicated: there are in fact "two Christian positions." That he does not acknowledge *more* than two may perhaps indicate a reluctance to sacrifice polemical force, but more likely reflects his belief that only two genuinely Christian accounts of humanity can be sustained in the current crisis. One is that of the great Swiss Protestant theologian Karl Barth, who, Maritain admits, was as evisceratingly dismissive of anthropocentric humanism as any theologian could possibly be. But the theological principles on which he based this dismissal arose from what Maritain called a "primitive Calvinism," a

Though Maritain would spend the war in America, those remaining in his homeland meditated on his ideas throughout the war. When France fell to the Wehrmacht in 1940, it was divided into two zones: an occupied zone in the north of the country and a "free" zone in the south, with the headquarters of its puppet government at Vichy. The largest city in Free France was Lyon, a hundred miles east of Vichy, and the leading theologian at the Institut catholique de Lyon was Henri de Lubac, a Jesuit priest. His superiors—including Fr. Norbert Boynes, the Assistant General of the whole Society of Jesus—made it clear that he and all other faculty of the Institut were to be obedient to the Vichy government, a command with which de Lubac took strong issue. Throughout the war he participated in the Catholic Resistance, and became a target of the Gestapo when German troops marched into Lyon in 1942. He was able to escape to a religious house farther south and continue his research and writing. This work consisted of an ambitious treatise on the meaning of the "supernatural" and an explanation and critique of the rise of an atheistic humanism in the nineteenth century: *The Drama of Atheist Humanism*. (These would be published after the liberation of France in 1944.)[15]

The essays that formed the latter book repeatedly made the same argument: that the biblical teaching that human beings are made in the image of God (Genesis 1:26), while elevating us to a great height within Creation, came eventually to be perceived, by many Western intellectuals, as a curb on our greatness: thus "the time came when man was no longer moved by" that account. "On the contrary, he began to think that henceforward he would forfeit his self-esteem and be unable to develop in freedom unless he broke first with the Church and then with the Transcendent Being upon whom, according to Christian tradition, he was dependent." That breaking with Transcendent Being began with "a reversion to even though she had great academic success. For instance, in 1931 she was one of only eleven people in France to pass the *agrégation* exam in philosophy—this was the primary means by which people qualified as teachers in the lycée system. Another successful examinee that year was Claude Levi-Strauss, and while he says in his great memoir *Tristes Tropiques* that he was the youngest successful candidate of his year, Weil was in fact two months younger.[17]

Another successful examinee that year was Weil's close friend and eventual biographer, Simone Pétrement. Pétrement's narrative of her friend's life remains the best available, but her intimacy with Weil lends a peculiar character to the book: it is simultaneously a modern scholarly biography, full of appropriate citations and documentation, and something like a saint's life, full of anecdotes illustrative of Weil's personal oddity and moral passion.

The idea of sainthood forms a penumbra around readers' responses to Weil, even when, as is frequently the case, that idea is accompanied by suspicion. Auden named her as one of those writers, along with Pascal, Nietzsche, and Kierkegaard, who tend to overwhelm readers with the brilliance and originality of their insights—but later, "one begins to react against their overemphasis on one aspect of the truth at the expense of all the others, and one's first enthusiasm may all too easily turn into an equally exaggerated aversion." Readers' thoughts about such writers' ideas can rarely be divorced from impressions of the character and style of their lives; for this reason, written treatments of them tend toward the hagiographical or anti-hagiographical. Thus Susan Sontag, writing in 1963, commented that Weil's life is an "exemplary" one, and that "[s]ome lives are exemplary, others not; and of exemplary lives, there are those which invite us to imitate them, and those which 'we regard from a distance with a mixture of revulsion, pity, and reverence.'" This is to see Weil as a kind of saint, "if one may use the . . . term in an aesthetic, rather than a religious sense." It may be that "[n]o one who loves life would wish to imitate her dedication to martyrdom nor would wish it for his children nor for anyone else whom he loves. Yet so far as we love seriousness, as well as life, we are moved by it, nourished by it."[18]

Moreover, such complex responses did not arise only after Weil's strange death, by something like self-starvation, at the age of thirty-four; during her lifetime, people often treated her as a curious or even bizarre psychological case, as she herself understood, and resented. In one of her last letters, to her parents, she notes that people always speculated about her mental health and the brilliance of her mind, but did so precisely in order to avoid asking the one question that really mattered: "Is what she says true?"[19]

* * *

During Holy Week of 1938, Weil went with her mother to the great abbey at Solesmes, where, she had heard, Gregorian chant was sung very beautifully. Weil attended every service she could during this time, despite being afflicted by the severe headaches she had been enduring for several years. She also met a young Englishman in whom she discerned a spiritual radiance—to Pétrement, she called him "angel boy"—and from whom she learned about the poetry of George Herbert. She would later tell her unofficial confessor, Father Joseph-Marie Perrin, that Herbert's "Love III" had a special power for her. "I learned it by heart. Often, at the culminating point of a violent headache, I make myself say it over, concentrating all my attention upon it and clinging with all my soul to the tenderness it enshrines. I used to think I was merely reciting it as a beautiful poem, but without my knowing it the recitation had the virtue of a prayer. It was during one of these recitations that . . . Christ himself came down and took possession of me."[20]

This experience sent Weil down a path of rethinking what it means to be a human being. But this would not, for her, result in a reclaiming of the notion of humanism. Also, though drawn to Catholicism, she would never receive baptism, and she never accepted Maritain's version of the faith. Indeed, as I will argue later, Maritain's thought became for Weil almost a *bête noire*, a nemesis— at best a false friend. She would not seek to correct and reclaim Catholic humanism. Even to speak of human*ism* is to place the human being at the center of his or her own story, which is precisely where we do not belong: to have Christ "take possession" of us is the true path. As she wrote in her notebook in 1941 or 1942, "The errors of our time come from Christianity without the supernatural. Secularization is the cause—and primarily humanism." This is not a movement that can simply be reversed: "Humanism and what has arisen out of it, is not a return to antiquity, but a development of poisons that are internal to Christianity." These poisons cannot be neutralized; they must be purged. To say this is still to think in terms of the human being, "the human being as such," to whom we owe some debt; but one must not place the human being at the *center* of discourse and understanding, for that is poisonous.[21]

Similarly, Auden in "New Year Letter," the long poem he wrote in the first months of 1940, sees the humanistic as a mode of comfortable optimism. In the aftermath of the Russian Revolution, some people dreamed that that "political upheaval / . . . / realised the potential Man, / A higher species brought to birth / Upon a sixth part of the earth." But those who sat down to read the writings that had inspired that revolution "found their humanistic view / In question": Marx "brought / To human consciousness a thought / It thought unthinkable." Genuine revolution in all its modes repudiates the comforts of any "humanistic view," and such comforts cannot now be restored.[22]

Indeed, Maritain is the only one of our *dramatis personae* for whom the concept of humanism is straightforwardly compelling. After two essays on the subject written around the time of his conversion to Christianity, each of which is both ambivalent and ambiguous, Eliot effectively abandons the term; and for Lewis, a scholar of the early modern period, it is a technical term used to describe an intellectual and literary movement for which he has little use or respect.[23] But as I noted at the outset of this chapter, all of them are engaged in projects of thought that arise from the humanist movement of the Renaissance and its reconfiguration in the aftermath of the encyclicals *Dei Filius* and *Aeterni Patris*. All of them believe that, to borrow once again Mark Greif's useful phrase, that they are living in "the age of the crisis of Man," and that that crisis can only be resolved by the restoration of the specifically Christian understanding of the human being as such. All of them would have endorsed, generally speaking, though perhaps not without slight amendment, John Milton's great statement in "On Education," which he in turn had derived from the early Christian humanists: "The end then of learning is to repair the ruins of our first parents by regaining to know God aright, and out of that knowledge to love him, to imitate him, to be like him, as we may the nearest by possessing our souls of true virtue, which being united to the heavenly grace of faith makes up the highest perfection." And they also share the conviction that this restoration will not be accomplished only, or even primarily, through theology as such, but also and more effectively through philosophy, literature, and the arts. It is through these practices, which I believe are best called "humanistic," that the renewal—or if necessary the revolutionary upheaval—of Western civilization will be achieved. That was the project that these figures, in the various ways and with their sometimes fierce disagreements, shared.

Chapter 3

Learning in War-Time

The primary task of this book is to explore this model of Christian humane learning as a force for social renewal. We have already seen why the model—especially in the more confrontational form advocated by Maritain, Adler, and Hutchins—was resisted by secularists and pluralists like Sidney Hook and John Dewey. But it is equally important to note that this approach was not the only Christian one on the scene at the outset of the war. One important alternative was the "Christian realism" of Reinhold Niebuhr.

To be sure, there is much overlap between Niebuhr's ideas and those of the protagonists of this book. In *Christianity and Power Politics*, the book he published in 1940 to mark his support for the war effort, and total rejection of the pacifism he had previously embraced, Niebuhr rejected the humanism of the Renaissance in terms very similar to those employed by Maritain and Weil: "The Renaissance . . . saw human history as a realm of infinite possibilities, but forgot that it is a realm of evil as well as good potentialities. In both its rationalism and its mysticism the Renaissance thought that it had found methods of extricating the universal man from the particular man, embedded in the flux of nature."[1] It thought wrongly.

This could be a quotation from Maritain. But in 1936 Niebuhr had reviewed Maritain's *Freedom in the Modern World* in the *Saturday*

Review and had been unimpressed by what he believed to be its nostalgia for an earlier social order that could never be restored. "A type of guild socialism seems to [Maritain] to conform best to the Christian ideal"—but the guild system is a relic of the Middle Ages. Therefore Maritain "is as unrealistic as the rationalistic liberals, whose approach he rejects, in explaining how that kind of a social order is to be created." Maritain wants to articulate a humane political philosophy that is prior and superior to economic concerns, but this, says Niebuhr, is precisely what one cannot achieve in the modern world: "He pleads for a priority of politics over economics but does not face the problem that a technical age has made economic power the most basic power, from which political power is derived." Maritain, Niebuhr thinks, "fails to recognize the dynamic and quasi-autonomous character of the various materials with which a modern statesman must deal." (His assumption of the perspective of the "modern statesman" is characteristic of Niebuhr and one of the chief ways he differs from Maritain and the other central figures of this book.) "One gains the impression that a Catholicism which once dominated a comparatively static agrarian society will have greater difficulty than it realizes in insinuating its ideals into the dynamic force of a technical age."[2]

This is the voice of what Niebuhr called Christian Realism. In contrast to a renewal of broadly based humane learning, Niebuhr offers a version of *Realpolitik* undergirded by a constant awareness of original sin and (consequently, he would say) unafraid to plunge into the give-and-take of "power politics" with the hope of getting something useful done.

In 1992, on the centennial of Niebuhr's birth, Arthur Schlesinger Jr. wrote of how bracing it had been to hear Niebuhr preach on this subject in the first years of the Second World War: "Traditionally, the idea of the frailty of man led to the demand for obedience to ordained authority. But Niebuhr rejected that ancient conservative argument. Ordained authority, he showed, is all the more subject to the temptations of self-interest, self-deception and self-righteousness. Power must be balanced by power."[3] *Power must be balanced by power*, and therefore any trust placed in the renewal of humane education to reshape the world can be little more than evasive nostalgia, a model of social action that simply fails to meet the need for a deeply Christian engagement with the "principalities and powers" of this world. A "technical age"—Niebuhr uses the phrase repeatedly—must be confronted on its own terms, not avoided by a shift sideways into an essentially private realm of personal formation. He draws a bright straight line between a Pauline and Augustinian theological anthropology and public policy.

Niebuhr was often a strong critic of some elements of the American political regime, but his critique came from within its walls. Some years ago, the sociologist Michael Lindsay wrote a book about Christian participation in politics called *Faith in the Halls of Power*. The title is susceptible to two very different construals. It could announce the story of how people of faith act when in the halls of power; it could also suggest the description of what happens when people *have* faith in what happens in the halls of power. Both possibilities fit Niebuhr. He never expected politics to achieve some utopian order—his pervasively skeptical anthropology forbade that—but he thought that Christians could intervene directly in the political order in powerful and valuable ways. He was, I think, less hopeful about attempts to alter society through intellectual transformation, though he used his own powerful intellect to produce critiques of modern society as incisive as any of his time. It can sometimes seem that Niebuhr's most theologically serious work merely laid the foundation for more direct modes of political intervention—precisely the modes that the protagonists of our story here shunned in favor of longer views and less direct interventions. Niebuhr's thinking owed little to the essentially humanistic tradition of which our protagonists are, in their admittedly varying ways, heirs and celebrants.

Auden was just getting to know Niebuhr and his wife Ursula when *Christianity and Power Politics* appeared. It was Ursula to whom he was closer—they were both English and missed their native land in similar ways—and in letters to her maintained a rather consistently bantering, not to say mocking, tone toward her husband. He described Reinhold as resembling a "benevolent eagle," and in a letter written in December 1941 said,

> I hope that that Christian Dynamo Reinhold will give you two or three days rest at Christmas, or rather that you will very firmly put him to bed and keep him there. How I laughed over your story about not getting anything DONE. I'm sure if Lutherans had confessors, his would say "Now, my son, as a penance for being an ecclesiastical Orson Welles, you shall sit in an arm-chair for 48 hours with NO RADIO and twiddle your thumbs."[4]

And when he reviewed *Christianity and Power Politics* for the *Nation* in January 1941, he allowed some of this tone to creep into his response. Acknowledging that the book is "lucid, just, and . . . theologically unexceptionable," he went on to say, "and yet it leaves me a little uneasy." The problem, for Auden, is that Niebuhr's eagerness to participate in the political arena, even under the banner of a belief in original sin, might allow him to lose sight of some of his own foundational beliefs. Auden illustrates his discomfort through a parable:

> A brother once came to one of the desert fathers saying, "My mind is intent on God." The old man replied, "It is no matter

that thy mind should be with God; but if thou didst see thyself less than any of his creatures, that were something." I am sure Dr Niebuhr knows this: I am not, sure, though, that he is sufficiently ashamed. The danger of being a professional exposer of the bogus is that, encountering it so often, one may come in time to cease to believe in the reality it counterfeits.

This is on the face of it a very peculiar response to a book on Christianity and politics. But I think Auden is suggesting, in as gentle a way as he can manage, that a vast chasm separates an Augustinian theological anthropology employed as a tool of social analysis and critique from an Augustinian theological anthropology that generates what would surely be a profoundly discomfiting self-knowledge. "The question is: does he believe that the contemplative life is the highest and most exhausting of vocations, that the church is saved by the saints, or doesn't he?"[5]

It is noteworthy that Auden does not defend the intellectual life—by implication a branch of the contemplative—by claiming that it is "a realm of infinite possibilities," as, in Niebuhr's account, did the Renaissance humanists; rather, he claims that it is the sphere that demands the most of its adherents, and the sphere in which the church itself is saved. What would it profit the church to engage effectively in "power politics" but lose its own soul through neglecting the witness, and the proper formation, of its saints? What would it profit a man, a theologian and a pastor, to articulate a convincing Augustinian critique of the whole social order while forgetting that he too is, as the *Book of Common Prayer* says, a "miserable offender"?

This is a question, as C. S. Lewis put it in an article he published in 1942, of distinguishing between first and second things. "You can't get second things by putting them first; you can get second things only by putting first things first. From which it would follow that the question, What things are first? is of concern not only to philosophers but to everyone." Lewis argues that throughout the twentieth century "our own civilization . . . has been putting itself first. To preserve civilization has been the great aim; the collapse of civilization, the great bugbear." And if "preserving civilization" really *is* the first order, then Niebuhr's Christian Realism is surely the political philosophy to follow. But, Lewis asks, "how if civilization has been imperilled precisely by the fact that we have all made civilization our *summum bonum*? Perhaps it can't be preserved in that way. Perhaps civilization will never be safe until we care for something else more than we care for it."[6]

To the question of what that "something else" might be, Lewis does not, in that essay, give an answer. But we may find a hint in "The Weight of Glory," the sermon he preached at Oxford's University Church of St. Mary the Virgin in June 1941. There he said, "There are no *ordinary* people. You have never talked to a mere mortal. Nations, cultures, arts, civilization—these are mortal, and their life is to ours as the life of a gnat. But it is immortals whom we joke with, work with, marry, snub, and exploit—immortal horrors or everlasting splendours."[7] To embrace this account of the human person, which is of course a traditional Christian one, is to decenter the world of politics—not to ignore it, but to shift it toward the periphery, to see it as among the second rather than the first things. To think from within this account is to accept the necessity of giving, before anything else, a proper account of *personhood*, and to understand oneself as bound as fully as anyone else by the account that one gives.

If Auden has rightly understood that Niebuhr neglected this account, and consequently failed to grasp his own place in the cosmos, then we might pose as the proper counterbalance to Niebuhr the self-understanding of Simone Weil. In the "spiritual autobiography" she wrote in 1942 for her informal personal confessor, Father Perrin, she describes a moment seven years earlier when she, "in a wretched condition physically," visited a Portuguese fishing village "which, alas, was very wretched too." She happened to arrive on the day of the festival of the village's patron saint.

> It was the evening and there was a full moon over the sea. The wives of the fishermen were, in procession, making a tour of all the ships, carrying candles and singing what must certainly be very ancient hymns of a heart-rending sadness. Nothing can give any idea of it. I have never heard anything so poignant unless it were the song of the boatmen on the Volga. There the conviction was suddenly borne in upon me that Christianity is preeminently the religion of slaves, that slaves cannot help belonging to it, and I among others.[8]

* * *

"The Weight of Glory" was the second wartime sermon Lewis preached at Oxford's University Church; the first had come a mere six weeks into the war. At that moment fraught with tension, he raised quite bluntly before the assembled students and dons the question of whether they should be attending the university at all. (This was also when he stated that he believed the Allied cause to be "very righteous.") Canon T. R. Milford, then the vicar of the church, discussed the topic with Lewis beforehand and got a copy of the address, with which he was so impressed that he had it mimeographed and handed out to everyone who came. The title on the handout was "None Other Gods: Culture in War-Time," though Lewis would later publish it under the title "Learning in War-Time." For this was Lewis's general question: What possible use could academic studies be in time of war?

His answer, in brief, is that such studies have the same use, and the same uselessness, in time of war as in time of peace, because "the war creates no absolutely new situation; it simply aggravates the permanent human situation so that we can no longer ignore it. Human life has always been lived on the edge of a precipice." He points out that the question of how people can possibly think of academic questions when the outcome of the war is at stake takes precisely the same form as the question raised everlastingly by some Christians: "How can you be so frivolous and selfish as to think about anything but the salvation of human souls?"[9]

Lewis's reply to the latter question is that whether or not it would be a good idea to think only explicitly "religious" thoughts, nobody does. "Before I became a Christian I do not think I fully realized that one's life, after conversion, would inevitably consist in doing most of the same things one had been doing before, one hopes, in a new spirit, but still the same things." And for Lewis, "in a new spirit" is the key concept: he takes his watchword in this sermon from the biblical injunction "Whether ye eat or drink or whatsoever ye do, do all to the glory of God" (1 Corinthians 10:31). The question, then, is whether academic work can be done to the glory of God, and Lewis's answer is that of course it can. "If our parents have sent us to Oxford, if our country allows us to remain there, this is *prima facie* evidence that the life which we, at any rate, can best lead to the glory of God at present is the learned life."[10]

There is some naïveté, or perhaps conscious exaggeration for the purposes of exhortation, in Lewis's assumption that his students understand themselves to be living "the learned life." Even for the most studious, learning is only part of undergraduate experience. But it could also be that Lewis was thinking of himself. When the previous war had come about, and he had fought in it, he was not a Christian and had no sense of religious obligation. Now he had to consider

whether this new war brought him any new responsibilities—
especially since it was to him a horror that he wanted only to sleep
through or, failing that, ignore. He was, I believe, sufficiently self-
aware to know that he was preaching a message that he himself
would like to hear; but he preached it anyway, because its message
was his genuine conviction.

For Lewis, then, trying to think in Christian terms, the life of
learning is like any other life: something that can be done "to the
glory of God" but not of any particular distinction—not different in
this respect from any other calling. As George Herbert had written
three hundred years earlier, "Who sweeps a room, as for thy laws,
/ Makes that and th' action fine." And Lewis had cause to develop
his thoughts further in an essay he wrote for the journal *Theology*
just a few weeks later, "Christianity and Culture." He wrote it in response to one George Every, who in an earlier contribution to the
same journal had argued that good literary taste is a Christian virtue
in need of cultivation. Lewis's essay initiated a controversy that went
on in the pages of *Theology* for several issues, and later in the disputation Lewis accepted Every's claim that Lewis had misunderstood
him; but the chief provocation of Lewis's side of the controversy
was his belief that Every did indeed contend that good aesthetic
taste was a Christian virtue and was very wrong so to contend.

Lewis says that his first response to Every's essay was to be "almost thankful for . . . bad hymns. It was good that we should have to
lay down our precious refinement at the very doorstep of the church."
But on further reflection he decided this that would be simply an
error in the opposite direction of Every's and that a more moderate
conclusion was needed. That conclusion, as he described it at a later
stage of the debate, "was that culture, though not in itself merito-
rious, was innocent and pleasant, might be a vocation for some, was
helpful in bringing certain souls to Christ, and could be pursued to

the glory of God." Some of these beliefs, especially his conviction of the value of activities that are *merely*, as some might say, "innocent and pleasant," find their way into much of his later writing; and generally he reinforces, throughout the dispute, the position he articulated in "Learning in War-Time" that cultural pursuits are permissible but not intrinsically good. There *may* be circumstances in which the cultivation of aesthetic excellence is misplaced, and in which its absence is not only justifiable but commendable: a given man may be uncultured "because he has given to good works the time and energy which others use to acquire elegant habits or good language." In almost the last words of Lewis's last contribution to the disputation, he writes, "I am stating, not solving, a problem."[11]

The "problem" comes into play because, as it turns out, there is no necessary and inevitable role for *any* element of human culture in relation to the "first things" of the Christian life. The first answer to the question of whether a given activity is for spiritual good or ill must always be that it depends. Thus when, a year after concluding this disputation in *Theology*, Lewis begins writing a series of fictional letters from a demon named Screwtape to his underling Wormwood, he has Screwtape say this: "I must warn you not to hope too much from a war."

> Of course a war is entertaining. The immediate fear and suffering of the humans is a legitimate and pleasing refreshment for our myriads of toiling workers. But what permanent good does it do us unless we make use of it for bringing souls to Our Father Below? . . . Let us therefore think rather how to use, than how to enjoy, this European war. For it has certain tendencies inherent in it which are, in themselves, by no means in our favour. We may hope for a good deal of cruelty and unchastity. But, if we are not careful, we shall see thousands turning in this tribulation to the

Enemy, while tens of thousands who do not go so far as that will nevertheless have their attention diverted from themselves to values and causes which they believe to be higher than the self.[12]

And of course Lewis means for his Christian readers to use the words of Screwtape as a kind of mirror in which they see their own priorities reversed.

But this means that Lewis here uses culture—more particularly, the literary genre of satire—to make what he believes to be vital theological and moral points. That is, he is striving to turn cultural instruments to good effect, so that one can say that in this case at least the pursuit of culture is commendable and helpful. In the disputation in *Theology*, Lewis had commented that literary reading had been for him an important vehicle for drawing closer to Christian faith, and believed that the same could be true for others, though some were of course led away from Christianity by their literary reading. ("It depends.") One of the questions he raised near the end of his last contribution to the debate in *Theology* was whether he had not just the opportunity but also the *duty* to use his literary gifts in that way, as a means of cultural critique and the illumination of tendencies. Having agreed with one of his interlocutors that one thing a good critic might do is tease out the hidden implications of a work of art, he asks, "Is it the function of the 'trained critic' to discover the latent beliefs and standards in a book, or to pass judgment on them when discovered, or both?"

I think that Lewis came to believe that this combination of inquiry and judgment was essential to his own public role, and that in pursuing that joint impulse he was bringing together his vocation as scholar and critic with his avocational pursuit of writing fiction. And this can be seen in the literary genres he chiefly employed in his writing during the war. He became expert in using storytelling as a form of cultural critique, and always with the war as a backdrop—incidental, in one sense, and yet essential. The experience of being in a country under siege turns up repeatedly in Lewis's work throughout the 1940s, from *The Screwtape Letters* at war's outset to *The Great Divorce* at its conclusion, and even after. In 1940, when he was hosting at his home in Oxford children who had been evacuated from London, he decided to write a children's story, but set it aside. When he returned to it a decade later, the setting he had originally envisioned remained the same: "Once there were four children whose names were Peter, Susan, Edmund, and Lucy. This story is about something that happened to them when they were sent away from London during the war because of the air-raids."[13]

In his storytelling and his polemical writings alike, Lewis understood himself to be bringing something distinctive to bear on the challenges of his world: an intimate knowledge of, and love for, the distant past. His academic training as a medievalist is not, in his mind, an irrelevance, still less an impediment, but a *qualification* for social commentary. As he says in "Learning in War-Time," "[W]e need intimate knowledge of the past. Not that the past has any magic about it, but because we cannot study the future, and yet need something to set against the present, to remind us that the basic assumptions have been quite different in different periods and that much which seems certain to the uneducated is merely temporary fashion." Moreover, since the twentieth century's powerful communications technologies have a tendency to reinforce those temporary fashions more powerfully than any culture could have imagined in the past, those who know other ways become especially vital: "the scholar has lived in many times and is therefore in some degree immune from the great cataract of nonsense that pours from the press and the microphone of his own age."[14]

On these grounds he freely commended the wisdom of the past, and filled his wartime stories with demons, transfigured and glorified souls, planetary Intelligences, unfallen beings radiant with wisdom and love . . . . One suspects, given his belief in the value of old books to correct "the great cataract of nonsense that pours from the press and the microphone," he would have told such tales even if he had not believed in the spiritual warfare that he continually portrays in them. But he did believe that such warfare was constant, and that an earthly war, even a worldwide one, was a small thing in comparison with the great cosmic conflict between a righteous and loving God and all those who aligned themselves against righteousness and love.

* * *

In July 1942, Auden wrote to his friend James Stern, "In 1912, it was a real vision to discover that God loves a Pernod and a good fuck, but in 1942 every maiden aunt knows this and it's time to discover something else He loves."[15] That sentence neatly encapsulates the intellectual and spiritual journey that Auden had openly embarked on soon after he came to America in January 1939.

In one sense, the journey had begun some years earlier. Looking back late in life on the steps that had led him to embrace Christianity, Auden recalled two events from the 1930s: his unexpected and inexplicably intense distress at seeing the destruction of churches in Barcelona during the Spanish Civil War; and his meeting with Charles Williams, the Oxford University Press editor and eccentric Christian writer, which gave to Auden the strong conviction that while he was with Williams he was "in the presence of personal sanctity."[16] But he was situated within English intellectual culture in a way that prevented him from absorbing whatever lessons were to be learned from those experiences, and it was only once he got to America that he began in a serious way to reconsider the foundations of his life.

This was not an easy task, especially since the move to America disrupted him in almost every way. That he had no fixed abode was nothing new—he had been peripatetic his entire adult life—but traveling about in a new and vast country was disorienting. Then he fell in love. As he wrote to his brother John, "Mr Right has come into my life. He is a Roumanian-Latvian-American Jew called Chester Kallman, eighteen, extremely intelligent and I think, about to become a good poet. His father who knows all and approves is a communist dentist who would be rich if he didn't have to pay two sets of alimony. This time, my dear, I really believe it's marriage."[17] But the relationship grew complicated very quickly, and Auden was forced to recognize that Kallman did not think of them as being married and fully intended to have sex with other men when so inclined (and he was often so inclined). Even as he sought to reckon with this ever-changing and unprecedentedly intense relationship, Auden was trying to figure out what he believed and why he believed it. He had never lived in a manner so closely approximating his intellectual preferences, but sorting through all that reading was immensely demanding. In December 1939, he gave a lecture at Harvard, and one of the attendees was the eminent English literary critic I. A. Richards, who reported to T. S. Eliot,

> Auden gave a Lecture here—very crowded audience, 300 seated, 20–30 standing throughout—and began by saying how proud he was to speak to the 1st University in the country in which he hoped to become, in a few years, a citizen . . . . He is an utterly changed man . . . thin, white, shrunk and tortured by something.[18]

Perhaps "tortured by something" is an exaggeration, but Auden was certainly struggling to find his way—and very consciously so. One of Auden's first New York friends was a much older woman, Elizabeth

Mayer, a German refugee whose father had been a Lutheran pastor. She began a correspondence with Auden's father, who wrote to her, with telling insight, "You know what a sense of Mission there has always been present in Wystan's plan of life from the time when he decided to leave England for America."[19] The Mission was, above all, to find his true vocation. And that proved an elusive Grail, not least because Auden's personal quest could not be disentangled from the events then tearing Europe apart.

He tried to disentangle it. "New Year Letter," the long poem he wrote in the first four months of 1940, is above all a defense of the new way of life he had chosen since coming to America: an aesthetic life, a life of reading and listening to music, as he sought to re-educate himself and to be open to new forms of art previously unknown to him (it was through Chester Kallman that he came to love opera). "New Year Letter" is perhaps not Auden's most learned poem, but it is his most *ostentatiously* learned one, with all the artists and thinkers whose works he had been reassessing featured prominently throughout the poem in small capitals:

> BLAKE shouted insults, ROUSSEAU wept,
> Ironic KIERKEGAARD stared long
> And muttered "All are in the wrong,"
> While BAUDELAIRE went mad protesting
> That progress is not interesting . . . .[20]

The poem is dotted from end to end with these typographic signals of a new emphasis: the local and the aesthetic now take precedence over the universal (it was a commitment to universal justice that had sent Auden to Spain in 1937) and the political—or what is usually taken to be the political. For Elizabeth Mayer's informal salon on Long Island—from which the poem emerges and which it continually commends—constitutes a counterpolitics. The world's sun, that true universal with its "neutral eye,"

> Lit up America and on
> A cottage in Long Island shone
> Where BUXTEHUDE as we played
> One of his passacaglias made
> Our minds a *civitas* of sound
> Where nothing but assent was found,
> For art had set in order sense
> And feeling and intelligence,
> And from its ideal order grew
> Our local understanding too.[21]

If the larger *civitas* is broken—"Defenceless under the night / Our world in stupor lies," he had written in "September 1, 1939"—this smaller one remains whole and beautiful. And those who both create and receive its wholeness are not that abstraction from the earlier poem, "the Just," but simply Elizabeth's friends, those who have been fortunate enough to come for a time within her orbit and under the protection of her house.

In the last pages of the poem, Auden muses that the external chaos from which they are temporarily protected has multiple causes, some of which are philosophical. "The flood of tyranny and force / Arises at a double source": "PLATO's lie of intellect" that allows philosopher-kings to arise and believe that they are born to rule over "the herd," or "ROUSSEAU's falsehood of the flesh" that creates a universal pride and confidence in the sane strength of "the Irrational."[22] But then he turns to what seems to be an even greater and more intransigent force, visible with particular clarity even in an America not yet at war:

More even than in Europe, here
The choice of patterns is made clear
Which the machine imposes, what
Is possible and what is not,
To what conditions we must bow
In building the Just City now.[23]

Twenty years earlier, Eliot had famously written, thinking of art, that Tradition "cannot be inherited, and if you want it you must obtain it by great labour."[24] Auden is translating that idea into the terms of politics. We must understand

That the machine has now destroyed
The local customs we enjoyed,
Replaced the bonds of blood and nation
By personal confederation.
To judge our means and plan our ends; . . .[25]

Another way to put this point is to say that nationalism and romantic individualism are equal and opposite errors: nationalism believes that the consoling and nurturing force of tradition can indeed be inherited—if you happen to be born in the right place—while romantic individualism believes that each of us can be wholly self-sufficient, self-made. Each of these errors is consolidated by "the machine": that is, enforced by a technological regime that makes "personal confederation" the only option for meaningful community. It is true that "Aloneness is man's real condition," but that merely sets each of us off as an adventurer, a "landless knight," a "GAWAIN-QUIXOTE," in quest of such community— which, again, must be consciously made, in local company, and neither inherited (which the machine had made impossible) nor done without (which the machine falsely tells you you can do, with its infinitely resourceful help).

So the ideas of Plato and Rousseau must be resisted, as well as the power (both concrete and ideological) of the machine. All very good. And yet hanging over the whole edifice is the question that Auden had faced at the theater in Yorkville: is this vision strong enough to oppose the forces tearing the world apart? In "the world we know / Of war and wastefulness and woe," it seems that "Ashamed civilians come to grief / In brotherhoods without belief."[26] Can brotherhoods be sustained without belief? Auden fears not; and so concludes his with a long and beautiful and yet also tentative prayer, "O Unicorn among the cedars." It is a prayer of petition rather than praise, and what it asks is for this Unicorn, this Dove, this Ichthus, this Wind, to

> Instruct us in the civil art
> Of making from the muddled heart
> A desert and a city where
> The thoughts that have to labour there
> May find locality and peace,
> And pent-up feelings their release,
> Send strength sufficient for our day,
> And point our knowledge on its way,
> O da quod jubes, Domine.[27]

The last phrase is adapted from Augustine's *Confessions*, probably by way of Charles Williams's *Descent of the Dove*: "O give what you command, Lord." Which is to say: Whatever you ask of us you must give us the strength to do.

"New Year Letter" is clearly an attempt to master internal disorder—given that external disorder was beyond Auden's control.

An especially telling account of his state of mind, in the dark last days of 1939, just before he began the poem, may be found in his review of an anthology edited by Walter de la Mare whose full title is *Behold, This Dreamer! Of Reverie, Night, Sleep, Dream, Love-Dreams, Nightmare, Death, the Unconscious, the Imagination, Divination, the Artist, and Kindred Subjects.* After but a few words concerning de la Mare's anthology, Auden, as was his habit, rose high into the intellectual sky to take a hawk's-eye view of the subject.

> We are confronted today by the spectacle, not of a utilitarian rationalism that dismisses all that cannot be expressed in prose and statistics as silly childish stuff, but rather by an ecstatic and morbid abdication of the free-willing and individual before the collective and daemonic. We have become obscene night worshippers who, having discovered that we cannot live exactly as we will, deny the possibility of willing anything and are content masochistically to be lived, a denial that betrays not only us but our daemon itself.[28]

In sum, he writes, "We are witnessing the dissolution of a historical epoch which may be called for convenience Protestant, one during which the day life and the night life were segregated from each other." The life of the daytime is represented by "the humanist tradition of the Renaissance"; the life of the night by "the Calvinist tradition of the Reformation making the contemplative man, whether as artist or as religious, the passive instrument of daemonic powers." It is impossible here not to think of *Finnegans Wake*, Joyce's "lingerous longerous book of the dark," which had appeared just a few months earlier and with which Auden would reckon in a 1941 essay. There, Auden imagines Joyce as "a man conscious of possessing great energy, who believes that order neither exists nor is possible." But it is hard to say what such a man would "think worth doing with his energy. If order cannot be created, then no *action* can be worthwhile." What is left, Auden says, is simply to "record the flux."

> One's taste for Joyce's work . . . will depend, therefore, on whether or not one accepts the flux as the Thing-in-itself. If one does, then Joyce must seem the supreme Master; but if, like myself, one does not, then, apart from the haunting beauty of accidental phrases with an accidental dream-like appeal, he ceases to interest as soon as he ceases to shock.[29]

All this is of course massively unfair to Joyce, whose ambitions are far greater and more complex (and far less "passive") than Auden recognizes, but unfair in understandable ways. For Joyce offers no clear path toward recognizing the psychological, social, and political dangers arising from the "dissolution" of the boundaries between the Day and the Night. One might say that, for Auden, Joyce's composition of *two* epics—one of the Day (*Ulysses*) and another of the Night (*Finnegans Wake*)—is a methodological failure to account for the bleeding of the "daemonic" forces of the Night into our daily lives.

At this period in Auden's development, he is caught between two vocabularies for describing these disorders, the Freudian and the Christian. This marks a pivotal moment in Auden's personal development, and it raises issues that are vital for any serious understanding of all five of the figures with whom we are here concerned. It is then, I think, necessary, to allow this account of Auden's thinking to lead us into a more general meditation on demons.

Chapter 4

Demons

In "September 1, 1939," Auden deploys Freudian categories to describe Hitler as a "psychopathic god" created by unresolvable psychodynamic conflicts in the German soul, whose sufferings had "driven a culture mad." Three weeks after the German invasion of Poland, Freud had died, in London, and from New York Auden wrote a brilliant and reverent elegy for him:

> One rational voice is dumb: over a grave
> The household of impulse mourns one dearly loved.
> Sad is Eros, builder of cities,
> And weeping anarchic Aphrodite.[1]

This "rational voice," Auden then believed, "would have us remember most of all / To be enthusiastic over the night," "because it needs our love." It is populated by "delectable creatures . . . exiles who long for the future / That lies in our power." They wish merely "to serve enlightenment like him," like Dr. Freud.

But his review of de la Mare's anthology, written at almost the same time as the elegy for Freud, reconceives the night not as a place inhabited by "delectable creatures" but as a realm ruled by demons. And this alternative account had been brewing in Auden's mind for several years. In 1936, he had written a sonnet ("And the age ended, and the last deliverer died") about the successful elimination of magical creatures, supernatural forces. The giants, the dragons, the kobolds are gone. What now? Alas: "The vanquished powers were glad / To be invisible and free." Now they "struck down the sons who strayed into their course, / And ravished the daughters, and drove the fathers mad." When they are no longer believed in, "the vanquished powers" but grow in malignity and influence.[2]

By late 1942, Auden had come fully to endorse this account, which sees Freudian psychoanalysis not as complementary to a Christian account of the afflicted human soul, nor even as a merely deficient alternative, but as something that obscures, in potentially deadly ways, the truths we need to know about ourselves. He wrote,

> Psychoanalysis, like all pagan *scientia*, says: "Come, my good man, no wonder you feel guilty. You have a distorting mirror, and that is indeed a very wicked thing to have. But cheer up. For a trifling consideration I shall be delighted to straighten it out for you. There. Look. A perfect image. The evil of distortion is exorcised. Now you have nothing to repent of any longer. Now you are one of the illumined and elect. That will be ten thousand dollars, please."
>
> And immediately come seven devils, and the last state of that man is worse than the first.[3]

That last sentence is a quotation from the Gospels, in which Jesus describes a demon who has been cast out but has the power to return, with "seven other spirits more wicked than himself" (Luke 11:24–26); and it is fair to say that in the period between 1936 and 1942, with the process accelerating dramatically with war's onset, Auden replaces a psychoanalytic account of human wickedness with a demonological one. And for him this demonological account was relevant both on the cultural and the personal level. If the societies of the democratic West had fallen into "an ecstatic and morbid abdication of the free-willing and individual before the collective and daemonic," Auden knew this experience in an intimate way: he would later write that, when faced with Kallman's infidelity to their "marriage," "I was forced to know in person what it is like to feel oneself the prey of demonic powers, in both the Greek and the Christian sense, stripped of self-control and self-respect, behaving like a ham actor in a Strindberg play."[4]

It is impossible to be sure, but I suspect that Auden's acquaintance with Charles Williams, as a person and as a writer, was key to his acceptance of this demonological account of human evil and pain. In all of Williams's writings, he accepts, and in his novels writes continually of, demonic forces at work in the world, and in the book of his that most profoundly influenced Auden, *Descent of the Dove*, just mentioned, he cites the very passage from the Gospels that Auden does: "There has never yet been found any method of driving out one devil—except by pure love—which does not allow the entrance of seven, as Messias had long ago pointed out.[5]

Eliot, whose response to Williams's personal charm and charisma was almost identical to Auden's, was taken by the matter-of-factness with which Williams accepted supernatural forces at work in our world. In an introduction to *All Hallows' Eve*, the novel that Williams completed just before his unexpected death in April 1945, Eliot wrote, "Williams seemed equally at ease among every sort and condition of men, naturally and unconsciously, without envy or contempt, without subservience or condescension. I have always believed that he would have been equally at ease in every kind of supernatural company; that he would never have been surprised or disconcerted by the intrusion of any visitor from another world, whether kindly or malevolent; and that he would have shown exactly the same natural ease and courtesy, with an exact awareness of how one should behave, to an angel, a demon, a human ghost, or an elemental." Eliot is struck by the evident fact that for Williams "there was no frontier between the material and the spiritual world .... To him the supernatural was perfectly natural, and the natural was also supernatural."[6]

Eliot only rarely suggested in print that he himself thought along these lines, but in the very first meeting of the Moot, Eliot warned that any attempt to provide a compelling socio-political organization "could let loose terrible demonic forces." In the second meeting, he said (in the secretary's summary), "We must bring to the surface these true religious impulses and guide thought so that their forces should not become demonic."[7]

Of all the figures studied here, it is of course Lewis who is most closely associated with writing about demonic powers, thanks largely to the enormous success of *The Screwtape Letters*. Giving a commencement address in 1944, he would wryly comment, "Everyone knows what a middle-aged moralist of my type warns his juniors against. He warns them against the World, the Flesh, and the Devil .... The Devil, I shall leave strictly alone. The association between him and me in the public mind has already gone quite as deep as I wish: in some quarters it has already reached the level of confusion, if not of identification."[8] Such "confusion" may best be illustrated by the clergymen who wrote to the magazine in which *Screwtape* originally appeared to complain that "much of the advice given in these letters seemed to him not only erroneous but positively diabolical."

But it is not just in *Screwtape* that Lewis writes about demons. In the first chapter of *Perelandra*, for instance, the narrator tries to get to a house, a place where he can offer aid to a good man, but has to do it "despite the loathing and dismay that pulled me back and a sort of invisible wall of resistance that met me in the face, fighting for each step"—and when he arrives, he discovers that he has made his way against the pressure of demonic opposition.[9] We will look later at *That Hideous Strength*, where the nature of this world as a battlefield, the site of ceaseless spiritual warfare between the forces who obey and those who repudiate God, is made explicit. And in the second talk in the second series of his BBC broadcast talks, delivered in early 1942, Lewis raises, with some trepidation, "all the difficult and terrible doctrines about sin and hell and the devil" that he knows many Christians are inclined to avoid.

He does this, interestingly enough, by using the current war to provide a set of metaphors that he hopes will make such "difficult and terrible doctrines" more comprehensible and ultimately more acceptable. He asks his readers to imagine that, in relation to eternal spiritual realities, they are already in the situation that the English had been fearing since September 1939: "Enemy-occupied territory—that is what this world is." And Christians are called "to take part in a great campaign of sabotage."

> When you go to church you are really listening-in to the secret wireless from our friends: that is why the enemy is so anxious to prevent us from going.... I know someone will ask me, "Do you really mean, at this time of day, to re-introduce our old friend the devil—hoofs and horns and all?" Well, what the time of day has to do with it I do not know. And I am not particular about the hoofs and horns. But in other respects my answer is "Yes, I do." I do not claim to know anything about his personal appearance. If anybody really wants to know him better I would say to that person. "Don't worry. If you really want to, you will. Whether you'll like it when you do is another question."[10]

But in the rest of *Mere Christianity*, Lewis says almost nothing about Satan or the demons, and I believe that is because he understands that no *argument* could be made, in the context of his own time and place, for traditional Christian teaching in these matters. Lewis once commented that reading, when he was a young atheist, the fantasies of George MacDonald had "baptized [his] imagination"—had given him a *feeling* for a world saturated by supernatural realities at a time when he would have poured scorn on any rational "case" made for them. It is for this reason that his major explorations of demonic activity are made in fiction. And it is on the basis of the same understanding, though with reversed moral priorities, that the demon Screwtape utters his very first words to his pupil Wormwood: "I note what you say about guiding your patient's reading and taking care that he sees a good deal of his materialist friend. But are you not being a trifle *naïve*? It sounds as if you supposed that *argument* was the way to keep him out of the Enemy's clutches." Lewis and Screwtape alike, then, hope to shape dreams before turning to the shaping of minds.[11]

* * *

In 1929, Raïssa Maritain had published a short treatise on Satan, *Le Prince de ce monde*, a translation of which ("Done into English by Gerald B. Phelan") was published by St Dominic's Press, the small publishing house Eric Gill had created at his communal retreat, Ditchling in Sussex, and from which he had published a translation of Jacques's *Art and Scholasticism*. In this curious pamphlet, she speaks of what she believes to be the chief work of the Evil One on human beings:

> Lucifer has cast the strong though invisible net of illusion upon us.... He persuades us that we can only love creatures by making Gods of them. He lulls us to sleep (and he interprets our dreams);

he makes us work. Then does the spirit of man brood over stagnant waters. Not the least of the devil's victories is to have convinced artists and poets that he is their necessary, inevitable collaborator and the guardian of their greatness. Grant him that, and soon you will grant him that Christianity is *unpracticable.* Thus does he reign in this world.[12]

What Henri de Lubac had called "atheist humanism" tends, then, to become a demonic humanism. What is required is a conversion of human imagination, and of our strongest conceptions of what art is, in order that we may understand who is our true Helper and who our true Enemy. One might say that what is first required is a redefinition of *imagination* itself, so that it is no longer valorized but rather feared as a source of illusion. Shelley had written in 1821 that "[t]he great instrument of moral good is the imagination"; but St. Paul had denounced those who are "vain in their imaginations" (Romans 1:21) and had declared that his apostolic work requires "casting down imaginations, and every high thing that exalteth itself against the knowledge of God" (2 Corinthians 10:5). The unbaptized imagination kills, but the baptized imagination giveth life. Thus Weil, in a rare comment on these matters, says, "Man has to perform an act of incarnation, for he is disembodied"—literally "disincarnated," *désincarne*—"by his imagination. What comes to us from Satan is our imagination."[13]

That unconverted imagination, then, *takes us out* of embodied life: for Weil this means, above all else, that we are deprived of the right understanding of human affliction, *malheur.* To imagine rightly is to be truly embodied; to be truly embodied is to imagine rightly. It is just this proper grounding in the world that the demons wish to deny us, and they deny it to us primarily through working in our dreams and visions. To be converted to true faith, then, is to be dis-illusioned—to be freed from a spell. In 1941, Lewis said, "Spells are used for breaking enchantments as well as for inducing them. And you and I have need of the strongest spell that can be found to wake us from the evil enchantment of worldliness which has laid upon us for nearly a hundred years." Similarly, Auden wrote in 1943: "Art is not Magic, i.e., a means by which the artist communicates or arouses his feelings in others, but a mirror in which they may become conscious of what their own feelings really are: its proper effect, in fact, is disenchanting."[14]

*   *   *

The "Christmas Oratorio" that Auden would write in the aftermath of his mother's death, in August 1941, is a poem above all about illusions, temptations, enchantments—and their possible remedies. The aesthetic models of *For the Time Being* are not musical but visual: the poem renders in verse and prose scenes from the Nativity narrative traditionally featured in Renaissance art. There is an "Annunciation," for instance, in which a soloist and chorus urge rejoicing: "*Let even the small rejoice*"; "*Let even the old rejoice.*" But the scene ends when "The Demolisher arrives"—and we are transferred to "The Temptation of St. Joseph."[15]

From offstage, voices sing doubts into Joseph's mind: "*Joseph, you have heard / what Mary says occurred; Yes, it may be so. / Is it likely? No.*" This is disillusionment in a more familiar sense: a loss of faith and trust in the beloved. And all Joseph wants from God is a single

> Important and elegant proof
> That what my Love had done
> Was really at your will
> And that your will is love.

But this double comfort—that Mary is virtuous and God good—is denied him. The angel Gabriel merely replies: "No, you must believe; / Be silent, and sit still."[16]

The existential paradoxes of faith and doubt—so familiar from Pascal and Kierkegaard and Karl Barth, all of whom Auden was reading with great attention at this time—might be expected to fill the remainder of the poem, but instead the poem takes a peculiar turn into the political realm: for, after all, what happened to Mary and Joseph and their baby happened not only within the history of Israel but within the history of the Roman Empire. The child born to these obscure Jews will teach and embody an ordering of the world that challenges and reproaches the claims of the Caesars.

The book that most thoroughly shaped Auden's thoughts on these matters is Charles Norris Cochrane's *Christianity and Classical Culture: A Study of Thought and Action from Augustus to Augustine*, which was published in 1940. Auden probably read it in the second half of that year, soon after completing "New Year Letter." By 1944, when he somehow convinced the *New Republic* to allow him to write a review of it, he claimed to have read it "many times," and at the end of the review explains one of the chief reasons he was so enamored with it:

> Our period is not so unlike the age of Augustine: the planned society, caesarism of thugs or bureaucracies, paideia, scientia, religious persecution, are all with us. Nor is there even lacking the possibility of a new Constantinism; letters have already begun to appear in the press, recommending religious instruction in schools as a cure for juvenile delinquency; Mr. Cochrane's terrifying description of the "Christian" empire under Theodosius should discourage such hopes of using Christianity as a spiritual benzedrine for the earthly city.[17]

Cochrane himself meant for all these analogies to be noted, and his ideas dominate the second half of *For the Time Being*. His study is enormously rich and complex, but it may perhaps be summarized thus, with the relevant page numbers indicated:

- Augustus, by uniting virtue and fortune in himself (pp. viii, 174), established "the final triumph of creative politics," solving "the problem of the classical commonwealth" (p. 32).
- For a Christian with Tertullian's understanding of human history, the "deification of imperial virtue" that accompanied this "triumph" was sheer idolatry: therefore *Regnum Caesaris, Regnum Diaboli* (pp. 124, 234).
- "The crisis of the third century ... marked ... an eclipse of the strictly classical ideal of virtue or excellence" (p. 166), and left people wondering what to do if the Augustan solution were not a solution after all. What if there is "no intelligible relationship" between virtue and fortune (p. 171)?
- Christians had remained largely detached during the crisis of the third century, neither wanting Rome to collapse nor prone to being surprised if it did, since its eventual fall was inevitable (p. 195).
- Then Constantine ascended the throne and "both professed and practiced a religion of success" (p. 235), according to which Christianity was a "talisman" that ensured the renewal of *Romanitas* (p. 236).
- After some time and several reversals (most notably in the reign of Julian the Apostate) and occasional recoveries (for instance in the reign of Theodosius), it became clear that both the Constantinian project and the larger, encompassing project of *Romanitas* had failed (p. 391).

- Obviously this was in many ways a disaster, but there was some compensation: the profound impetus these vast cultural crises gave to Christian thought, whose best representatives (above all Augustine) understood that neither the simple denunciations of the social world of Tertullian nor Constantine's easy blending of divergent projects were politically, philosophically, or theologically adequate.
- Thus the great edifice of the *City of God*, Cochrane's treatment of which concludes with a detailed analysis of the philosophy of history that emerges from Augustine's new account of human personality (pp. 502, 536, 542, 567–69).

We have already seen in our look at "New Year Letter" that for Auden both nationalism and romantic individualism had failed, and had thrown us back on the formation of local communities of understanding; but he had also suggested that the sustaining of such communities is impossible in the absence of religious belief: thus the poem's great concluding prayer. So far, his thinking might be seen as an echo of Maritain's, or that of Mortimer Adler and Robert Maynard Hutchins. But Cochrane's book had taught him that such a program of Christian social renewal has its own dangers and temptations—and its own characteristic illusions. For it is a massive misunderstanding of the claims of Christianity to see it as "spiritual benzedrine for the earthly city," as a means to an end, that end being social cohesion and perhaps even victory against totalitarianism. This is to re-enact the Constantinian error, which was to "profess and practice a religion of success": now Christianity becomes once again a "talisman," not for *Romanitas* but for the successor of *Romanitas*, liberal Western democracy. Meet the new Caesar, same as the old Caesar.

In *For the Time Being*, the claims of Caesar are first announced in a great "Fugal Chorus," each stanza of which begins with the claim that Caesar has "conquered seven kingdoms": "Abstract Idea," "Natural Cause," "Infinite Number," "Credit Exchange," "Inorganic Giants," "Organic Dwarfs," and "Popular Soul." These correspond to the signal achievements of democratic societies: for instance, the "Organic Dwarfs" are the microorganisms conquered by the modern pharmaceutical industry, and the "Popular Soul" is equally subject to Caesarist control.[18] And what is Caesar? What President Eisenhower, in his farewell address to the nation in 1961, called the "military-industrial complex"; what Michel Foucault called the "power-knowledge regime"; what Auden himself in "New Year Letter" had called "the machine." In a word, Caesar is force—a word to which we will soon return.

The one figure in *For the Time Being* who grasps this, and the relation of the Christ Child to it, is King Herod. It should first be said that "The Massacre of the Innocents" is by far the funniest section of this poem. After the model of the commemoration of good influences that lead off Marcus Aurelius's *Meditations* ("From my grandfather Verus I learned good morals and the government of my temper"), Herod begins his own reflection thus:

> To Fortune—that I have become Tetrarch, that I have escaped assassination, that at sixty my head is clear and my digestion sound.
> To my Father—for the means to gratify my love of travel and study.
> To my Mother—for a straight nose.
> To Eva, my coloured nurse—for regular habits.
> To my brother, Sandy, who married a trapeze artist and died of drink—for so refuting the position of the Hedonists.[19]

It it useful when reading Auden, who learned from Kierkegaard the strategy of "indirect communication," to assume that the broader the humor, the more serious the point he wishes to make. Herod's long complaint is comical almost throughout, which should alert readers that its concerns lie at the very heart of this poem.[20]

Herod, reflecting on his long career as Tetrarch, sees that he has governed well in Judaea, has brought the province into ever greater order and conformity to the rule of Reason.

> Yes, in twenty years I have managed to do a little. Not enough, of course. There are villages only a few miles from here where they still believe in witches. There isn't a single town where a good bookshop would pay. One could count on the fingers of one hand the people capable of solving the problem of Achilles and the tortoise. Still it is a beginning. In twenty years the darkness has been pushed back a few inches.[21]

Yet news has come to him that makes him fear that the whole edifice he has so carefully constructed could fall like a nest made of twigs. Three ancient scholars have announced that "God has been born . . . we have seen him ourselves. The World is saved. Nothing else matters."

Herod immediately sees the danger: "One needn't be much of a psychologist to realise that if this rumour is not stamped out now, in a few years it is capable of diseasing the whole Empire." But why? Because the proclamation of these Wise Men addresses something his people that no legal structures can ever address: "Legislation is helpless against the wild prayer of longing that rises, day in, day out, from all these households under my protection." If that prayer has been answered, or if people believe it has been answered, then

"Reason will be replaced by Revelation. Instead of Rational Law, objective truths perceptible to any who will undergo the necessary intellectual discipline, and the same for all, Knowledge will degenerate into a riot of subjective visions." But more than the intellectual life will be degraded: the political realm will be corrupted beyond recognition:

> Justice will be replaced by Pity as the cardinal human virtue, and all fear of retribution will vanish. Every corner-boy will congratulate himself: "I'm such a sinner that God had to come down in person to save me. I must be a devil of a fellow." Every crook will argue: "I like committing crimes. God likes forgiving them. Really the world is admirably arranged." . . . The Rough Diamond, the Consumptive Whore, the bandit who is good to his mother, the epileptic girl who has a way with animals will be the heroes and heroines of the New Tragedy when the general, the statesman, and the philosopher have become the butt of every farce and satire.

And therefore he concludes: "Naturally this cannot be allowed to happen." The Child must be found, and destroyed, and Herod will give the necessary orders because he lives by Necessity—though he grieves at what his actions will do to his reputation: "I've tried to be good. I brush my teeth every night. I haven't had sex for a month. I object. I'm a liberal. I want everyone to be happy. I wish I had never been born."[22]

What Herod realizes is that this Child and the message he brings of universal forgiveness and reconciliation with God do not offer a rival source of power and order but a radical alternative to what the classical world understands as "power" and "order." They do not seek to replace him on the throne of his kingdom but to usher in a wholly new Kingdom, not providing "spiritual benzedrine for the earthly city" but replacing that city with a new one: the City of Man passes away, the City of God abides forever. This Child marks the end of the machine, the end of the military-industrial complex, the end of *force*.

* * *

In December 1943, a young scientist then doing research for the Royal Air Force, primarily on the development of radar, wrote to C. S. Lewis, "I wish to disagree, somewhat violently, with you over a passage" in Lewis's new novel *Perelandra*. The passage concerns a scientist named Weston, whom the protagonist, Ransom, had met on Mars in Lewis's previous science fiction novel *Out of the Silent Planet*. Now Weston is interested in Venus—in conquering and controlling it. The passage that Lewis's correspondent objected to is this:

> He was a man obsessed with the idea which is at this moment circulating all over our planet in obscure works of "scientifiction," in little Interplanetary Societies and Rocketry Clubs, and between the covers of monstrous magazines, ignored or mocked by the intellectuals, but ready, if ever the power is put into its hands, to open a new chapter of misery for the universe. It is the idea that humanity, having now sufficiently corrupted the planet where it arose, must at all costs contrive to seed itself over a larger area.

Weston, thinks Ransom, is one of the few who openly embraces this dream of conquest, which is "fondled in secret by thousands of ignorant men and hundreds who are not ignorant. The destruction or enslavement of other species in the universe, if such there are, is to these minds a welcome corollary."[23]

To Lewis's correspondent, "The whole passage seems to be an outburst of unreasoning and emotional panic rather surprising after the acute penetration of 'The Screwtape Letters' which, incidentally, appealed considerably to me notwithstanding the fact that I have never felt much sympathy towards the Christian tradition." Lewis replied in a conciliating tone, though reaffirming the essential claim, which the correspondent had rightly identified as Lewis's own:

> I don't of course think that at the moment many scientists are budding Westons: but I do think (hang at all, I *live* among scientists!) that a point of view not unlike Weston's is on the way . . . . I agree Technology is *per se* neutral: but a race devoted to the increase of its own power by technology with complete indifference to ethics *does* seem to me a cancer in the universe. Certainly if he goes on his present course much further man can *not* be trusted with knowledge.[24]

It is a shame that the correspondence, it appears, went no further; it would have been especially interesting to hear Lewis's correspondent's thoughts on what happens to Weston: his body is possessed by a demon while his soul is cast into Hell.

A decade later that correspondent—his name was Arthur C. Clarke—published a novel of his own, *Childhood's End*, which is a mirror image of *Perelandra*: humans do not reach and conquer other worlds, but a powerful alien race comes to conquer us. They are the Overlords, and they bring powerful technological gifts—though these gifts serve chiefly to sap human creativity and energy: as one character says, "The world's now placid, featureless, and culturally dead: nothing really new has been created since the Overlords came. The reason's obvious. There's nothing left to struggle for, and there are too many distractions and entertainments."[25]

There is reason to suspect that humans may have met the Overlords before, at some long-forgotten period of our history, and held in their minds a collective memory of the event. This suspicion is based on the Overlords' appearance: "There was no mistake. The leathery wings, the little horns, the barbed tail—all were there. The most terrible of all legends had come to life, out of the unknown past. Yet now it stood smiling, in ebon majesty, with the sunlight gleaming upon its tremendous body, and with a human child resting trustfully on either arm."[26]

After a century of rule, the Overlords begin to explain themselves, and their view of human beings, and in their apparently demonic form, they say this: "In the centuries before our coming, your scientists uncovered the secrets of the physical world and led you from the energy of steam to the energy of the atom. You had put superstition behind you: Science was the only real religion of mankind. It was the gift of the western minority to the remainder of mankind, and it had destroyed all other faiths."[27]

When *Childhood's End* appeared, Lewis wrote to Joy Gresham, who would later become his wife, and called it "AN ABSOLUTE CORKER." "It is a strange comment on our age that such a book lies hid in a hideous paper-backed edition, wholly unnoticed by the *cognoscenti*, while any 'realistic' drivel about some neurotic in a London flat—something that needs no real invention at all, something that any educated man could write if he chose, may get seriously reviewed and mentioned in serious books—as if it really mattered. I wonder how long this tyranny will last? Twenty years ago I felt no doubt that I should live to see it all break up and great literature return: But here I am, losing teeth and hair, and still no break in the clouds."[28]

(Clarke and Lewis eventually met, perhaps around 1960, as Francis Spufford has narrated: "Clarke contacted Lewis and they arranged to meet in the Eastgate Tavern, Oxford. Clarke brought Val Cleaver as his second; Lewis brought along J. R. R. Tolkien. They saw the world so differently that even argument was scarcely possible. As Orwell said about something completely different, their beliefs were as impossible to compare as a sausage and a rose. Clarke and Cleaver could not see any darkness in technology, while Lewis and Tolkien could not see the ways in which a new tool genuinely transforms the possibilities of human awareness. For them, machines at very best were a purely instrumental source of pipe tobacco and transport to the Bodleian. So what could they do? They all got pissed. 'I'm sure you are very wicked people,' said Lewis cheerfully as he staggered away, 'but how dull it would be if everyone was good.'"[29])

Lewis of course understood just what new mythology Clarke was weaving in *Childhood's End*, and applauded it not because he agreed with it but because he admired its audacity and imaginative power. And Clarke, also of course, knows precisely what he is doing in portraying his Overlords so: if, as Blake famously said, "Milton was of the Devil's party without knowing it," Clarke, if he does not quite take the Devil's side, at least acknowledges that the Devil's claims and purposes are as valid as our own. Certainly Clarke believes that what Christians call sinful disobedience is in fact intellectual liberation. When in *Paradise Lost* the angel Raphael warns Adam, "Solicit not thy thoughts with matters hid, / Leave them to God above, him serve and fear" (VIII.167–68), he is, by Clarke's lights, merely forging manacles for Adam's mind. By contrast, Lewis, in his brilliant little book on *Paradise Lost*, says, "What we see in Satan is the horrible co-existence of a subtle and incessant intellectual activity with an incapacity to understand anything."[30] And therefore when Satan transmits his ideas to Eve and Adam, he does not liberate them but infect them with his own incapacity. Clarke and Lewis could not disagree more about the effects of these supposedly demonic forces on human well-being; but they agree in this at least, that what the demons bring to our world is indeed force.

Chapter 5

Force

Jacques Maritain and his wife Raïssa had come to America in January 1940. Like Auden, who had arrived a year earlier, they found lodgings in New York—though while Auden had to make do with rather Bohemian digs in Brooklyn Heights, where he shared a house with other expatriate artists and a famous "exotic dancer" named Gypsy Rose Lee, the Maritains were installed on Fifth Avenue.

According to Jacques's biographer Ralph McInerny, in *The Very Rich Hours of Jacques Maritain*, they settled at 30 Fifth Avenue. Another great French exile, the anthropologist Claude Levi-Strauss, lived just around the corner at 51 West 11th Street, in the same apartment building as Claude Shannon, the creator of information theory, who worked for Bell Labs. (Shannon's theory of information bears a curious affinity to the structural anthropology that Levi-Strauss, under the influence of his fellow exile, the structural linguist Roman Jakobson, developed during the war.) Even by Manhattan standards, that is a remarkable accumulation of intellectual fire-power in one small area. Since I learned about this synchronicity, I have longed for Tom Stoppard to write a play about Maritain, Levi-Strauss, and Shannon—along the lines of what he did with Joyce, Lenin, and Tristan Tzara in *Travesties*.

Maritain had crossed the Atlantic only in order to give some lectures at the Pontifical Institute in Toronto and then in New York; it was the fall of France later in 1940 that forced him to remain in the States. Though a leading French Catholic thinker since the period of World War I, he had in his adolescence been an atheist, like Raïssa Oumançoff, a Russian-Jewish immigrant he met at the Sorbonne in 1901, when they were both still teenagers. They fell in love, and the tightness of their bond—which would last until Raïssa's death in 1960—was intensified by their shared longing for something absolute, something transcendent, which in their student days neither of them could then grasp. They certainly did not receive anything sustaining from their professors at the Sorbonne: many years later, Raïssa would write that their only teacher "inspired with ardent faith" was Emile Durkheim, and his faith was in sociology.

One day, walking after class through the Jardin des Plantes on the Left Bank, they said to each other—as Raïssa recalled in 1940, writing from their apartment in New York—"that if our nature was so unhappy as to possess only a pseudo-intelligence capable of everything but the truth, if, sitting in judgment on itself, it had to debase itself to such a point, then we could neither think nor act with any dignity. In that case everything became absurd."[1]

"I wanted no part in such a comedy," Raïssa recollected. "I would have accepted a sad life, but not one that was absurd." She and Jacques agreed that for a certain period they would continue the "experiment" of living, to see if "the meaning of life would reveal itself."

> But if the experiment should not be successful, the solution would be suicide; suicide before the years had accumulated their dust, before our youthful strength was spent. We wanted to die by a free act if it were impossible to live according to the truth.

In the end the experiment *was* successful. "It was then," Raïssa writes at the beginning of her memoir's next chapter, "that God's pity caused us to find Henri Bergson." Bergson, a Jew whose beliefs were unorthodox by any standard, was not seeking to win people to religious faith; but he was working at the time on the ideas that would lead to his most famous book, *L'Évolution créatrice* (*Creative Evolution*), which posited an *élan vital* saturating the whole of life and drawing it ever onward toward perfection. Jacques and Raïssa's encounter with those ideas, in 1901, was enough to save them from suicide, even though they would not long hold to Bergson's general point of view: five years after they first attended his lectures, and two years after their marriage, they were received into the Roman Catholic Church.

Jacques's first book would be a critique of Bergson and *Bergsonisme*. Much later in life he came to feel that he had been ungenerous, and should have expressed more gratitude for what Bergson did to bring him out of the slough of despond. And indeed his work as a theologian would always be marked by that early spiritual crisis. Long before Camus wrote that the one truly serious philosophical problem is whether to commit suicide—indeed, a dozen years before Camus was even born—the Maritains had faced this decision and come out on the other side as Catholics, and he as a theologian. But he had not pursued the priesthood, indeed as a married man could not have, and this meant that his theological orientation was always that of a layperson, a Catholic in the pew, not presiding at the altar. It was the task of every person, he thought, to follow and to practice what in the 1930s, as we have seen, he came to call "integral humanism"—an account of the human being that, unlike the truncated humanism of the Renaissance and Enlightenment, took into full account our proper relationship to God. The last book he published before leaving the Continent, *The Twilight of Civilization*, lamented the failure of France and Europe more generally to achieve such a humanism and their consequent descent into spiritual torpor—a torpor that made the whole continent vulnerable to the utopian visions of Communism and Fascism alike.

It is noteworthy that Raïssa began her memoir, to which she gave the title *We Have Been Friends Together*, after their exile to New York, at a time when they were separated from their native land and from those friends, when Jacques was still trying to find a role with the Free French and she had no public role at all. In March 1940, she wrote in her journal, "For me this exile is a terrible trial"—and she even contemplated suicide, for the first time since those dark days in the Jardin des Plantes.[2] The writing of her memoir, then, was an exercise in what St. Augustine called *memoria*: not memory in any passive sense, but the willed realization, through the study of one's past, of the pattern of one's life. It was a reminder to herself, and perhaps to Jacques, that the "experiment" had after all been successful, that genuine meaning had been found, and that even in unpropitious times there was still useful work to do.

When she was in the midst of telling their story to herself, she learned, in January 1941, that Bergson had died. "Great pain for us. I think of all that we owe him, and that many others do as well. We heard in a letter from France that he had been baptized and did not want to declare it publicly out of consideration for the Jews subject to persecution in recent years. Our master, lost and found."[3] In fact, Bergson's biographers doubt whether he ever converted. According to his widow, he said late in life that he might have converted were it not for the rise of European anti-Semitism, which made it a moral necessity for him to remain in full solidarity with France's Jews. But in any case he did not wish to be baptized.[4]

But for the Maritains, Bergson remained always their "master," because he had been the one to suggest to them that the world just might be ruled by something other than blind force.

*   *   *

Around the time that the Maritains arrived in New York and Raïssa began work on her memoir—almost immediately after the fall of France to the German armies—Simone Weil wrote an essay about the *Iliad*. It remains her most famous piece of writing. Here is how it begins:

> The true hero, the true subject, the center of the *Iliad* is force. Force employed by man, force that enslaves man, force before which man's flesh shrinks away. In this work, at all times, the human spirit is shown as modified by its relations with force, as swept away, blinded by the very force it imagined it could handle, as deformed by the weight of the force it submits to. For those dreamers who considered that force, thanks to progress, would soon be a thing of the past, the *Iliad* could appear as an historical document; for others, whose powers of recognition are more acute and who perceive force, today as yesterday, at the very center of human history, the *Iliad* is the purest and the loveliest of mirrors.[5]

The word "loveliest" arrests the reader: but for Weil anything that reveals the truth to us is lovely. And it is supremely true that "the subjection of the human spirit to force . . . is the common lot, although each spirit will bear it differently, in proportion to its own virtue. No one in the *Iliad* is spared by it, as no one on earth is."[6]

It is perhaps for this reason that when human beings gain power over other human beings, they are unable to use it moderately. "The moderate use of force, which alone would enable man to escape being enmeshed in its machinery, would require superhuman virtue, which is as rare as dignity in weakness." The human being does not settle on the employment of extreme force after careful deliberation, but rather "dashes . . . to it as to an irresistible temptation."[7]

We must, then, ask: What may profitably be opposed to force? What, if anything, could be stronger than it? We can only answer, Weil thinks, after sustained contemplation of ourselves in this "purest and loveliest of mirrors." The Western world has not yet found the *Iliad*'s counterepic: Perhaps the people of Europe "will yet rediscover the epic genius, when they learn that there is no refuge from fate, learn not to admire force, not to hate the enemy, nor to scorn the unfortunate." But, she adds, in the final words of her essay, "How soon this will happen is another question."[8] In the three remaining years of her life, Weil would devote much of her intellectual energy to the attempt to ask what might prompt and ground an authentic and adequate answer to Homer's "poem of force," an epic of another power, another ethos.

A year or so after writing about the *Iliad*, while living in Marseille and writing for *Les Cahiers du Sud*, Weil sought to find that alternative power in what she called the "Romanesque Renaissance." Her essay is a strange and subtle one that creates curious variations on an all-too-familiar theme: the idealization by nineteenth- and twentieth-century Christians, especially Catholic ones, of medieval Christendom.

The opening sentences of the essay could flow directly from the conclusion of her thoughts on the *Iliad*: "Why dwell upon the past, instead of directing one's thoughts to the future? If people are turning, for the first time in hundreds of years, to contemplate the past is this because we are weary and close to despair? Indeed we are so." And reflection on a poem that teaches us the ultimate and inescapable power of force over us all might, if unaccompanied by other reflections, bring on that despair. "But there are better grounds for contemplating the past." Those grounds arise from recognition of this fact: "We cannot be made better except by the influence upon us of what is better than we are." Now, it may be that in the future there will be societies better than ours, but we do not have access to them—nor will it do any good to exhort us to imagine them, for that just presents us with the intractable problem that *we* are the ones doing the imagining: "the future is empty and is filled by our imagination . . . it is just as imperfect as we are." Therefore we must turn to the past, not because it is necessarily better than our own world, but because it is *different.*[9]

Weil here offers a version of an argument that C. S. Lewis made in his 1939 sermon on "Learning in War-Time." He would return to the point, and expand it, in an introduction to a new English translation of Athanasius's *On the Incarnation of the Word of God.* There he argues, "Every age has its own outlook. It is specially good at seeing certain truths and specially liable to make certain mistakes." All writers of a given period—"even those, like myself, who seem most opposed to it"—"share to some extent the contemporary outlook." We therefore "need the books that will correct the characteristic mistakes of our own period. And that means the old books." Like Weil, Lewis does not believe that there was "any magic about the past. People were no cleverer then than they are now; they made as many mistakes as we. But not the same mistakes." And he adds, again like Weil, "To be sure, the books of the future would be just as good a corrective as the books of the past, but unfortunately we cannot get at them."[10]

Weil's argument in "The Romanesque Renaissance" certainly rhymes with Lewis's, but it is in certain respects more subtle. "The past offers us a partially completed discrimination," she writes. "Our attachments and our passions do not so thickly obscure our discrimination of the eternal in the past." For Weil, the great task of thought is just this, to *discern the eternal*, that which is always and everywhere true but also always and everywhere obscured by the "attachments and passions" of a given person or a given culture. What has survived from the past is the discrimination of the eternal achieved by that time and place, a discrimination that is never complete and never directly mappable onto our own moment but that nevertheless remains of inestimable value. What the past saw clearly is a pearl of great price for us.

However, it is not always easy for us to *read* with clarity the past's achievements. Those same attachments and passions that blind us to the eternal blind us also, and for the same reasons, to the wisdom of our ancestors. This is why for Weil the power of the past to offer us the needful discriminations "is true above all for the past which is temporarily so dead that it offers no food for our passions."[11] No stage of the past is permanently dead; any moment of it can rise up again into full and dramatic life, as the *Iliad* did in the opening months of the war. But the "temporarily dead"—the past that has lost its relevance for us, that seems to bear no analogies to our current situation—we may have the power to read discerningly. Its voice we may just be able to hear.

In this essay, Weil is, I believe, setting her thoughts subtly but firmly apart from those of Maritain. She knew well his 1920 book *Art and Scholasticism*, in which, as we have seen, he celebrated the high Gothic as the pinnacle of Christian art and lamented the cultural fall into the naturalistic humanism of the so-called Renaissance and so-called Enlightenment. Weil does not wholly disagree with this narrative. She speaks, for instance, of "the false Renaissance, which is called by that name today."[12] Like Maritain, she traces a kind of decline. Yet her story takes a very different course, and again, as we saw with the comparison to Lewis on "old books," her account offers subtleties and surprises that the more standard narratives, especially narratives of secularization, lack.

Weil contends that the Romanesque civilization of the tenth and eleventh centuries "was the true Renaissance. The Greek spirit was reborn in the Christian form which is its truth." And for her, one of the key marks of its truth was the ease with which it lived in the midst of, and peacefully tolerated, profanity and error. The center of the Romanesque Renaissance, in Weil's reading, was Languedoc; and Languedoc was also the center of Cathar Christianity, or, from another point of view, the Albigensian heresy. The Albigensian Crusade of the early thirteenth century, which resulted not only in the suppression of the Cathars but the absorption of Languedoc into France, amounted to the "murder" of a country, the "decisive crime" that not only ended the Cathars but also ended the true Renaissance. It was this destruction of a vibrant if chaotic culture that ushered in the Gothic era; and for Weil the whole of the Gothic world should be seen as shadowed by the massive crime that brought it into being. "The Gothic Middle Ages," so praised and celebrated by major European artists and intellectuals from Ruskin to Maritain, were, in Weil's deliberately shocking phrase, "an essay in totalitarian spirituality."[13]

Interestingly, a very similar argument had been made a few years earlier by Charles Williams, in a book that had a major effect on Auden's return to Christianity: in *Descent of the Dove* (subtitled *A Short History of the Holy Spirit in the Church*), he writes of the desire to create "a dominant culture, an achieved society" via "the method of the imposition of belief." These impulses produce "totalitarian minds."[14] It was this temptation to impose belief that, in Weil's view, the Romanesque era resisted. In pre-Gothic Languedoc, "leaving the profane intact, the supernatural thereby retained its purity." But within the new Gothic regime, "the profane as such had no rights any more." This was a disaster not only for the Cathars and other representatives of the profane, but for Christendom itself: "spirituality is necessarily degraded by becoming totalitarian. This is not what Christian civilization is."[15]

Weil knows that her view of that period has massive implications for any account of a subsequent history, and she embraces those implications without flinching. It is true that at the time of what is usually called the Renaissance, "humanism" was produced, and as we have seen, Weil believed that humanism was "poisonous"— and a distinctively Christian kind of poison, or, perhaps it is better to say, one to which Christianity is distinctively prone. Humanism "consists in treating the bridges bequeathed to us by the Greeks as if they were permanent habitations." To be sure, "Humanism was not wrong in thinking that truth, beauty, liberty, and equality are of infinite value"; but it was tragically wrong "in thinking that man can get them for himself without grace."[16] What is usually called humanism, in what is usually called the Renaissance, lost sight of the possibility of a truly Christian culture toward which the insights of Greek paganism pointed, and "from then onwards, the spiritual life of Europe has diminished until it has almost shrunk to nothing." But this diminishment was the unwitting creation of the "spiritual totalitarianism" of the Gothic era: it was against this tyranny that the early modern spirit revolted, and in so doing it was bound to fall into error. In Weil's view, we should not fail to see how the early modern era ushered in a great spiritual decline; but we should assign the causes more accurately, and see that nonreligious, or antireligious, humanism was a genuine attempt, however misguided and doomed to failure, to seek spiritual freedom from the oppression imposed by the "imposition of belief" of the Gothic era. "Today, in the grip of affliction, we feel a loathing for the process which has led to the present situation. We vilify and would reject that humanism which was developed by the Renaissance, the eighteenth century, and the Revolution. But by doing that, so far from raising ourselves, we are throwing away the last faint, confused image that remained to us of man's supernatural vocation."[17] For Weil, *l'humanisme athée* decried by de Lubac, Maritain, and Gilson was an error, but it was an understandable error, and an authentic attempt to reclaim freedom that had been taken away by the "spiritual totalitarianism" of the twelfth and thirteenth centuries. The Church of that time had unwittingly created its own nemesis.

Weil states the conclusion of her brief history flatly and boldly: "It may be that in those early years of the thirteenth century Christianity was faced with a choice. She made an evil choice. She chose evil, and the evil bore fruit and now we are suffering evil."[18] In other words, we find ourselves subject to *force*. Indeed, the totalitarianism of the Gothic era was a kind of contract with force, and effected the transformation of the Church into "the social beast" that "alone possesses force."[19] In a very strong sense, the *Iliad*, the "poem of force," is "the purest and loveliest of mirrors" for twentieth-century Europe because thirteenth-century French kings united in a single course of action a passion for eliminating heresy and an equally strong passion for expanding the reach of their empire. Weil lays her finger on that moment in European history and calls for repentance; and "repentance means going back to the moment which preceded the wrong choice." It means going back beyond the celebrated High Gothic era to the relatively neglected Romanesque era, when leaders of Christendom found they could live in peace with error; when force was at their command but they chose not to employ it. In reading this history, modern Europeans may escape despair by discerning the eternal. In reading it, they may "learn not to admire force, not to hate the enemy, nor to scorn the unfortunate."[20]

* * *

In the misery of France's fall, in May and June 1940, the one bright spot was the successful evacuation of nearly 350,000 soldiers from Dunkirk, on the English Channel. Perhaps it should be called merely a less dark spot: as Churchill—appointed as Prime Minister just a few weeks earlier—commented in the House of Commons, "We must be very careful not to assign to this deliverance the attributes of a victory. Wars are not won by evacuations."

Dunkirk gripped the imagination of Britons in a peculiar but powerful way. The soldiers themselves tended toward anger and resentment at having been effectively abandoned on the beach, but the English people were amazed that they had been rescued at all, and especially by the role that ordinary citizens had played in the rescue. In a BBC radio broadcast, the novelist and playwright J. B. Priestley said of the *Gracie Fields*, a ferryboat from the Isle of Wight that was sunk in the Channel, that "this little steamer . . . is immortal. She'll go sailing proudly down the years in the epic of Dunkirk." And a headline in the *Daily Mirror* read simply, "BLOODY MARVELLOUS."[21]

A less enthusiastic observer of the scene was T. S. Eliot, who from his flat in Kensington wrote a melancholy meditation on the events. E. McKnight Kauffer, of the Ministry of Information, had come up with the idea of an exhibition of photographs of the British war effort, to be displayed in New York with the evident hope of generating American sympathy. Eliot was asked to provide a kind of commentary, and he called it "Defence of the Islands." He would later say that he had Dunkirk on his mind as he wrote. Echoing Thomas Gray's famous "Elegy Written in a Country Churchyard"— "The paths of glory lead but to the grave"—he wrote of those "for whom the paths of glory are the lanes and the streets of Britain," and also those who "fight the power of darkness in air and fire." In a foreshadowing of the great poem he would write two years later, "Little Gidding," he invokes the traditional four elements and discerns those elements as the stage on which history is enacted. What the photographs of the exhibition "say, to the past and the future generations of our kin and of our speech," is merely this: "we took up our positions, in obedience to instructions."[22]

We took up our positions. Eliot by this point had identified himself completely with Englishness, and wished to take up whatever position might be assigned to him—though he knew that at his age his options were limited. In February 1940, he had said of himself and his fellow writers, "We can have very little hope of contributing to any immediate social change; and we are more disposed to see our hope in modest and local beginnings, than in transforming the whole world at once . . . . We must keep alive aspirations which can remain valid throughout the longest and darkest period of universal calamity and degradation."[23]

What those proper "aspirations" might be is a question partly answered by Eliot's ongoing participation in Oldham's Moot, which was making its own "modest and local beginnings" of an inquiry into the restoration of Christian intellectual leadership in Britain. But Eliot was also thinking of the "modest and local beginnings" of his own ancestors in the Somerset village of East Coker, which he had visited in 1937 and about which he had been thinking ever since. He was composing the poem bearing the name of that village as he wrote of the hopes he and his fellow writers should and should not have; and the poem was published just two months before Dunkirk.

In her *Composition of Four Quartets*, Helen Gardner commented that at that dark hour the poem had an extraordinary consoling and encouraging effect on the British reading public: it was reprinted several times in 1940, and in its first year in print sold twelve thousand copies.[24] Seen as a poetic self-assessment, the poem is discouraging: "That was a way of putting it—not very satisfactory," he writes

in immediate response to one of the poem's lyrical movements; and
then, later, more summarily,

> So here I am, in the middle way, having had twenty years—
> Twenty years largely wasted, the years of *l'entre deux guerres*
> Trying to learn to use words, and every attempt
> Is a wholly new start, and a different kind of failure
> Because one has only learnt to get the better of words
> For the thing one no longer has to say, or the way in which
> One is no longer disposed to say it.

This makes "each venture . . . a raid on the inarticulate / With shabby
equipment always deteriorating" and "under conditions / That
seem unpropitious." And yet he continues to work: "For us, there is
only the trying. The rest is not our business."

The ethic undergirding this beautiful and elegant poem is something rather homely: the English self-conception at the time of
Dunkirk, the mustn't-grumble stoicism that allows the people of a
besieged nation to to their duty in "conditions / That seem unpropitious"—a suitably English litotes for being subjected to ceaseless
aerial bombardment.

That stoicism is generally thought to have had its best expression in the rhetoric of the new Prime Minister. In his most famous
speech—just before he expresses his hope that future generations
will say of that moment in British history that "[t]his was their finest
hour"—he presents the moment not as an opportunity for triumph
but rather of effective resistance:

> The whole fury and might of the enemy must very soon be turned
> on us. Hitler knows that he will have to break us in this Island or
> lose the war. If we can stand up to him, all Europe may be free and

the life of the world may move forward into broad, sunlit uplands. But if we fail, then the whole world, including the United States, including all that we have known and cared for, will sink into the abyss of a new Dark Age made more sinister, and perhaps more protracted, by the lights of perverted science.[25]

The language of "perverted science" indicates the general belief that the Nazis were masters of new and unprecedentedly dangerous technologies; this belief is accompanied, as it usually was, by the conviction that the only forces capable of offering meaningful resistance to such technologies were moral, were forces of character.

"East Coker" is, more than anything else, a reinterpretation of the events of the war as spiritual trial and discipline. Section 4 in particular counsels acceptance of suffering as necessary to restoration: if the poem's speaker is "to be warmed," then he must first "freeze / And quake in frigid purgatorial fires." Such harsh measures are "the sharp compassion of the healer's art."[26] It is possible to read the poem without regarding the "unpropitious" moment of its composition—indeed, most of its readers surely have—and Eliot would surely have agreed with Lewis, in his sermon on "Learning in War-Time," that "the war creates no absolutely new situation; it simply aggravates the permanent human situation so that we can no longer ignore it. Human life has always been lived on the edge of a precipice."[27] But at the time of its first publication, so general a reading would have been effectively impossible. "East Coker" was an expression in specifically Christian terms of a stoic fortitude that almost everyone in Britain aspired to achieve, and it was an attempt to be simultaneously universal and topical. The last line of part 4 concludes, "in spite of that, we call this Friday good"—and the poem was published on Maundy Thursday 1940: the day before that year's Good Friday.

A similar doubleness of vision characterizes the next poem in the sequence, "The Dry Salvages," which appeared eleven months later. It would not be wrong to say that the metaphorical environment of the poem is determined by its being the Quartet of Water ("Burnt Norton" being of Air, "East Coker" of Earth, "Little Gidding" of Fire); but it is also a poem written in an island nation, surrounded by the sea, traditionally dependent on its Navy rather than its Army—simultaneously protected and endangered by its maritime character (thus the earlier "Defence of the Islands"). So when Eliot addresses

> O voyagers, O seamen,
> You who come to port, and you whose bodies
> Will suffer the trial and judgment of the sea

—or pleads, "Lady, whose shrine stands on the promontory, / Pray for all those who are in ships"[28]—we should remember the war-time efforts of the British Navy; we should remember Dunkirk; we should remember that an entire section of the Book of Common Prayer is devoted to "Forms of Prayer to Be Used at Sea." The poem is simultaneously elemental, Christian, British, and highly topical.

* * *

Just after Eliot had published "East Coker," and only a few days before delivering the celebrated "Their Finest Hour" speech of June 18, 1940, Churchill had uttered what would prove to be his most lastingly famous words: he said that he had "nothing to offer but blood, toil, tears and sweat." The following March, when "The Dry Salvages" was newly in print and he was preparing a speech for the BBC to be called "Towards a Christian Britain," Eliot remembered Churchill's phrase. Writing to Philip Mairet, he commented, "I was, and am, wanting to give them blood and sweat, and not promise them a Christian happy land as the reward for the Churchill blood and sweat."[29]

"Towards a Christian Britain" might be seen as the first of several prose sequels to his 1939 book *The Idea of a Christian Society*, which had been, even for Eliot, a masterpiece of vagueness and evasion. One of the book's most persistent and curious tics involves its disavowals: "this book does not make any plea for a 'religious revival' in a sense with which we are already familiar"; "what I am concerned with here is not spiritual institutions in their separated aspect"; "I am not at this moment concerned with the means for bringing a Christian Society into existence; I am not even primarily concerned with making it appear desirable"; "[w]ith religious Liberalism, however, I am no more specifically concerned than with political Liberalism.... Nor am I concerned with the politics of a revolutionary party"; "I am not concerned with the problem of Christians as a persecuted minority"; "I am not here concerned with the problem of how radically [the parish system of the Church of England] must be modified to suit a future state of things"; "I am not here concerned with the means by which a Christian society could be brought about"; "[w]ith the reform of the Establishment I am not here concerned"; "I am not here concerned with what must occupy the mind of anyone approaching the subject of Education directly, that is the question of what should be done *now*."[30]

Even when Eliot confesses a "concern," he may then immediately disavow it:

I am not concerned with rationalistic pacifism, or with humanitarian pacifism, but with Christian pacifism—that which asserts that all warfare is categorically forbidden to followers of Our

Lord. This absolute Christian pacifism should be distinguished again from another: that which would assert that only a *Christian* society is worth fighting for, and that a particular society may fall so far short, or may be so positively anti-Christian, that no Christian will be justified or excused for fighting for it. With this relative Christian pacifism I cannot be concerned, because my hypothesis is that of a Christian Society.[31]

To this point in his career, Eliot had been a poet and literary critic, with only occasional forays into larger matters of public concern; and he cannot have failed to be aware of the ambiguities of his status as, though a subject of the King, a *metoikos*, a resident alien—"the American gentleman" (see note 23 in this chapter). And yet he has allied himself with those who "take up our positions, in obedience to instructions." So he oscillates between speech and the withdrawal of speech; this is understandable enough, but a rather maddening dance for the reader to attempt to track.

With considerable relief, then, this reader turns from these oscillations and evasions to "Towards a Christian Britain." It is a short talk, but serves as an effective bridge between the obliquities of *The Idea of a Christian Society* and the more highly developed critique Eliot would articulate in 1942 and 1943, in a series of essays that eventually lead to *Notes towards the Definition of Culture* (1948). The British people had been schooled, since 1939, in the need for sacrifice, and indeed "a Christian Britain demands sacrifice from all," he writes, but this sacrifice is "beyond our power as human beings." However, "this knowledge should bring not discouragement but a greater hope," at least for Christians who understand that human influence is not the only influence at work in the world. But we need "prophets" to help us grasp this hope, prophets "who have lived through the mind of this dark age, and got beyond it."[32]

Eliot cites as an example of such a prophet Charles de Foucauld, a French priest who lived for years with the Tuareg in southern Algeria and was killed by bandits in 1916. "I think that is it through such men as Foucauld that the reborn Christian consciousness comes; and I think that from the point of view which we should take, there is no higher glory of a Christian empire than that which was here brought into being by a death in the desert"—a direct reference to Robert Browning's poem of that name, and perhaps particularly to these words: "For I say, this is death and the sole death, / When a man's loss comes to him from his gain."

It is rather curious, to say the least, that in a talk on "Christian Britain" Eliot would hold up as an exemplary figure a French Catholic priest who died in a foreign land. Yet Charles Foucauld, like Eliot's listeners, was no soldier but rather an ordinary citizen, endangered in time of war through no choice of his own, shot dead as he was merely pursuing his calling—something that could happen to any of those listeners, as it happened to Wormwood's "patient" in *The Screwtape Letters*, struck down in his youth and health by a German bomb in the streets of London. Eliot seems to be suggesting that "Christian Britain" will only become possible if his listeners become seriously and primarily Christian—if their national identity, even in time of war, plays a secondary role. To orient oneself to the Christian life is to realize that "the reward for the Churchill blood and sweat" may not be "a Christian happy land" but rather a martyr's death. To *refuse* such martyrdom is, as Browning puts it, "death and the sole death."

In "The Dry Salvages," published, again, just a few weeks before Eliot gave this address, he wrote,

But to apprehend
The point of intersection of the timeless

With time, is an occupation for the saint—
No occupation either, but something given
And taken, in a lifetime's death in love,
Ardour and selflessness and self-surrender.[33]

Surely Charles Foucauld is one of the saints he thought of as he wrote those lines. The ordinary person will not experience the full grace within which the saint lives, however painfully, but will have "only hints and guesses, / Hints followed by guesses"; anything more will come only through "prayer, observance, discipline, thought and action." Eliot often said that the three *Quartets* that he wrote during the war—"East Coker," "The Dry Salvages," and "Little Gidding"—"are primarily patriotic poems," and this is, as we have seen, true; but it leaves unspoken the degree to which they revise and decenter the typical impulses of patriotism.[34]

* * *

Throughout the war, Eliot led an unsettled life. He had no home: he left the flat in Kensington he had lived in for several years and lived chiefly as a paid lodger in the village of Shamley Green, in Surrey near Guildford, with the writer Hope Mirrlees and her extended family, commuting by train to his job at Faber in London. When commuting was impractical, he stayed with Geoffrey Faber and family in Hampstead, or, later in the war, in a tiny flat at the office. Meanwhile he kept up an extraordinary range of social and intellectual commitments: he continued to participate in the Moot as well as a similar gathering, focusing more on economic and sociological issues, called the Chandos Group; he wrote for the Oldham-associated periodical called the *Christian News Letter*; he gave lectures to all sorts of groups throughout England, made a lecture tour to Sweden in 1942, served on Church of England committees—an astonishing whirl of activity for someone who often, in his letters, complains about illness and exhaustion. Ezra Pound even wanted him to collaborate with George Santayana on a project envisioning "the ideal University," though nothing came of that.[35] But when he began to work seriously on the poems that became the *Four Quartets*, he stayed away from London as much as possible. While he had in some odd sense enjoyed serving as an air raid warden in Kensington—an experience that, as we shall see, made its way into "Little Gidding"—the chaos and the crush of daily London life had been at best enormously challenging for him. Once he wrote to the Greek poet George Seferis that he hated having to take shelter in an underground station during an air raid: "I would feel the need to get out as quickly as possible, to escape all those faces gathered there, to escape all that humanity."[36]

Retreating to Shamley Green, he could focus on those things that were, rather than fleeting and unpredictable, permanent or repetitive. As Lyndall Gordon has rightly noted, "Repetition is the very message of *Four Quartets*: to try again and yet again for the perfect life, and not to look for the fruits of action, an end to the pilgrimage."[37] It was necessary for him to connect himself to the long past—to the Somerset village of East Coker where his ancestors had lived for centuries, to the New England coast where they had come in the seventeenth century—and deep in that past find a wellspring of meaningful action, or stability, in the present moment.

> All this begins with waiting.
> I said to my soul, be still, and wait without hope
> For hope would be hope for the wrong thing; wait without love,
> For love would be love of the wrong thing; there is yet faith
> But the faith and the love and the hope are all in the waiting.[38]

In the long slow martyrdom of waiting and listening, one stands a chance of hearing the word of consolation, or the word of authority. "We took up our positions, in obedience to instructions." It is in this frame of mind that one may possibly perceive a spiritual world that transcends the rule of force that governs everyday wartime life.

* * *

From the spring of 1942 until her death in August 1943, Simone Weil's travels took her on a great arc from Marseilles to Casablanca to New York to London. Once she saw to it that her parents were safe in New York, she would have returned, had she had her way, to France; but this proved impossible, and her circuit remained incomplete. In her mental life, this period traced not a parabola but an expanding circle, as her attempt to understand her own spiritual autobiography led her outward toward questions of the largest social and political consequence. It may seem strange that an internal debate on whether to undergo baptism would lead to something like a fully articulated political philosophy, but in Weil's mind this is precisely what happened.

In May 1942, Weil wrote a series of letters to her unofficial confessor, Father Perrin, in which she tried to explain to him, though perhaps more to herself, why she had not asked for the sacrament of Holy Baptism and why she might not in the future. The letters oscillate between a confessional and a lecturing tone, and were it not for Weil's terrifyingly intense earnestness, there would be something comical about her desire to instruct the priest in a range of theological topics. "I have been wondering lately about the will of God, what it means, and how we can reach the point of conforming ourselves to it completely—I will tell you what I think about this." "I have also been thinking about the nature of the sacraments, and

I will tell you what I think about this subject as well." It is hard to imagine that she would have *asked* Father Perrin for his or his Church's views on these matters; indeed, at the end of her first letter, she seems to warn the priest away from any attempt to correct her: "It may well be that some of the thoughts I have just confided to you are illusory and defective. In a sense this matters little to me; I do not want to go on examining any more."[39]

Sacraments are traditionally understood to be "means of grace," and while Weil acknowledges that she is in need of God's grace and is willing to ask for it, she effectively dissociates that need from her thoughts about whether to be baptized. "I think that only those who are above a certain level of spirituality can participate in the sacraments as such." She understands herself not to have reached the requisite level and on those grounds declines baptism. And she further believes that this shortcoming is her fault and must be amended by the full exercise of her own powers: "God rewards the soul that thinks of him with attention and love, and he rewards it by exercising a compulsion upon it strict and mathematically proportionate to this attention and this love."[40] The idea that God might freely and graciously reveal himself to someone who has not fully earned that revelation is simply alien to Weil's strenuous theology.

This articulation of a spiritual algebra comprised of cold and inflexible equations may call to mind Weil's complex (though always affectionate) relationship with her mathematician brother, André. "The exceptional gifts of my brother," she writes in a later letter, "who had a childhood and youth comparable to those of Pascal, brought my own inferiority home to me."[41] The particular pain she felt at her inferiority "was the idea of being excluded from that transcendent kingdom to which only the truly great have access and wherein truth abides." She says, and I think without exaggeration, that she would prefer to die than to live so excluded from those truths accessible only to the great. But she did not die; and her strategy for living seems to have involved as a central component the redescription of her "exclusion" as an opportunity and even a vocation:

> I suddenly had the everlasting conviction that any human being, even though practically devoid of natural faculties, can penetrate to the kingdom of truth reserved for genius, if only he longs for truth and perpetually concentrates all his attention upon its attainment. He thus becomes a genius too, even though for lack of talent his genius cannot be visible from the outside.[42]

She acquired this "everlasting conviction" when she was fifteen, and it clearly stayed with her: it provides the foundation for the talk she gave, at about the same time as her letters to Father Perrin, "Reflections on the Right Use of School Studies with a View to the Love of God," where she speaks of the ways that even academic failures, if the student is fully attentive and works diligently, can bear fruit in other dimensions of life, such as prayer.[43] But she clearly believed this idea to be of special importance for her, an insight into her distinctive religious vocation. Just as she was called to be one who without genius longed to enter the kingdom of truth, so too, and in much the same way, was she called to remain always *outside* the household of the Church while nevertheless seeking with all her heart and soul what is to be found only there. "I cannot help still wondering whether . . . God does not want there to be some men and women who have given themselves to him and to Christ and who yet remain outside the church." And then, in the next letter, she writes no longer speculatively but conclusively: "I feel that it is necessary and ordained that I should be alone, a stranger and an exile in relation to every human circle without exception."[44]

She is at pains to insist, to Father Perrin, that she does not stay outside because she is "of a very individualistic temperament"—on the contrary: "I am aware of very strong gregarious tendencies in myself. My natural disposition is to be very easily influenced, too much influenced, and above all by anything collective. I know that if at this moment I had before me a group of twenty young Germans singing Nazi songs in chorus, a part of my soul would instantly become Nazi." And this confession leads her to another dimension of her resistance to the Church: "I am afraid of the Church patriotism existing in Catholic circles . . . . I am afraid of it because I fear to catch it."[45] The danger of this infection, she believes, may be seen in the tendency of even great saints to approve of such manifest injustices as the Crusades or the Inquisition—acts of, to recall her phrase about the edifice of Christendom in the high Gothic era, "spiritual totalitarianism." It is partly, perhaps chiefly, in order to bear witness against such patriotic perversity—and such a rule of force in the one place from which force should be exiled—that she is called to a love *of* the Church expressed only *outside* it.

Here we might recall her treatment of the Cathars in "The Romanesque Renaissance," where she suggests that in suppressing them Christendom suppressed some uncomfortable truths: the Cathars' "horror of force was carried to the point of practicing non-violence and to the doctrine which sees everything associated with the domain of force as originating in evil: namely, everything carnal and everything social. That was going far," she concedes, "but not further than the gospel."[46] Weil makes it clear, in the "Spiritual Autobiography" that she wrote for Father Perrin, that in her own outsider status she identifies with the Cathars, in both the truths that they perceived and the heresies for which they were condemned: "In my eyes Christianity is catholic by right but not in fact. So many things are outside it, so many things that I love and do not want to give up, so many things that God loves . . . all the traditions banned as heretical, those of the Manicheans and Alibgenses [another name for the Cathars] for instance; all those things resulting from the Renaissance"—that despised "humanist" Renaissance—"too often degraded but not quite without value."[47]

For Weil, the Church's "right" to determine within and without—the power it claims from Christ's promise to his apostles, "what you bind on earth will be bound in heaven; what you loose on earth will be loosed in heaven"—generates a logic of exclusion that Weil, in her relentless identification with the excluded, cannot endorse except *as* one of those the church excludes. In New York, a few months after composing her spiritual autobiography, she wrote a letter to a priest in which she listed her own heresies: the total came to thirty-five. One suspects that she would have made it a thousand if she could have.[48]

Weil's reasoning on these matters leads her to extreme conclusions, but as usual she embraces the extremity. She grounds her position in a reading of Jesus's temptation by Satan in the wilderness (Luke 4). For her, the fact that Satan offers Jesus dominion over "all the kingdoms of the world"—that he has the *power* to make such an offer—demonstrates that "the social is irremediably the domain of the devil."[49] Thus her most common designation throughout her work of the social order: the Social Beast, the Beast. Not just her view of the Church but also the entire political philosophy she elaborates in the final year of her life emerges from this single decisive point. She acknowledges that "the Church must inevitably be a social structure"; nevertheless, "in so far as it is a social structure, it belongs to the Prince of this World." It is just because she discerns this truth that it is "necessary and ordained" that she should be "a stranger and an exile in relation to every human circle without exception." From the outside of the Church, she can remind the

Church of what it must (but dare not) know about itself. And she does this for love of the Church; indeed, she is so constituted that it is *only* in such critique that she can manifest that love.

And yet despite this fear and loathing of the social Beast, this suspicion of all the kingdoms, ecclesial and political, that belong to the Prince of this World who is also therefore the Prince of force, Weil loved France and, when driven away from it, longed to return. In the few months that she lived in New York—her brother André had arranged for their parents to be resettled there for the duration of the war, and Simone had accompanied them—she sought desperately to get back to France by any means possible. But her ideal, her great goal, was to establish what seemed to others a bizarre institution, a kind of sacred company of front-line nurses: women who would treat wounded soldiers on the battlefield, not in a hospital safely behind the lines. Almost as soon as she arrived in New York she wrote to Jacques Maritain, seeking his help: she seems to have wanted him to arrange for her to meet with President Roosevelt. (She also told him a bit about her own peculiar spiritual situation, and he put her in touch with the priest to whom she made her list of heresies.)

Needless to say, Weil did not meet with the president. (Eventually her plan for a front-line nursing corps was put before General de Gaulle, who simply declared her insane.) She spent all her time in New York seeking for ways to get back to France, consoling herself only with weekly attendance at a Baptist church in Harlem—and once, a visit to a synagogue of Ethiopian Jews: the only time in her life she ever entered a synagogue. To an English soldier she had heard on the radio, she wrote a typically passionate letter: "Now I find myself among comfort and security, far from the danger and the hunger, and I feel a deserter. I cannot bear that . . . . I would welcome *any* degree of danger if only I could do something really useful. My life is of no value to me so long as Paris, my native city, is subject to German domination. Nor do I wish the town to be freed only with the blood of others."[50]

* * *

Weil's self-accusing confession of her susceptibility to "anything collective"—"I know that if at this moment I had before me a group of twenty young Germans singing Nazi songs in chorus, a part of my soul would instantly become Nazi"—is a reminder both of the enormous power of collectivist ideologies and of a general sense, among the intelligentsia of the Western democracies, that such power had to be resisted. And yet the war could not be fought if some analogue to the power of collectivism were not found. Auden experienced some of the complexities of this situation in early 1939, soon after his arrival in the United States. He gave a speech at a dinner in New York convened to raise money for refugees from the Spanish Civil War, and, as he later reported to an English friend, "I suddenly found I could really do it, that I could make a fighting demagogic speech and have the audience roaring. So exciting but so absolutely degrading. I felt just covered with dirt afterwards."[51] From then on, he gave no political speeches, a decision that left him open to charges of indifference to the great cause of the war—charges intensified when he declined to return to England after war broke out. In 1940, a Member of Parliament proposed that Auden and his friend Christopher Isherwood be forcibly returned to England and conscripted into the military, or, if that proved impossible, be deprived of their citizenship. Auden simply ignored these and other provocations. He wrote to his brother John, "All that we can do, we who are spared the horrors, is to be happy and not pretend out of a sense of guilt that we are not, to study as hard as we can, and keep our feeble little lamps burning in the big wind."[52] And this he surely believed. But he also knew the temptations his quiet study was protecting him from.

A comical version of Weil's anxiety about her vulnerability to the pressures of the collective may be found in a letter C. S. Lewis wrote to his brother Warnie in July 1940. He reports that their friend Humphrey Havard paid him a visit and "we listened to Hitler's speech together. I don't know if I'm weaker than other people: but it's a positive revelation to me how *while the speech lasts* it is impossible not to waver just a little. I should be useless as a schoolmaster or a policeman. Statements which I *know* to be untrue all but convince me, at any rate for the moment, if only the man says them unflinchingly."[53] In this case, and crucially, what was being articulated so unflinchingly was a vision of a chaotic world brought to order by a shared obedience to a single Leader. And while Lewis was just as convinced as Weil that opponents of totalitarianism had to be attentive to the danger of replacing Hitler's authoritarian collectivism with one of their own— we may recall his discomfort at the war's outset with prayers in church that God prosper "our righteous cause"—his response to that danger was quite dramatically different than hers. He remained *within*— within the familiar English social order, within the walls of an ancient college in an ancient university, within the Established Church of his adopted homeland—a homeland for which he had fought in the previous war, though as a native of Ireland he had not been required or even expected to. And from within he served as faithfully as he knew how. But such a road was not for Weil.

In a wonderful book on reading and interpretation, *The Genesis of Secrecy*, Frank Kermode writes eloquently about one of the most peculiar and troubling cruxes in the text of the Gospels. In Matthew's Gospel, Jesus, after explaining one of his parables to his disciples, refers to the great crowds that gather to listen to him: "The reason I speak to them in parables is that 'seeing they do not perceive, and hearing they do not listen, nor do they understand'" (13:13; the quotation there is from the prophet Isaiah). But in Mark's Gospel, he says that "to those outside, everything comes in parables, *in order that* 'they may indeed look, but not perceive, and may indeed listen, but not understand; so that they may not turn again and be forgiven'" (4:12; emphasis added). In the first text, people exclude themselves by their indifference; in the second, they are forcibly excluded from the beginning. The dedication of Kermode's book reads, simply and without explanation: *To Those Outside.* To "those outside," Simone Weil dedicated not a book but her whole life.

Interlude

Other Pilgrims, Other Paths

January 1943

Just after Pearl Harbor, Dorothy Day had reaffirmed the Catholic Worker movement's commitment to pacifism: "Our manifesto is the Sermon on the Mount, which means that we will try to be peacemakers . . . . We will not participate in armed warfare or in making munitions, or by buying government bonds to prosecute the war, or in urging others to those efforts." Now, in New York City, she writes in her newsletter, with some satisfaction, that she and her colleagues had been at their work of maintaining "houses of hospitality where the works of mercy can be practiced through voluntary poverty" for a full decade. She is grateful for what has been achieved, but pleads for more help. She quotes Eric Gill, the English Catholic artist who had died in 1940, claiming Gill's goal as her own: "to make a cell of good living in the chaos of our world."[1]

*   *   *

In Sumter County, Georgia, two couples—Clarence and Florence Jordan, Mabel and Martin England—are in the first full month of their experiment in intentional interracial community, Koinonia Farm. (*Koinonia* is a New Testament Greek word meaning "fellowship.") By living with people of all races, growing their own food, and bearing daily witness to the possibility of living according to the teachings of Jesus, they hope to build a "demonstration plot for the kingdom of God."[2]

* * *

In Berlin, Dietrich Bonhoeffer is spending the Christmas season with his parents and other family members. He too commemorates a one-decade anniversary: the rise of Hitler to power in Germany. He sits down to write a summary of what he and his fellow German Christians have learned in that decade: he calls it, "After Ten Years: A Reckoning Made at New Year's 1943." In it he says, "We have been the silent witnesses of evil deeds. We have become cunning and learned the arts of obfuscation and equivocation." But though "the huge masquerade of evil has thrown all ethical concepts into confusion," some things have been seen clearly: "that evil [appears] in the form of bright, good deeds, historical necessity, social justice"; and, above all, "the failure of '*the reasonable ones*'—those who think with the best of intentions and in their naive misreading of reality, that with a bit of reason they can patch up the structure that has come out of joint." In such circumstances, "Who stands firm?" His answer: "Only the one whose ultimate standard is not his reason, his principles, conscience, freedom, or virtue; only the one who is prepared to sacrifice all of these when, in faith and in relationship to God alone, he is called to obedient and responsible action." Soon after he writes these words, the Gestapo begin to prepare a case against him for his role in plots against Hitler. In April they will arrest him and take him to prison; in a different prison, two years later, he will be shot.[3]

* * *

In Freetown, Sierra Leone, in the middle of 1942, Graham Greene had found enough free time from his work in military intelligence—his boss back in London is Kim Philby, later to be notorious as one of the "Cambridge Spies" for the Soviet Union— to write an "entertainment" centered on the experience of the Blitz. Fearing that the typescript might not make it safely to London, he had sent it off in three parts between September and November. By January, *Ministry of Fear* is out, reviews are appearing, and movie rights are assigned. (The movie, directed by the German émigré Fritz Lang and starring Ray Milland, will appear in 1944.) Greene is languishing in Freetown, hoping for a quick return to London. "I felt sick in the stomach when I heard the Germans had started on London again," he writes to his mother on January 19, as the Casablanca Conference was proceeding father up the West African coast. "I feel I'd be of much more use back [serving as an air warden]. One feels out of it in this colony of escapists with their huge drinking parties and their complete unconsciousness of what war is like."[4]

In *Ministry of Fear*, the protagonist, a man named Rowe, finds himself in a London auction room scanning a row of books:

Just on the level of his eyes was a Roman missal of no particular value .... The missal was ornamented with ugly colored capitals; oddly enough, it was the only thing that spoke of war in the old quiet room. Open it where you would, you came on prayers for deliverance, the angry nations, the unjust, the wicked, the adversary like a roaring lion .... The words stuck out between the decorated borders like a cannon out of a flower bed. "Let not man prevail," he read—and the truth of the appeal chimed like music. For in all the world outside that room man had indeed prevailed; he had himself prevailed. It wasn't only evil men who did these things. Courage smashes a cathedral, endurance lets a city starve, pity kills .... We are trapped and betrayed by our virtues.[5]

Later in the story, Rowe opens a suitcase with a bomb inside it. He survives, but loses his memory. He no longer remembers that he had killed—a "mercy killing"—his own wife. He does not know who Hitler is, or that his country is in the midst of a war. The section of the book describing Rowe's amnesiac experience is entitled "The Happy Man."

* * *

In the northern Chinese city then known as Tientsin (now Tianjin), a Scottish missionary mulls over the ever-spreading gossip: people say the occupying army of Japan will soon round up all foreign nationals in the city and place them in an internment camp. He realizes that he has already missed his chance to return to the West, to his wife and daughters, then living in Toronto. This Scotsman had been born in Tientsin in 1902 and had returned there to serve after being educated in England and Scotland, and after having won a gold medal at the 1924 Paris Olympics in the 400-meter run and a bronze in the 200 meters. His name is Eric Liddell, and in March he will be taken to the Weihsien internment camp, and will die there, of a brain tumor, in February 1945. Decades later, Langdon Gilkey, an American interned with Liddell, will offer a recollection: "Often in an evening I would see him bent over a chessboard or a model boat, or directing some sort of square dance—absorbed, weary and interested, pouring all of himself into this effort to capture the imagination of these penned-up youths. He was overflowing with good humour and love for life, and with enthusiasm and charm. It is rare indeed that a person has the good fortune to meet a saint, but he came as close to it as anyone I have ever known."[6]

Chapter 6

The Year of Our Lord 1943

In December 1942, writing a foreword to an English translation of *The Twilight of Civilization*, Jacques Maritain commented on the apparent despair of his title: "If twilight ushers in night, night itself precedes day. And in human history it often happens that the first rays of a dawn are mingled with the twilight." This was his hope. Perhaps "the present trials endured by civilization" prepare the Western world for "a *new humanism*," which can in turn help bring about "the renewal of civilization."[1] The Terry Lectures he gave at Yale were, then, a looking-forward to what might be done when the long night of Europe is over and the day comes again, bringing the light in which one can work.

In the opening moments of his first lecture, on January 14, 1943, Maritain moves with remarkable swiftness to identify the issues that must underlie any valid account of what education is and what it does. The first step he takes in this endeavor is to identify his own period as, to borrow again a phrase from Mark Greif, "the age of the crisis of Man": education, Maritain asserts, "cannot escape the problems and entanglements of philosophy, for it supposes by its very nature a philosophy of man, and from the outset it is obliged to answer the question: 'What is man?' which the philosophical sphinx is asking."[2]

Therefore, he says, in thinking about education, we must choose between the two generally possible pictures of Man, that offered by science and that offered by religion, more particularly Christianity. And if we opt for the scientific picture, we shall soon find ourselves at sea, since "to ask what is the nature and the destiny of man"—I assume that the invocation of Niebuhr's recent book of that title is deliberate—is to attempt "to draw from [science] a kind of metaphysics," which runs contrary to the nature of science. The *theoretical* result would be "a spurious metaphysics disguised as science and yet deprived of any really philosophical insight"—that is, a metaphysics that *claimed* a scientific warrant without the power to justify itself scientifically. Even worse would be the *practical* result: "a denial or misconception of those very realities and values without which education loses all human sense or becomes the training of an animal for the utility of the state."[3]

That a putatively, but not actually, scientific model of the human being would transform us into animals trained "for the utility of the state" is a constant theme of writers in this period: obviously it generates the governing allegory of Orwell's *Animal Farm*. But less than the animal is the numerical: thus Auden's "The Unknown Citizen," written in March 1939, just after his arrival in the States, presents an inscription dedicated thus:

(To JS/07 M 378
This Marble Monument Is Erected by the State)

The model is of course the creation of a Tomb of the Unknown Soldier, a practice that began in England after the Great War and spread to France and the United States. John Keegan, in his magisterial account of that earlier war, suggests that the victors' refusal to allow Germans to honor their own dead in a similar way was instrumental to the growing resentment in Germany that led to the rise of Hitler. Indeed, Hitler and his propagandists referred to him as "the living embodiment of the 'unknown soldier.'" But the rest had to be content to be *numbered* rather than *named* among what the Cenotaph in London calls "The Glorious Dead"; and Auden imagines a future in which every citizen, as well as every lost soldier, can aspire to no more than numerical identification.

> He was married and added five children to the population,
> Which our Eugenist says was the right number for a parent of his generation,
> And our teachers report that he never interfered with their education.
> Was he free? Was he happy? The question is absurd:
> Had anything been wrong, we should certainly have heard.[4]

It is against the animal and numerical modes of accounting for human beings—two ways of "losing all human sense"—that Maritain wants to resist by grounding education in a commitment to personalism. "To say that a man is a person is to say that in the depth of his being he is more a whole than a part and more independent than servile. It is this mystery of our nature which religious thought designates when it says that the person is the image of God."[5]

Maritain was very aware, when speaking to his American audience, of the great tradition of American individualism, so a key distinction Maritain makes at the outset of his lectures is that between the individual and the person. An individual, in Maritain's usage, is merely a *material* individual, "a fragment of a species, a part of the physical universe, a single dot in the immense network of forces and influences, cosmic, ethnic, historic, whose laws we must obey." (The individual is, to use a phrase C. S. Lewis makes much of in his great lecture on "Membership," a member of a set, interchangeable for all practical purposes—emphasis on "practical"—with other members of the same set. Or, in the language that Auden often uses, the individual belongs to nature, whereas only persons dwell in history.[6])

Maritain does not want to deny that human beings are animals, and that their animal nature may be taken into account and in certain respects trained. What he wants to deny is that our animal nature is the whole of us. "A kind of animal training, which deals with psychophysical habits, conditioned reflexes, sense-memorization, etc., undoubtedly plays its part in education: it refers to material individuality, or to what is not specifically human in man. But education is not animal training. The education of man is a human awakening." And what one awakens *to* Maritain calls aspiration, and what the human person aspires to is freedom. Though Maritain acknowledges that some attention needs to be given, in education, to enabling people to make a living—"the children of man are not made for aristocratic leisure"—he believes that "this practical aim is best provided by the general human capacities developed" through education. "Thus," Maritain writes, "the prime goal of education is the conquest of internal and spiritual freedom to be achieved by the individual person, or, in other words, his liberation through knowledge and wisdom, good will, and love."[7]

Like Lewis and Weil, Maritain is concerned that too much emphasis can be placed on subordination to what Weil calls the social Beast. While "it is obvious that man's education must be concerned with the social group and prepare him to play his part in it," and therefore it is true in a sense that "[m]an finds himself by subordinating himself to the group," nevertheless, "[t]he ultimate end of education concerns the human person in his personal life and spiritual progress, not in his relationship to the social environment." It is vital, Maritain believes, to grasp "that man has secrets which escape the group and a vocation which is not included in the group."[8]

It is not easy for Maritain to say exactly how important education is to human freedom. On the one hand, he wants to insist that "for man and human life there is indeed nothing greater than intuition and love," and moreover that "neither intuition nor love is a matter of training and learning." We all know this, which is why, as he points out, "there are courses in philosophy, but no courses in wisdom." That is because "wisdom is gained through spiritual experience," which in turn is why "the saints and martyrs are the true educators of mankind"—not the teachers. And yet Maritain nevertheless wants to insist that, though intuition and love cannot be taught, "education should be primarily concerned with them." The best summary I can make of Maritain's subtle argument goes like this: Though intuition and love cannot be taught directly, it is the task of the teacher to help form young people so that when the opportunity comes, outside of school, for them to acquire intuition and love, they will be prepared to do so. Teachers, then, play a pivotal role in the building and sustaining of meaningful human culture: if they do not intervene in young people's lives, in the indirect yet distinctive way that only they can, the culture will surely, if slowly, fall. Therefore "it is . . . with the art of medicine that the art of education must be compared." Doctors heal "by imitating the ways of nature herself in her operations, and by helping nature, by providing appropriate diet and remedies that nature herself uses, according to her own dynamism, toward a biological equilibrium." When this method is understood, it will become clear that "medicine is *ars cooperativa naturae*, an art of ministering, an art subservient to nature. And so is education."[9]

In Maritain's account, what the well-educated person is healed from is *bondage*—bondage to "bad energies." He talks throughout *Education at the Crossroads* about freedom: "Education must center on the development and liberation of the individual person." "The task of the teacher is above all one of liberation. To liberate the good energies is the best way of repressing the bad ones."[10] But it is vital to distinguish between this radical freedom and "the mere freeing of the material ego." The radical freedom which is so vital to the person can only be achieved with "discipline and asceticism, as well as the necessity of striving towards self-perfection." If you ignore that and focus on freeing the material ego, then "instead of fulfilling himself, man disperses himself and disintegrates." But as bad as this false notion of freedom may be, promoting anarchy rather than freedom, it is perhaps less tragic than the "despotic conception" that moves "first to take out our heart, with anesthetics if possible, and next to replace it by some perfect organ standardized according to the rules of what everyone ought to be . . . . Instead of a genuine human personality, sealed with the mysterious face of its creator, there appears a mask, that of the conventional man or that of the rubber-stamped conscience, 'incorporated.'"[11]

In these lectures, Maritain spells out this vision for education with particular reference to the impediments he sees to its realization—impediments in the form of these two alternative conceptions of what education is for, or, more precisely, what education is meant to *produce*. The *despotic* model he associates with the deformations of totalitarianism; the *anarchic* model with the Western democracies at their worst, which is to say, when they are unable to conceive of freedom as anything other than the absence of constraint. If we remember that Maritain was speaking at the moment of the Casablanca Conference, when the American entry into the war on both fronts had permanently altered the balance of military power in favor of the Allies, his double focus makes sense. The despotic European present was even then giving way to a possibly anarchic American future, something that Maritain saw with particular clarity as he took temporary refuge in the New World while awaiting the material death and—he devoutly hoped—spiritual resurrection of the Old.

Maritain seems to be thinking that American educators must learn from the cultural collapse of Europe, not because they are likely to repeat the European mistakes, but because they may well commit others that arise from the very different but equally heedless momentum of their society. That is, what Americans need to learn from Europe's catastrophe is the danger of failing to cultivate intellectual and spiritual aspirations beyond what one's everyday culture encourages. In Europe, what had primarily impeded genuine education was a false and ultimately poisonous model of group identity—as manifested, for instance, in the belief in an intrinsically "German physics" that had led the Nazi regime to expel most of its Jewish scientists. In America, the chief impediment to genuine education was technocratic pragmatism. Both paths led, in their different ways, to the death of deep education and therefore, ultimately, to the death of genuine human culture.

Maritain believed that these challenges needed to be faced with moral clarity and intellectual energy because, at the moment when he was speaking, and on all political sides, education was assuming what he believed to be an unnaturally and inappropriately central role:

> As a result of the present disintegration of family life, of a crisis in morality and the break between religion and life, and finally of a crisis in the political state and the civic conscience, and the necessity for democratic states to rebuild themselves according to new patterns, there is a tendency, everywhere, to burden education with remedying all these deficiencies.[12]

In a properly functioning society, those other institutions (family, church, politics broadly conceived) play a role in forming persons for service to the community and for their own inner flourishing. But those institutions had been gravely damaged by those anarchic and despotic forces that he sees as enemies to true personhood. It is surely unfair to expect education to heal such vast and complex afflictions, especially since the very attempt "involves a risk of warping educational work"; moreover, as we have seen, Maritain believed that "the saints and martyrs are the true educators of mankind." But in these exceptional circumstances "extraneous burdens superadded to the normal task of education must be accepted for the sake of the general welfare."

It is, however, vital not to accept these "extraneous burdens" on behalf of the state and its interests: "the state would summon education to make up for all that is lacking in the surrounding order in the matter of common political inspiration, stable customs and traditions, common inherited standards, moral unity and unanimity." But if education is recruited *by the state* "to compensate for all the deficiencies in civil society," then "education would become . . . uniquely dependent on the management of the state," and as a direct consequence "both the essence and the freedom of education would be ruined." The well-educated person will always and necessarily, in an age afflicted by both anarchic and despotic tendencies, be in tension with the surrounding society: "The freedom enjoyed by education . . . will not be a quiet and easygoing, peacefully expanding freedom, but a tense and fighting one." There will be, especially in the years following the war, a danger of shaping people not in a "truly human" way, but rather making them merely into "the organ of a technocratic society." He sums up this element of his argument in a passage that might have been written by Simone Weil:

Technology is good, as a means for the human spirit and for human ends. But technocracy, that is to say, technology so understood and so worshipped as to exclude any superior wisdom and any other understanding than that of calculable phenomena, leaves in human life nothing but relationships of force, or at best those of pleasure, and necessarily ends up in a philosophy of domination. A technocratic society is but a totalitarian one.[13]

* * *

"Technology is good," says Maritain, knowing that he will be accused of saying that it is not. And near the end of the Riddell Memorial Lectures, which he gave in Newcastle at almost the precise moment that Maritain was completing the Terry Lectures, C. S. Lewis says, "Nothing I can say will prevent some people from describing this lecture as an attack on science. I deny the charge, of course."[14] But when reading these writers, it is impossible not to suspect that their suspicions of science and technology run deeper than they are willing to acknowledge. That is to say, the development they trace in their accounts of social and intellectual history—from the creation of the scientific method, to an increasingly powerful set of technologies, to technocracy or rule by those who command the machines—certainly *appears* inevitable. It is hard to imagine how technocracy might be undone without the undoing of modern technology itself. And that would not be a matter merely of taking away machines, even if such direct action were possible. What J. R. R. Tolkien, who thought in these respects much as his friend Lewis did, called The Machine is an ideology, a set of unconfronted assumptions deeply embedded in human psyches and social structures alike. And indeed what distinguishes Lewis from Maritain in their thinking about technology is just this, that Maritain treats technological modernity as an explicit philosophy, whereas Lewis understands that it functions most powerfully in its subterranean mode. In treating scientism and technocracy, Lewis becomes a Nietzschean or Foucauldian genealogist, a subtle tracer of hidden histories.[15]

His key insight into this genealogy may be found in the bravura introduction to his history of English poetry and prose in the sixteenth century, a book that he agreed to write in 1935 but did not complete until 1953. Along the way he condensed some of that project's major themes into the 1944 Clark Lectures at Cambridge, and those themes overlap strongly with those of his novel *That Hideous Strength*, which he began at the end of 1942, just as he was writing the Riddell lectures. As was typical of Lewis—his friend Owen Barfield once commented that "what he thought about everything was secretly present in what he said about anything"—he was, just as the war's momentum permanently shifted, working out a single set of ideas in multiple genres and for multiple audiences. It is therefore helpful to explore *The Abolition of Man* in conjunction with these other texts that are so closely related to it. And the one that makes the key argument most pointedly is *English Literature in the Sixteenth Century, Excluding Drama*.[16]

The book's introduction is entitled "New Learning and New Ignorance," and in it Lewis strives to sketch the many and powerful intellectual cross-currents in the age whose literature he was tasked to write about. One of the most interesting moments comes when he describes the beginnings of modern science, which, he points out, is a chapter in the history of magic—or, if you prefer, magic is a chapter in the history of science. (In a similar vein, the American historian Lynn Thorndike published, between 1923 and 1958, eight magisterial volumes on the *History of Magic and Experimental Science*.) Lewis states forthrightly that "the serious magical endeavour and the serious scientific endeavour are twins: one was sickly and died, the other strong and throve." The method of science, Lewis continued,

> is no doubt contrasted in our minds with that of the magicians: but contrasted only in the light of the event, only because we know that science succeeded and magic failed. That event was then still uncertain. Stripping off our knowledge of it, we see at once that [Sir Francis Bacon, one of the founders of experimental science] and the magicians have the closest possible affinity . . . . Nor would Bacon himself deny the affinity: he thought the aim of the magicians was "noble."[17]

What lies at the heart of this "affinity"? "Both seek knowledge for the sake of power (in Bacon's words, as 'a spouse for fruit,' not a 'curtesan for pleasure'), both move in a grandiose dream of days when Man shall have been raised to the performance of 'all things possible.'" What we now call magic and what we now call science find their place "among the other dreams of power which then haunted the European mind"—including those of Machiavelli.

It has often been said of Bacon that he advocated "putting Nature on the rack" in order to extract her secrets by torture. As Peter Pesic has argued in a series of essays, this is not quite right: it was Leibniz who spoke of "the art of inquiry into nature itself and of putting it on the rack—the art of experiment which Lord Bacon began so ably." But Bacon often wrote of nature as Proteus, the shape-shifting god, and noted that if you wished to get the truth out of Proteus, "the only way was first to secure his hands with handcuffs, and then to bind him with chains." Human "art"—by which Bacon means something like "ingenuity"—"endeavours by much vexing of bodies to force Nature to its will and conquer and subdue her."[18] This is what Lewis means by "dreams of power": not submission to an ordained place within a God-made cosmos, but the pursuit by the world's apex predator of "all things possible." We are back within the realm of force, to which all of us are subject, as described in the *Iliad*.

The third and last chapter of *The Abolition of Man* begins with the idea of the human "conquest of Nature":

> "Man has Nature whacked," said someone to a friend of mine not long ago. In their context the words had a certain tragic beauty, for the speaker was dying of tuberculosis. "No matter," he said, "I know I'm one of the casualties. Of course there are casualties on the winning as well as on the losing side. But that doesn't alter the fact that it is winning." . . . I must proceed to analyse this conception a little more closely. In what sense is Man the possessor of increasing power over Nature?[19]

And the conclusion that Lewis comes to almost immediately is this: "What we call Man's power over Nature turns out to be a power exercised by some men over other men with Nature as its instrument." Lewis makes this claim because the most powerful technologies are never universally distributed, but are always in the hands of some powerful few—who typically use them in order to maintain and extend their control over the many. The airplane is an amazing invention, but at the time Lewis wrote, airplanes were being used to bomb people who neither owned nor controlled airplanes.

Those with the most complete control over technology Lewis calls, bluntly enough, the Controllers, and the chief purpose of the concluding chapter of *The Abolition of Man* is to ask what moral commitments are likely to direct the decisions of the Controllers. His answer is that the Controllers of our time have adopted an account of what human beings are—a theory of Man—that undercuts every possible motive for action except the "dream of power." The argument is structurally identical to the one he would make a couple of years later in his book *Miracles*, in a chapter called "The Cardinal Difficulty of Naturalism." There he argues that if human reason is a product of the blind, undirected forces of natural selection, and unrelated in any necessary or intrinsic way to the way things actually are, then we cannot trust the claims made by the use of human reason, including the claim that human reason is a product of the blind undirected forces of natural selection. Naturalism, then, says Lewis, undoes itself. In the same way, he argues in *Abolition*, the claim that "traditional moral values" are but socially constructed— Lewis does not use the term, which is a recent coinage of course, but it is what he means—and unrelated in any necessary or intrinsic way to the way things should be, to a universally binding moral law, undercuts any ground on which the Controllers might justify their rule except that of "might makes right." For if all values are socially constructed and in relation to Nature arbitrary, then even the claim that some act is necessary for the perpetuation of the human race is also arbitrary. For why should the human race survive? Lewis's term for the natural law is the *Tao*, and his term for those who have rejected its authority the Innovators, and we are all required, he argues, to choose one of those two paths: "Either we are rational spirit obliged for ever to obey the absolute values of the *Tao*, or else we are mere nature to be kneaded and cut into new shapes for the pleasures of masters who must, by hypothesis, have no motive but their own 'natural' impulses. Only the *Tao* provides a common human law of action which can over-arch rulers and ruled alike."[20]

Lewis is at pains to insist that this abolition of an objective and absolutely binding standard of value—which is also in effect "the abolition of Man"—has not just happened among the evidently monstrous like the Nazis. We may discern the loss of the *Tao* even in everyday language: "Once we killed bad men; now we liquidate

Lewis's response to these claims begins with the note that Gaius and Titius have, though they are not aware of it, set themselves quite apart from Coleridge. For while Coleridge surely would have acknowledged that sometimes people indeed speak of their feelings rather than of the object they are nominally attending to, he did not think that such a condition was either necessary or good. For Coleridge, the tourist who says that the waterfall is "pretty" simply has not perceived the waterfall properly, whereas the one who calls it "sublime" had said something *correct*: "The reason why Coleridge agreed with the tourist who called the cataract sublime and disagreed with the one who called it pretty was of course that he believed inanimate nature to be such that certain responses could be more 'just' or 'ordinate' or 'appropriate' to it than others."[23] Kant in his *Critique of Judgment* had defined the absolute sublime as that in relation to which everything else seems small, but of course there are also degrees of sublimity, and the *proper* response of a human being to a mighty waterfall is to be cognizant of its size and power, and indeed to *feel* its magnificence and our corresponding smallness.

For Lewis, the further point to be made here is that such proper response is not inevitable: it does not come naturally to all of us— as can be seen in the tourist who called the waterfall "pretty"—but often must be the product of careful training. And, Lewis goes on to argue, one of the primary objects of pedagogical attention, especially in a child's early years, will be the training of such responses: "St Augustine defines virtue as *ordo amoris*, the ordinate condition of the affections in which every object is accorded that kind or degree of love which is appropriate to it . . . . The little human animal will not at first have the right responses. It must be trained to feel pleasure, liking, disgust, and hatred at those things which really are pleasant, likeable, disgusting and hateful."[24] But of course this training will not occur if the teachers do not believe that any given emotional

Nature means the power of some men over other men with Nature as the instrument."[26]

The character spoken of in that first quotation from *That Hideous Strength*, and spoken to in the second, is Mark Studdock, whose descent into an inferno of evil is one of two major strands of the novel's plot (the other being his wife Jane's ascent to a far higher life than she had previously known). Immediately after the wicked man, named Filostrato, speaks to Mark about what "Man's power over Nature" means, he conveys Mark to a kind of inner chamber where the inmost secret of his organization—or what he claims and believes to be the inmost secret—is revealed. It may be a lesser secret; it may be irrelevant to the organization's deepest purposes. But in any event, Mark is floored by what he sees, and by the increasingly explicit threats of violence against him if he does not obey the commands of the leaders. And as Mark quakes in fear, Lewis comments,

> It must be remembered that in Mark's mind hardly one rag of noble thought, either Christian or Pagan, had a secure lodging. His education had been neither scientific nor classical—merely "Modern." The severities both of abstraction and of high human tradition had passed him by: and he had neither peasant shrewdness nor aristocratic honor to help him. He was a man of straw, a glib examinee in subjects that require no exact knowledge (he had always done well on Essays and General Papers) and the first hint of a real threat to his bodily life knocked him sprawling.[27]

Lewis describes here the consequences of a comprehensive failure of *moral formation*, a failure that has left Mark utterly vulnerable to the draw of what appears to him to be the "Inner Ring" of Filostrato's organization, the National Institute of Co-ordinated Experiments.

Now he begins to see what N.I.C.E. is really like—but too late for him to withdraw from it. The heart of Mark's problem is that he had never before this point suspected the intentions of those around him, at least not to the degree that he should have: he had had no firm evidence, but a better-trained heart would have been uncomfortable from the beginning. To one habituated to the *Tao*, the whole place would have had an unpleasant and unsettling odor. We should be reminded here of Maritain's argument in *Education at the Crossroads* that certain vital elements of moral and spiritual formation cannot be straightforwardly inculcated but must nevertheless always be aimed at. None of Mark's education has acknowledged this necessity.

The educational failure Lewis describes here is not one merely of schools, though indeed the formal educational system had failed Mark by allowing him to evade "the severities both of abstraction and of high human tradition" (the natural sciences, mathematics, and analytical philosophy on the one hand, the proper humanities on the other) and left him "a glib examinee in subjects that require no exact knowledge." It is telling that the job N.I.C.E. finds for Mark to do is writing propagandistic op-eds for newspapers. But the failure is social as well: Lewis shares with Eliot (see, for instance, the latter's eulogy of the famous music-hall performer Marie Lloyd[28]) the belief that the lower and upper classes have managed to retain and transmit some ethical orientation that the middle class has completely forgotten: "neither peasant shrewdness nor aristocratic honor."

Mark's wife Jane, by contrast, whose education is little different than her husband's, retains just enough residual understanding of the *Tao* that when she meets a genuinely holy man she is strongly drawn by who he is and what he stands for. (Jane's receptiveness might be a function of what used to be called "female intuition," but more probably is a result of her being the last in a long line of spiritual sensitives or clairvoyants. In any case, Lewis is openly dismissive of Jane's intellectual stature and potential.) If Mark is drawn inexorably into a voracious Inner Ring, Jane is offered the possibility of genuine Membership. And gradually, hesitatingly, she accepts it, and is thereby saved from destruction. If Mark too finds rescue, that is less because of any inherent virtue than because of the mad overreach of N.I.C.E.

N.I.C.E. is of course a technocratic organization. As one enthusiastic supporter of its endeavors says early in the book, "The N.I.C.E. marks the beginning of a new era—the *really* scientific era. Up to now, everything has been haphazard. This is going to put science itself on a scientific basis."[29] That the organization's ambitions are, as Maritain predicted, totalitarian goes almost without saying: its every action demonstrates its determination to seize absolute control of everything within its grasp; Lewis finds this aspect of its character so inevitable as to be uninteresting. What he wishes to emphasize about it—to return to the theme of an earlier chapter—is that it is *demonic*.

That is, while its leaders have become Controllers in relation to everyone around them, in relation to forces far greater than themselves, they are the Controlled. A few of them understand that they receive instructions from invisible but masterful beings they call the Macrobes; none of them understand, until it is too late, that the Macrobes are demons like Screwtape, but, it seems, far more powerful. In short, the Controllers are precisely like Mark Studdock: having received no moral education or having forgotten what they once knew—having set aside the *Tao*, which is to say, the only orientation that would have revealed to them the danger they were courting—they give themselves to forces they not only do not fear but do not even believe in, and are consumed. The scientist-magicians have dreamed their dreams and have conjured powers they cannot control. Thus those chilling words of Auden's cited earlier: "The vanquished powers were glad // To be invisible and free; without remorse / Struck down the sons who strayed into their course, / And ravished the daughters, and drove the fathers mad."

Lewis commented on these matters quite directly in *The Screwtape Letters*, and these words, perhaps, shall be a proper conclusion to the renewal of our demonological meditations. Screwtape notes that the official policy of "Our Father Below" is that the demons should conceal their existence, which has certain advantages—it enables the demons to make people into "materialists and skeptics"—but also certain disadvantages—primarily the inability to practice "direct terrorism" and to produce dark magicians. But perhaps, he muses, there may be ways to combine the two approaches: "I have great hopes that we shall learn in due time how to emotionalise and mythologise their science to such an extent that what is, in effect, a belief in us (though not under that name) will creep in while the human mind remains closed to belief in the Enemy." Eventually, he hopes, "If once we can produce our perfect work—the Materialist Magician, the man, not using, but veritably worshipping, what he vaguely calls 'Forces' while denying the existence of 'spirits'—then the end of the war will be in sight."[30]

*   *   *

Auden's feelings about Swarthmore were mixed. "Everyone is very nice but not very lively," he wrote to a friend soon after his arrival in the fall of 1942. "The place is a dump without either a bar or a movie house and the trains are so bad that going to Philadelphia is an excursion." The only place to eat in town was a little diner where the jukebox blared unremittingly: "I thought I'd go out of my mind if

I heard 'I'm Dreaming of a White Christmas' one more time." A certain Quaker abstemiousness still permeated the college's culture at that time, and Auden wrote to Ursula Niebuhr, "My seminar on Romanticism starts tomorrow. Quakers or no Quakers, I shall serve bread and cheese and beer at four o'clock."[31] But the quietness of the place also offered him the opportunity to continue the complete remaking of his intellectual equipment that he had begun when he came to America in 1939.

It was while teaching at Swarthmore that Auden completed his Christmas oratorio, *For the Time Being*, and wrote almost all of what may be his masterpiece, *The Sea and the Mirror*. That poem's subtitle, "A Commentary on *The Tempest*," disguises its ambition: it is, as he told Ursula Niebuhr, a poem about the relationship between Christianity and art, and therefore corresponds in curious yet important ways to the poem Eliot was writing at the same time: "Little Gidding." Though Eliot was twenty years older than Auden, an elder statesman of poetry rather than a Young Turk, their poems share a valedictory air.[32]

When Eliot is confronted, in the Dantesque second section of "Little Gidding," by the specter of "some dead master," "a familiar compound ghost / Both intimate and unidentifiable," that figure says to him that "our concern was speech, and speech impelled us / To purify the dialect of the tribe"—speaking in the past tense, as though marking Eliot too as one of the dead. (Eliot was Auden's editor at Faber and Faber, and when he visited Eliot there, he typically found him playing patience at his desk. When Auden asked him why he liked the game, Eliot replied, "Because it's the nearest thing to being dead."[33]) The ghost then advises Eliot how to bring his work and his life to a conclusion—"Let me disclose the gifts reserved for age / To set a crown upon your lifetime's effort"—and the poem's famous final lines address "the end of all our exploring."

Auden, in his mid-thirties, would scarcely be expected to sound such a note, and yet in choosing Shakespeare's aged magician Prospero—who at the end of *The Tempest* says that he will break his staff and drown his book and retire to Milan, "where / Every third thought shall be my grave" (V.i.)—as his protagonist, he enters the same environment of feeling. And there is no question that Auden identifies with Prospero, who, in this "Commentary," tells Ariel that he "knows now what magic is: / The power to enchant that comes from disillusion."[34] Auden had come to understand that his own poetic magic, a magic that had captivated the English poetic world in the previous decade, had hidden from him his own disillusionments; and he had come to believe that to have any real hope of seeing himself and his world truly, he needed like Prospero to break his staff and drown his book. Looking back on the great change in Auden's career, Seamus Heaney commented, shrewdly and incisively, that Auden in his reinvention of his poetic self wished to ensure that his verse "keep a civil tongue"—in all senses of the word "civil"—but "the price of all this is a certain diminution of the language's autonomy, a not uncensorious training of its wilder shoots."[35] This is more than fair, and one can sympathize with any reader who laments the training, indeed often the rigorous pruning, of those shoots. Auden's more civil, and civic, and broadly religious (in the etymological sense of *religio*) later verse is not to everyone'e taste.

These attempts by Eliot and Auden to articulate a disciplined Christian poetics, a role for poetry within the broader framework of the Christian life, are beyond the scope of this book; but it would be wrong not to acknowledge that these poets were pursuing these matters alongside the more public meditations that we explore here. As Auden wrote in the first months of 1942, "To be living in the greatest revolutionary epoch since the Reformation means . . . that the external conflict of classes and nations and political systems is paralleled by an equally intense internal conflict in every individual."[36]

If *The Sea and the Mirror* is the one major work that belongs wholly to Auden's Swarthmore years, the place and the period mark a kind of hinge or pivot in Auden's career. More than a decade later he would write of his time spent on the island of Ischia in the Bay of Naples as one characterized by "hoping to twig from / What we are not what we might be next," and the less romantic venue of Swarthmore was that for him also. He completed *For the Time Being* there; there he began his last long poem, *The Age of Anxiety*; and in the midst of all that, he even gave thought to what it means to be a teacher, and what it means to be educated.

The talk he gave on January 15, 1943—the second day of the Casablanca Conference, and the day after Maritain had given the first of his Terry Lectures at Yale—is called "Vocation and Society," and it seems slight and casual but is not. He begins by using a scene from *The Magic Flute*—by this point Chester Kallman had taught him to make opera central to his aesthetics—to critique the vacuity of ordinary middle-class life (as we have seen Eliot and Lewis do).

> To all of us the gods offer a similar choice between two kinds of existence, between remaining Papageno the lowbrow, and becoming Tamino the highbrow. What they permit to none of us, is to be a middlebrow, that is, to exist without passion and without a willingness to suffer.[37]

And to bring this immediately home to his audience, comprised largely of students, he continues by noting that the middlebrow "does not wish to *become* wise, only to *be* wise, to graduate cum laude." He thereby drives a wedge between the quest for genuine wisdom and the desire to be academically (and then, of course, socially and economically) successful.

To have a vocation, Auden says, is to be in a state of "subjective requiredness": your vocation is something you are required to do, but the requirement comes from within. You are the one who is called, not necessarily anyone else, and likewise you alone are the discerner of the call. "For this reason Vocational Guidance is a contradiction in terms. The only reasons another can give me why I should adopt this career rather than that are that I should be more successful or happier or it pays better, but such matters are precisely what I must not think about if I am really to find my vocation."[38]

But the freedom to shun "Vocational Guidance" and seek my own calling is not something that I can take for granted. Indeed, in many societies it is impossible. Fascism, Auden argues, refuses to acknowledge any place for *subjective* requiredness: in its social model, what is required is always *objective*, imposed from without by the State. Fascism further contends that no given society, at least in the world of the modern, highly armed nation-state, can flourish unless the only requiredness is objective and state-determined. Confronted by this view, Auden replies, the Western democracies must "defeat our enemies in the field," yes, but also disprove their implicit (and sometimes explicit) "assertion that . . . war is the natural state of an industrialised society, by proving that a peaceful society can function under modern conditions. For those of us who are concerned with education, this means that our first problem is what, if anything, can we do to make a sense of vocation the normal instead of the exceptional thing."[39]

In other words, a humanistic education that encourages students to think vocationally is in itself a refutation of Fascism—perhaps one of the more lastingly powerful refutations imaginable. Enemies defeated on the field of battle can rearm and resume hostilities, as the Germany that lost in 1918 had done. But a model of the state cannot be so easily revived if its ideas are conclusively refuted by the flourishing of persons in a radically different social structure. In his lecture, Auden was asking the undergraduates of Swarthmore to seek their own vocations not only for themselves but also for the sake of democracy.

At the end of his talk, however, he introduces a new and complicating thought—a destabilizing one in many respects. Is democracy, after all, sustainable? Or, to put the question more precisely, and as it was often put in the debates surrounding Finkelstein's Conference, is it *self*-sustaining? Auden echoes a famous essay by E. M. Forster in offering "Two Cheers for Democracy," but he withholds the third cheer for rather different reasons than the atheist Forster had. "Two cheers for Democracy," says Auden: "one because it admits vocation, and two because it permits contrition. Two cheers are quite enough. There is no occasion to give three. Only Agape, the Beloved Republic, deserves that."[40] What he would later call "our dear old bag of a democracy" is sustained, not by itself, but by belief in something deeper and greater than itself. So Auden concludes his talk not with those cheers, but with the reading of a few lines of a very recent poem.

Just four months earlier, T. S. Eliot had published "Little Gidding," the last of his *Four Quartets*, and Auden finished his talk by reading the poem's concluding lines, culminating in this famous affirmation:

And all shall be well and
All manner of thing shall be well
When the tongues of flame are in-folded
Into the crowned knot of fire
And the fire and the rose are one.[41]

Auden sometimes expressed ambivalence about Eliot's poetic achievement and influence, but not on this occasion. He called Eliot "the greatest poet now living, one in whom America and England may both rejoice, one whose personal and professional example are to every other and lesser writer at once an inspiration and a reproach."[42] And it was surely Eliot's calm vision of an ultimate restoration of all broken things that called forth Auden's highest praise.

Auden's vision, then, is of a vocation-based education sustained by a democratic polity, and a democratic polity sustained by Christian faith. This vision stood (as did Maritain's in *Education at the Crossroads*, as did Lewis's in *The Abolition of Man*) against the commanding power of the nation-state, against pragmatism, against modern technocratic canons of efficiency—against Weil's Social Beast.

*   *   *

The last three of the *Four Quartets* appeared in the *New English Weekly*, a periodical edited by a literary and Christian entrepreneur named Philip Mairet. With the encouragement and interlocution of Mairet, Eliot began, in late 1942, to articulate some of the convictions that he had reached in conversations within the Moot and within an even more informal organization called the Chandos Group, because it typically met at the Chandos Restaurant. (Mairet was involved in this group too.) Its purpose was to seek "certain absolute and eternal principles"—which is to say, Christian principles—"of true sociology."[43] Stimulated by the Chandos conversations, Eliot began to think that what was needed, even prior to reflections on a "Christian society" or a "Christian Britain," was some more general conceptual framework—some elementary and yet flexible definition of the objects of inquiry. So, in the first weeks of 1943, just as Maritain was delivering his Terry lectures, and Lewis his Riddell lectures, and Auden his talk on "Vocation and Society," Eliot published a series of essays under the general title "Notes toward the Definition of Culture."

Later in the year, Eliot and Mairet convened still more meetings, at St. Anne's Church in Soho, to explore the question of how "culture" should be defined, and these meetings helped him to refine his concepts. He eventually published *Notes toward the Definition of Culture* in book form in 1948, but the book does not differ in its basic framework from the original essays, so I think it is acceptable, even at the risk of time travel, to treat the finished product of 1948 as a reasonably faithful account of what Eliot was thinking in early 1943.

Eliot says at several points in the book that he is writing not as a poet or a critic but as a sociologist—thus showing his debt to the interests of the Chandos Group—though he does not seek to define "society" but rather "culture." This decision stems in part from conversations going on around him in which much debate about how to shape and form culture is accompanied by a complete lack of interest in what the word means: "I have observed with growing anxiety the career of this word culture during the past six or seven years."[44] It is perhaps odd that, though claiming to be a sociologist, Eliot does not define "society" or explain precisely how culture is to be distinguished from it. We have to guess, but it seems reasonably evident that for Eliot culture is comprised of the meaning-bearing elements of society. At one point he says, "Culture may even be described simply as that which makes life worth living."[45]

This description clearly calls into question the relationship between culture and religion, and Eliot's chief difficulty in *Notes* is to negotiate this relationship. With the neurotically discriminating hypersubtlety we have seen in his earlier writing on these topics, he wants to emphasize in certain ways the absolute indissolubility of religion and culture, while in other ways, and in other contexts, emphasizing the danger of treating them as simply identical. He is not perfectly clear on these matters, but I think he mistrusts the tendency to *separate* religion and culture for two reasons: first, it violates the sociological definition of culture that he uses throughout the book—again, he claims to be writing as a sociologist—and second, he denies that you can have genuinely healthy and sustainable cultural developments that are not related to a healthy practiced religion. Conversely, he mistrusts the tendency to *unify* the two because this leads all too easily to the conflation of religious duties with patriotic and economic (in the sense of the *oikos*, the household) impulses.[46]

Two contrasting separatist errors, Eliot argues, must be avoided: the belief "that culture can be preserved, extended and developed in the absence of religion"; and "the belief that the preservation and maintenance of religion need not reckon with the preservation and maintenance of culture."[47] He tries to avoid these errors, and also those of simple unification, by describing culture as the *incarnation* of religion: the embodiment in a wide series of practices, from harvest festivals to fox-hunting, of a set of core beliefs, convictions, and obligations. "Bishops are a part of English culture, and horses and dogs are a part of English religion."[48]

And yet it would not be a good sign if bishops were nothing more than culture, and horses and dogs occupied the heights of religious practice: "when this identification [of religion and culture] is complete, it means in actual societies both an inferior culture and an inferior religion."[49]

I have expressed my frustration with the vague evasiveness from which Eliot's prose too often suffers, but I do not believe he is evading anything here, nor is he any more vague than necessary. "The way of looking at culture and religion which I have been trying to adumbrate is so difficult that I am not sure I grasp it my-self except in flashes, or that I comprehend all its implications."[50] His difficulty can be better understood if we reflect on his use of the term *incarnation* to describe culture's relation to religion. At the end of the chapter in which he proffers this word, he says, "While I am aware of the temerity of employing such an exalted term, I cannot think of any other which would convey so well the inten-tion to avoid [mere] relation on the one hand and [absolute] iden-tification on the other."[51] It is perhaps useful here to trace the term back to its theological usage: the complications introduced into the doctrine of God by saying that God became Man are indeed very similar. The Athanasian Creed says, "And the catholic faith is this: That we worship one God in Trinity, and Trinity in Unity; neither confounding the persons nor dividing the substance." Eliot argues that we may not confound the persons by treating religion and culture as merely and simply identical; nor may we divide the substance by treating them as capable of completely independent development. To make either mistake is to fall into sociological heresy.

Having established these coordinates, Eliot then sets out to re-flect on the conditions that must be in place in order for culture to *rightly* embody the religion of a given society. This will require establishing further coordinates, primarily involving the elite who will be charged, either implicitly or explicitly, with the direction of the culture. (This is the burden of chapter 2.) In brief, Eliot considers the differences between a hereditary aristocracy in which elite status is conferred by birth and, alternatively, something like a meritocracy.[52] His primary argument is that while the elite may not be confined to any particular social class, that does not make them any less the elite, the shapers and directors of culture. Eliot insists that even a wholly classless society will still have an elite, and that

that elite will have the chief burden of *transmitting* culture. A failure to recognize the role of the elite will eviscerate our social criticism.

All this leads, inevitably and as a kind of culmination of the whole book, to reflections on the role of education in creating or sustaining culture. Eliot begins by noting something I mentioned in the preface to this book: "During the recent war an exceptional number of books were published on the subject of education; there were also voluminous reports of commissions, and an incalculable number of contributions on this subject in periodicals."[53] Eliot adds to this flood with some trepidation, in large part because he knows that his views run strictly against its current: and that happens because the role he has assigned to the cultural elite is altogether unacknowledged, indeed is repudiated, by most other writers, and especially within the "voluminous reports of commissions." In his first mention of this subject in *Notes*, he writes, "All that concerns me at the moment is the question whether, by education alone, we can ensure the transmission of culture in a society in which some educationists appear indifferent to class distinctions, and from which some other educationists appear to want to remove class distinctions altogether."[54] And it cannot surprise anyone to learn that Eliot thinks the transmission of culture is impossible if "class distinctions," and more particularly the cultivation and sustaining of a genuine elite, are neglected.

One of Eliot's chief concerns is that the "educationists," assuming the part of what Lewis called the Controllers, will necessarily diminish the role of the family in education, within which Eliot includes moral formation. "In the society desired by some reformers, what the family can transmit will be limited to the minimum, especially if the child is to be, as Mr. H. C. Dent hopes, manipulated by a unified educational system 'from the cradle to the grave.'"[55] Dent had been since 1940 the editor of the *Times Education Supplement* and had written one of the most widely read of the many wartime books on education, *A New Order in English Education* (1942).[56] The phrase "from the cradle to the grave" was associated with the Beveridge Report, also from 1942, which laid the foundation for the postwar creation of the National Health Service and other elements of a comprehensive welfare state, and Dent understood a new national educational scheme as necessarily and intimately related to this larger social program. All this simply appalled Eliot, who—to borrow Lewis's language—foresaw education being detached from the *Tao* (which the family traditionally taught and transmitted) and turned over to moral "Innovators" like Gaius and Titius.

Little of the protest against such a model that Eliot registers in *Notes* is obviously derived from Christian thought: it arises from a kind of conservatism that was even then archaic. For instance, Eliot worries what such state-controlled education might do to the children of poor and uneducated parents: "to be educated above the level of those whose social habits and tastes one has inherited, may cause a division within a man which interferes with happiness; even though, when the individual is of superior intellect, it may bring him a fuller and more useful life." He is, moreover, not convinced that every member of a society needs formal education: "A high average of general education is perhaps less necessary for a civil society than is a respect for learning."[57]

When education has worked well in England, he asserts, such circumstances "were not brought about by equality of opportunity. They were not brought about, either, by mere privilege; but by a happy combination of privilege and opportunity . . . of which no Education Act will ever find the secret."[58] (This is a reference to the Education Act of 1944, mentioned in my preface.) This is as much as to say—in defiance of the nearly universal commitment to planning that Mannheim endorsed and that Tony Judt saw as one of the chief markers of the postwar world—that successful educational regimes can never be planned, can never be systematic, must inevitably be fortuitous when they exist at all. This is not a conclusion for which Eliot argues; it seems to be something closer to an axiom for him.

For Eliot, what is missing from the rhetoric of the "educationists" is an acknowledgement that they believe that "we have arrived at a stage of civilisation at which the family is irresponsible, or incompetent, or helpless; at which parents cannot be expected to train their children properly; at which many parents cannot afford to feed them properly, and would not know how, even if they had the means; and that Education must step in and make the best of a bad job." But for Eliot, "the instructive point is this, that the more education arrogates to itself the responsibility, the more systematically will it betray culture."[59] It is striking at this stage, near the very end of his book, how powerfully Eliot veers from his habitual calmness of approach, detachment of style:

> We know now that the highest achievements of the past, in art, in wisdom, in holiness, were but "stages in development" which we can teach [young people] to improve upon. We must not train them merely to receive the culture of the past, for that would be to regard the culture of the past as final. We must not impose culture upon the young, though we may impose upon them whatever political and social philosophy is in vogue. And yet the culture of Europe has deteriorated visibly within the memory of many who are by no means the oldest among us. And we know, that whether education can foster and improve culture or not, it can surely adulterate and degrade it. For there is no doubt that in our headlong rush to educate everybody, we are lowering our standards, and more and more abandoning the study of those subjects by which the essentials of our culture—of that part of

it which is transmissible by education—are transmitted; destroying our ancient edifices to make ready the ground upon which the barbarian nomads of the future will encamp in their mechanised caravans.[60]

Eliot knows he has lapsed into jeremiad here: His next sentence reads, "The previous paragraph is to be considered only as an incidental flourish to relieve the feelings of the writer and perhaps of a few of his more sympathetic readers."

It is a curious and unsatisfying performance, to say the best that can be said. And what is most striking about it, in relation to the other critiques and models of education that we have been exploring in this chapter, is how utterly uninformed it is by distinctively Christian reflection. It seems, rather, the cry of a man who has traded in his egalitarian American birthright for a class-based British traditionalism that now seems to be dissolving just at the moment that he comes fully into his inheritance of it.

* * *

When the writings of the last months of Simone Weil's life were collected in book form and published in English, in 1952, they appeared with an introduction by Eliot. He acknowledges at the outset that "the reader of her work finds himself confronted by a difficult, violent and complex personality"; he notes her tendency to "immoderate affirmations" and admits that these will surely "tax the patience of the reader." But he exhorts us to master any impatience and keep reading. He centers his comments on an observation by Father Perrin: "Je crois que son âme est incomparablement plus haute que son génie" (I think her soul is incomparably greater [or, more literally and perhaps better, *higher*] than her genius). Eliot does not think we should understand this as a disparagement of Weil's intellect. Rather, one should read *The Need for Roots* in the conviction that Weil's intellectual gifts were enormous, but also with the constant awareness that she died young and "had a very great soul to grow up to."[61]

The writing that Weil did in the last eighteen months of her life, in *The Need for Roots* and in miscellaneous essays, circles endlessly around a single word, *malheur*, commonly translated in ordinary circumstances as "unhappiness," but often rendered by Weil's translators as "affliction." It is not suffering (*souffrance*): In one essay Weil writes, "La plus grande énigme de la vie humaine, ce n'est pas la souffrance, c'est le malheur" (The greatest enigma of human life is not suffering, it is *malheur*). It is a kind of stamp or permanent inscription: "It takes possession of the soul and marks it through and through with its own particular mark, the mark of slavery." The form of *malheur* to which she calls particular attention is that created when force—as we see in the *Iliad*—reduces a person to a thing. To know that you have been reduced to the status of a mere thing and cannot undo this violation of your being—this, perhaps, is the experience of *malheur*. "In the best of cases, the one who is marked by [*malheur*] will only keep half his soul."[62]

We who see others in the grip of *malheur* are obliged, first and foremost, to *pay attention*—to pay the same absolute attention that God deserves, and which, as we have seen, Weil did not think herself successful in giving. Love of God and love of neighbor—the twofold commandment that Jesus said summed up all the law and the prophets[63]—begins and in a sense also ends in attention. To attend to God is difficult because he is absent; to attend to the person marked by *malheur* is equally difficult but for the opposite reason: she is too present. Everything in us wants to turn away. It is this temptation that *must* be resisted. The *Iliad* is great, and is for us "a pure and lovely mirror," precisely because it "never tires of showing us" the scandalous image of human beings transformed into things.

(In 1946 Auden recalled the poems—"versified trash"—that had been written about the Lidice massacre in 1942: by way of reprisal for the assassination of a German official, the Nazis executed every man in the village of Lidice, near Prague, and sent almost all of the women and children to the Chełmno concentration camp, where they were killed with poison gas. Auden could not "avoid the conclusion that what was really bothering the versifiers was a feeling of guilt at not feeling horrorstruck enough. Could a good poem have been written on such a subject? Possibly. One that revealed this lack of feeling, that told how when he read the news, the poet, like you and I, dear reader, went on thinking about his fame or his lunch, and how glad he was that he was not one of the victims."[64])

If God and the afflicted neighbor are opposites according to the logic of presence and absence, they are according to another logic precisely the same: they are silent. They do not and cannot communicate, through language, what it is like to be them. ("As for those who have been struck by one of those blows that leave a being struggling on the ground like a half-crushed worm, they have no words to express what is happening to them."[65]) Attention, then, not speech, is the means by which understanding of wholly alien experience may be achieved. And to take on this costly obligation to attend, to forego the privilege of looking away or offering easy words, is a kind of spiritual poverty—one much to be desired.

That searing meditation on *malheur*, and the possible responses to it, was probably written in Marseilles in the spring of 1942.[66] A year later, in England, she returned to this theme, but playing it now in a political key: "Enslaved and oppressed Europe will not see better days, when she is liberated, unless spiritual poverty has first taken root in her." And how might such spiritual poverty be encouraged? Weil, like Eliot, sees that the practices of the social elite are key to the spiritual and moral formation of the culture—but the practices she recommends are considerably stricter and more self-abnegating than anything Eliot had envisioned: "What is needed today is an elite to inspire the virtue of spiritual poverty among the ill-used masses; and for this it is necessary that the elite shall be poor not just in spirit but in fact." That is, the European elite must not see the actual, material poverty that the war has brought to them as lamentable condition to be overcome as soon as possible, but must rather *embrace* it as a means by which to pursue a spiritual poverty that they can manifest to the masses. They must, to borrow and transfigure another of Eliot's notions, *incarnate* poverty. Only in a spiritual renewal brought about by poverty may Europe be saved: "If we are only saved by American money and machines we shall fall back, one way or another, into a new servitude like the one which we now suffer."[67] Once again, we see the argument that entrusting technocracy with our salvation is a recipe for winning the war while losing the peace; but Weil's preferred alternative to technocracy is far more radical than that proposed by any of the other figures studied in this book.

In the last months of her life, in London, Weil wrote so much that her biographer Simone Pétrement wonders how it was physically possible. Indeed, the workload she imposed on herself must surely have been incompatible with taking proper care of her body and therefore may well have hastened her death. The primary document that emerged from that period of frantic energy, the book known in English as *The Need for Roots*, but which she called *Enracinement* (Rootedness), is perhaps the most extreme, idealistic, and uncompromising statement by this most extreme, idealistic, and uncompromising of writers. Eliot described it as a young person's book, not primarily in the sense that only a young person could have written it but rather in the sense that only a young person can read it: "This is one of those books which ought to be studied by the young before their leisure has been lost and their capacity for thought destroyed in the life of the hustings and the legislative assembly; books of the effect of which, we can only hope, will become apparent in the attitude of mind of another generation."[68]

Eliot also wrote in that introduction of Weil that she "was three things in the highest degree: French, Jewish and Christian."[69] It seems likely that she would have agreed only with the first. Her rejection of Judaism was consistent and fierce. In a letter to the Minister of Jewish Affairs in the Vichy regime in October 1941, she wrote, "I do not consider myself a Jew, since I have never set foot in a synagogue, have been raised by my free-thinking parents with no religious observances of any kind, have no feeling of attraction to the Jewish religion and no attachment to Jewish tradition." (As noted earlier, the following year when she was in New York she attended a synagogue for the only time in her life—a congregation of Ethiopian Jews.)[70]

The greatest blot on Weil's thought and character is her extreme anti-Semitism. Many of her statements about Jews are nearly indistinguishable from the utterances of Hitler. Of the history of Israel, Weil wrote that "from Abraham onwards," and only "excepting some of the prophets," "everything becomes sullied and foul, as if to demonstrate quite clearly: Look! There it is, evil!" Even the courageous resistance of the Jews to Roman tyranny is, bizarrely, portrayed by her as a vice: "The religion of Israel was not noble enough to be fragile." Her comment on the idea that the Jews are the Chosen People of God: "A people chosen for its blindness, chosen to be Christ's executioner."[71]

Weil's hatred of Judaism centered on the idea of the Chosen People—which is to say, it bears a close kinship to her repudiation of the Roman Catholic Church's practices of exclusion. For some to be chosen, others must remain not chosen; for some to be orthodox, others must be designated as heterodox. Such ideas are for Weil the logic of the Inner Ring writ in world-historical capitals. As she had said, insistently, in one of her letters to Father Perrin,

> I should like to draw your attention to one point. It is that there is an absolutely insurmountable obstacle to the Incarnation of Christianity. It is the use of the two little words *anathema sit*. It is not their existence, but the way they have been employed up till now. It is that also which prevents me from crossing the threshold of the Church. I remain beside all those things that cannot enter the Church, the universal repository, on account of those two little words. I remain beside them all the more because my own intelligence is numbered among them.[72]

Conor Cruise O'Brien has, I think, summed up this element of Weil's thought with great clarity and concision. He comments that her "repulsion" at the idea of a chosen people

> is a fundamental and abiding element in her mind and character. It could both carry her to strange extremes and stop her dead in her tracks. At one time it made it possible for her to counsel the acceptance of an anti-Semitic state in France as a lesser evil than war; at another it made it impossible for her to accept baptism into the Catholic Church. Both that acceptance and that refusal are significant expressions of what I call her antipolitics; her radical rejection of all limited associations.[73]

In an earlier chapter I described Lewis's central distinction between the destructive power of the Inner Ring and the healing, restorative power of genuine membership in a genuine community.

Weil did not in any way acknowledge such a distinction. To accept on *any* grounds "limited associations" is to worship what she called the Great Beast. In notebooks she wrote during her last months in France, she pressed this point repeatedly: "The collective is the root of all idolatry. This is what chains us to the earth . . . . It is only by entering the transcendental, the supernatural, the authentically spiritual order that man rises above the social." To accept a social meaning for the person is a form of "service of the false God (of the social Beast under whatever form it may be)" which "purifies evil by eliminating its horror."

She hammers relentlessly: "The social order is irreducibly that of the prince of this world." "Rootedness [*enracinement*] lies in something other than the social." "Conscience is deceived by the social." All *belonging* is idolatrous, evil, opposed to the message of Christ. Weil does not notice that Jesus tells his disciples, "To you has been given the secret of the kingdom of God, but for those outside, everything comes in parables" (Mark 4:11). It is always, as I have noted, "those outside" with whom Weil identifies—outside the Abrahamic and Mosaic covenants, outside the magisterially defined boundaries of Christian orthodoxy—and it is those who police those boundaries from within whom she most energetically and angrily resists. For such policing to her was one of the manifestations of force and therefore a mighty contributor to *malheur*.[74]

It is in light of these considerations that we may consider a key passage in *The Need for Roots*:

How often, for instance, we hear the following commonplace repeated: "Whether Catholics, Protestants, Jews or Free-Thinkers, we're all Frenchmen," exactly as though it were a question of small territorial fragments of the country, as who should say, "Whether from Marseilles, Lyon or Paris, we're all Frenchmen."

In a document promulgated by the Pope, one may read: "Not only from the Christian point of view, but, more generally, from the human point of view . . . ," as though the Christian point of view—which either has no meaning at all, or else claims to encompass everything, in this world and the next—possessed a smaller degree of generality than the human point of view. It is impossible to conceive of a more terrible admission of religious bankruptcy. That is how the *anathema sit* have to be paid for. To sum up, religion, degraded to the rank of a private matter, reduces itself to the choice of a place in which to spend an hour or two every Sunday morning.[75]

This seems to contradict, quite directly, her resistance to orthodoxy—and indeed it may. It is often difficult to tell with Weil whether she is contradicting herself or making a point of great subtlety. This passage may be read to say that religious institutions, if they must exist at all, should manifest humility in *deed*, but should be uncompromising in *proclamation*. It appears that she did not mind the Church declaring unambiguously and unhesitatingly its beliefs; she minded the "spiritual totalitarianism" of what Charles Williams, again, called "the method of *imposition* of belief."

In this she wished for religious institutions to be as she herself was. Father Perrin said of her that she was a person of the most extraordinary humility, but also that he had never seen her give an inch in an argument. Eliot, in his introduction to *The Need for Roots*, comments on this apparent paradox: "One is struck, here and there, by a contrast between an almost superhuman humility and what appears to be an almost outrageous arrogance." He accounts for this by noting, shrewdly I believe, that "all her thought was so intensely lived, that the abandonment of any opinion required modifications in her whole being: a process which could not take place painlessly, or in the course of a conversation."[76] But it is not obvious that this particular complex of attitudes can be practiced at all by institutions. This much is clear, however: institutions can do harm. They can uproot. And throughout *The Need for Roots* Weil assigns blame to *educational* institutions for the deracination she laments. Her analysis of this situation is, as was typical for her, more deeply historical than that of other critics—though building an argument along many of the same lines as the other figures we have studied. She points to the Renaissance as the period that "brought about a break between people of culture and the mass of the population," a break that had the effect of "abstracting culture from national tradition." However, to some degree it compensated for this by causing that culture "to be steeped in Greek tradition." Weil, as an evident Hellenophile but also someone compelled by the Christian Gospel, has mixed feelings about this: as we saw in her essay on "The Romanesque Renaissance," the later movement usually called the Renaissance offered a "faint, confused image ... of man's supernatural vocation"—but it was a genuine image nonetheless. When, in subsequent centuries, "links with the national traditions have not been renewed, but Greece has been forgotten," something of great value was lost.

> The result has been a culture which has developed in a very restricted medium, removed from the world, in a stove-pipe atmosphere—a culture very strongly directed towards and influenced by technical science, very strongly tinged with pragmatism, extremely broken up by specialization, entirely deprived both of contact with this world and, at the same time, of any window opening on to the world beyond.[77]

Thus, "what is called today educating the masses" is a matter of "taking this modern culture, evolved in such a closed, unwholesome atmosphere, and one so indifferent to the truth, removing what-ever it may still contain of intrinsic merit—an operation known as popularization—and shovelling the residue as it stands into the minds of the unfortunate individuals desirous of learning, in the same way as you feed birds with a stick." Such a model clearly cannot be called genuine education.

Returning to this theme late in the book, Weil echoes Maritain and Lewis in calling for an education that trains the sensibility and affections at least as seriously as it attends to the mind: "To show what is beneficial, what is obligatory, what is good—that is the task of education. Education concerns itself with the motives for effective action. For no action is ever carried out in the absence of motives capable of supplying the indispensable amount of energy for its execution."[78] We are back, then, to Augustine's *ordo amoris*: education is a disciplining of the affections to make them "ordinate," appropriate, and adequate to the circumstances.

In *The Abolition of Man*, Lewis had written, "You can hardly open a periodical without coming across the statement that what our civilization needs is more 'drive,' or dynamism, or self-sacrifice, or 'creativity.' In a sort of ghastly simplicity we remove the organ and demand the function. We make men without chests and expect of them virtue and enterprise. We laugh at honour and are shocked to find traitors in our midst. We castrate and bid the geldings be fruitful."[79] Weil makes the same point by way of, ironically enough, a technological metaphor: "To want to direct human creatures—others or oneself—towards the good by simply pointing out the direction, without making sure the necessary motives have been provided, is as if one tried, by pressing down the accelerator, to set off in a motor-car with an empty petrol tank."[80]

The chief problem for Weil is to understand what social institutions could be adequate to providing this kind of formation, especially given her insistence that every kind of collectivity is a manifestation of the social Beast. We know that she does not trust the institutional Church. Eliot had suggested that the family must be the essential source for moral formation, but Weil has little to say about the family except to note that the progress of modernity has effectively eliminated it as a constructive agent: "The family doesn't exist. What nowadays goes by that name is a minute collection of human beings grouped around each of us: father and mother, husband or wife, and children; brothers and sisters being already a little remote . . . . From the point of view of the collectivity and its particular function, the family no longer counts."[81] It is impossible to tell whether she even regrets this diminishment.

We find, therefore, in Weil's critique of education, a diagnosis without a prescription—or, to be more precise, a prescription without a delivery system. For she makes clear, first, what she believes to be the chief enemy of genuine education, and second, the general form that true education should take. About these matters she is consistent from the early pages of her book to the very end.

The enemy is technocracy: "it is inevitable that evil should dominate wherever the technical side of things is either completely or almost completely sovereign." Weil accepts that "Technicians always tend to make themselves sovereign, because they feel they alone know what they are about"; this is a given. Those who are not technicians must therefore refuse to "allow them full rein." But this we cannot do unless we keep "continually in mind a clear and absolutely precise conception of the particular ends to which this, that or the other technique should be subordinated."[82]

And here is where Weil goes beyond those who would simply say (as Lewis does) that science is good, or (as Maritain does) that technology is good. She argues that an education worthy of the name must be "inspired by the conception of a certain form of

human perfection"; and then, moving a step back in the logical sequence, that "the inspiration for such an education must be sought,
like the method itself, among the truths eternally inscribed in the
nature of things."[83] It is *Platonist science*, as it were, that she counsels.

> The spirit of truth can dwell in science on condition that the
> motive prompting the savant is the love of the object which
> forms the stuff of his investigations. That object is the universe
> in which we live. What can we find to love about it, if it isn't its
> beauty? The true definition of science is this: the study of the
> beauty of the world.[84]

To think otherwise is to identify science with the study—and
therefore the worship—of "matter, blind force." But by what means
could people in general, as opposed to the odd peculiar individual
like Weil herself, come to see, and be drawn to, this pursuit? What
institutions could possibly teach us that true science is the study, by
people oppressed by force, of the beauty of the world?

*   *   *

In the final pages of *The Need for Roots*—which is to say, at the very
end of her brief life's work—Weil returns to her skeptical interroga-
tion of what I have called the neo-Thomist interpretation of history.
"But a Christian civilization in which the light of Christianity would
have illuminated the whole of life, would only have been possible
if the Roman conception of enslaving people's minds adopted by
the Church had been cast aside."[85] It is important to recall here that
she had told Father Perrin that "my own intelligence is numbered
among" those things that cannot enter the Church because of those
two words, *anathema sit*: she could not enter the Church because
that would have been to accept intellectual "enslavement"—to, as

she puts it in her essay on the *Iliad*, bow her neck to force. Those who embrace the High Gothic era as the high point in the history of the Church, who therefore endorse what she calls "spiritual totalitarianism," have exchanged the suffering Christ for a version of Jupiter. "The Roman conception of God still exists today, even in such minds as that of Maritain"—one of her few explicit references to the philosopher with whom, as I have tried to show, she is often in implicit controversy.[86]

But the Church had not always and everywhere made such demands. There was at one time, especially in the south of France, and as we saw in an earlier chapter, a more generous accommodation at work. But "at the beginning of the thirteenth century, this civilization still in process of formation was destroyed by the ruin of its principal centre, that is to say, the lands to the south of the Loire, the setting up of the Inquisition and the stifling of religious thought under the sign of orthodoxy."[87]

This stifling produced consequences that were massive, unforeseen—and inevitable, given the assumptions that underlay this "spiritual totalitarianism": the very "conception of orthodoxy" is effectively, functionally, generated by "rigorously separating the domain relating to the welfare of souls, which is that of an unconditional subjection of the mind to external authority, from the domain relating to so-called profane matters, in which the intelligence remains free." This distinction is, for Weil, utterly tragic, because it "makes impossible that mutual penetration of the religious and the profane which would be the essence of a Christian civilization." A mind that is free only in some areas, having bowed its neck to force in others, can never be whole. Therefore "[i]t is in vain that every day, at Mass, a little water is mixed with the wine."

At this stage, her writing became more fragmentary, aphoristic. She was working very quickly. Throughout the spring of 1943 her health had been declining, probably because she had been working at the Free French offices all day and writing all night. So much needed to be said; there was so much to do. In those last months, her whole life was work; it is significant that the last problem she raises in her unfinished book is the problem of *labor*, labor with and without dignity, which had concerned her all her life.

Eventually she was diagnosed with tuberculosis and was taken to a sanatorium in Kent, where she insisted that she did not want, or deserve, more food than people in occupied France were likely to have. When she died of cardiac failure on August 24, 1943, the coroner ruled that "the deceased did kill and slay herself by refusing to eat whilst the balance of her mind was disturbed." The verdict was rashly and unfairly reached: her body was failing, and it is unlikely that even with the best care she could have held out much longer. She had always opposed to the force of the world the force of her own personality—she had heard the idea of grace freely given and freely, but such a notion was at the deepest levels of her being inaccessible—and so unequal a contest could not have lasted long.

She was thirty-four when she died. She was buried in the Catholic section of Bybrook Cemetery in Ashford, Kent, but did not receive—as an unbaptized person, could not have received— Catholic burial. A friend, Maurice Schumann, read prayers over her grave. She never entered the Church, and her body rests in a strange land. In death, as in life, she remained one of those outside.

Chapter 7

Approaching the End

Around the time Auden gave his Swarthmore talk on "Vocation and Society," he wrote an essay entitled "Purely Subjective" that began with these words:

> I wake into my existence to find myself and the world that is not myself already there, and simultaneously feel responsible for my discovery. I can and must ask: "Who am I? Do I want to be? Who do I want and who ought I to become?" I am, in fact, an anxious subject. That is my religious problem.[1]

And as the war drew to its close and the great civilizational problems it forced upon everyone began to recede, the condition of being "an anxious subject" came to the fore. This is the great theme of Hannah Arendt's book *Between Past and Future*, in which she describes people whose lives had been governed by a great and all-consuming cause—the French Resistance, for example—who now must strive to return to normalcy, only to find that the "normal" can no longer be found. Arendt quotes René Char, who anticipated this choice before having to face it directly: "If I survive, I know that I have to break with the aroma of these essential years, silently reject my treasure"—his "treasure" being the complete identification with the work of resistance, the existential security that labor offered to him and to everyone else who participated.[2] Indeed, one might argue that the obsession with education that I have traced throughout this book is moved by an anticipation of the experience Char describes, an awareness that the end of the war, even in victory, would necessarily be personally destabilizing, and that people so destabilized would need to be fixed in new social roles.

Auden wrote four long poems during the war years. The first, "New Year Letter," served him as a kind of intellectual orientation, a sorting through of his reading (and to a lesser extent his musical listening). The second, *For the Time Being,* marked his return to the Christian faith and worked to situate Christian belief and practice historically and politically. Among the four, it most closely tracks the concerns I have been exploring here. The third, *The Sea and the Mirror,* mapped the possible coordinates for a theological aesthetics and served to establish Auden's self-understanding as a poet under the rule of faith. And the fourth, *The Age of Anxiety,* describes the psychological consequences of "war-time, when everybody is reduced to the anxious status of a shady character or displaced person."[3]

The phrase "displaced person" had a very particular meaning at the end of World War II: it was apparently coined by the Russian-American sociologist Eugene Kulischer to describe those who, as a result of war or other catastrophic social disruption, were forced to leave their native land and had no clear path to return. (It is noteworthy that Kulischer, between 1920 and 1941, was forced to flee newly Soviet Russia for Germany, Germany for Denmark, Denmark for France, and France for the United States—the last move occurring at approximately the same time that the Weil family and Claude Levi-Strauss came to America.) For Auden, the civilizational disruptions of the war had displaced everyone in some respect.

Auden would not have equated the life-endangering horrors of displaced persons in Europe with the purely interior confusions of the four New Yorkers he describes in *The Age of Anxiety*. While working on the poem, he visited a ruined Germany as part of the US Strategic Bombing Survey and was shocked and grieved by what he saw. To his friend Elizabeth Mayer—herself a refugee from Nazi Germany—he wrote, "I keep wishing you were with us to help and then I think, perhaps not, for as I write this sentence I find myself crying."[4] He understood perfectly well what he had gained by living free and safe in America during the war years. But this did not mean that the merely psychological displacements were unimportant or unworthy of his attention. Indeed, given his concern with the future of the Western democracies—a concern he shared with the other figures whose destinies I have traced in this book—attention to the state of affairs on the home front was especially important for him.

In *For the Time Being*, Auden had introduced the Four Faculties, a quartet borrowed from Carl Jung's *Psychological Types*: Thought, Feeling, Sensation, Intuition—and had suggested that their differentiation is a product of the Fall: "We who are four were / Once but one / Before his act of / Rebellion."[5] But in *The Age of Anxiety*, the Faculties become individual characters, three men and a woman, with different personalities, histories, and occupations, an expansion of the original appropriation of Jung that suggests a need not just for personal reintegration but also some strategy by which persons of strongly varying tendencies and preferences could be reconciled with one another. Auden once made up a "parlor game" he called Purgatory Mates, which required players to imagine two people of radically alien personalities—and then to imagine the means by which they might come to be at peace with each other. Each of the four characters in *The Age of Anxiety* needs interior healing; but the poem is also a massively complex game of Purgatory Mates.

After Malin, Emble, Rosetta, and Quant meet in a Manhattan bar, they pass together through a series of allegorical landscapes that test them and reveal their fears, their repulsions, their affinities, their virtues, in a narrative that Auden seems to have thought of as a "Dream Quest" but whose purpose is never straightforwardly articulated. And then, having made their way through the most harrowing of their challenges, they find themselves back in what is recognizably our world. They hail a taxi and make their way toward Rosetta's apartment, and on their way there, reflecting on their experiences of the evening and on the state of the whole world, they sing a great dirge.[6]

When Auden published this dirge separately, in *Horizon* magazine, he called it "Lament for a Lawgiver." As war comes to an end, and its exigencies ease, and people return to a freedom absent for so long that its return is discomfiting, they think of the apparent lawlessness of Nature and Man alike: "it seemed impossible to them that either [Nature or humanity] could have survived so long had not some semi-divine stranger with superhuman powers, some Gilgamesh or Napoleon, some Solon or Sherlock Holmes, appeared from time to time to rescue both, for a brief bright moment, from their egregious destructive blunders."[7]

The forms of lawgiving suggested here are various and go well beyond those like Napoleon and Solon, who specified and enforced actual laws. Also invoked is a hero, Gilgamesh, who fought—and (surely this is significant in the time of the Marshall Plan) later befriended—the wild man Enkidu, and built great walls to protect the city of Uruk; and then Sherlock Holmes, whose successful deductions prove that even the most chaotic and unexpected events are susceptible to rational explanation. There are a thousand ways to bring order out of chaos, or reveal the order that is always there but hidden from mortal eyes. "Mourn for him now, / Our lost dad, / Our colossal father."[8]

What shall we do now, without "The didactic digit and dreaded voice / Which imposed peace on the pullulating / Primordial mass"? The gods themselves "are wringing their great worn hands / For their watchman is away, their world-engine / Creaking and cracking."[9]

Having sung their great dirge and arrived at Rosetta's apartment, they collectively enter into a strange psychological state: "Alcohol, lust, fatigue, and the longing to be good, had by now induced in them all a euphoric state in which it seemed as if it were only some trifling and easily rectifiable error, improper diet, inadequate schooling, or an outmoded moral code which was keeping mankind from the millennial Earthly Paradise." Are not all wars fought in the name of achieving just this perfected state of social order? And is not this current war—it should be remembered that Auden began this poem in 1944—on its way to successful resolution? "Just a little more effort, perhaps merely the discovery of the right terms in which to describe it, and surely absolute pleasure must immediately descend upon the astonished armies of this world and abolish for ever all their hate and suffering."[10]

And then: "So, such efforts as at that moment they could, they made." It is a poignant moment, for there is little they *can* do. In the concluding pages of the poem, Emble goes to sleep and Quant disappears in a flutter of comical song. But Rosetta is a Jew; and her thoughts necessarily take a darker turn. As Auden knew that he had been spared the sufferings of his fellow English, so Rosetta knows that she has been spared the horrors of the Shoah. Those Jews who remain are indeed, she thinks, "His People still," and have a role, however vexed and complicated, yet to play:

> We'll point for Him,
> Be as obvious always if He won't show
> To threaten their thinking in their way,

Nor His strong arm that stood no nonsense,
Fly, let's face it, to defend us now
When we bruised or broiled our bodies are chucked
Like cracked crocks onto kitchen middens
In the time He takes. We'll trust. He'll slay
If His Wisdom will. He won't alter
Nor fake one fact. Though I fly to Wall Street
Or Publisher's Row, or pass out, or
Submerge in music, or marry well,
Marooned on riches, He'll be right there
With His Eye upon me.[11]

Like "Our lost dad, / Our colossal father," He seems to have fled or failed: "His strong arm" does not defend His People. Yet, Rosetta says, she and the rest of scattered Israel will continue to "point for Him."

"Though I fly to Wall Street" is a clear echo of Psalm 139: "If I ascend up into heaven, thou art there: if I make my bed in hell, behold, thou art there. If I take the wings of the morning, and dwell in the uttermost parts of the sea; Even there shall thy hand lead me, and thy right hand shall hold me." Such was not the thinking of every Jew in the aftermath of the Shoah, and it was either bold or reckless, wise or foolish, for a Gentile like Auden to imagine himself into Rosetta's lifeworld. But he takes this risk. "We'll trust," he has her think, and, in her final words: "*Shema' yisra'el: / 'adonai 'elohenu, 'adonai 'echad.*"[12]

If Rosetta reflects on the long history of the children of Israel, Malin, as the sun rises over Manhattan, thinks toward the future:

His Question disqualifies our quick senses,
His Truth makes our theories historical sins,
It is where we are wounded that is when He speaks

Our creaturely cry, concluding His children
In their mad unbelief to have mercy on them all
As they wait unawares for His World to come.[13]

And in the poem's concluding lines, the narrator tells us that "creation lay in pain and earnest"—an echo not of the Hebrew Bible but of the New Testament, Paul's letter to the Romans: "For we know that the whole creation groaneth and travaileth in pain together until now. And not only they, but ourselves also, which have the firstfruits of the Spirit, even we ourselves groan within ourselves, waiting for the adoption" (Romans 8:22–23). This created order, the narrator says, is "once more reprieved from self-destruction, its adoption, as usual, postponed." As the narrator of an earlier poem had said,

To those who have seen
The Child, however dimly, however incredulously,
The Time Being is, in a sense, the most trying time of all.[14]

* * *

"We ourselves groan within ourselves," Paul had said, "waiting for the adoption"—but what adoption? He answers by continuing, "to wit, the redemption of our body."

A few years later, Auden would reflect again on the experience he describes at the outset of "Purely Objective": "I wake into my existence to find myself and the world that is not myself already there," and understand it not as a cause for anxiety but rather for rejoicing:

Holy this moment, wholly in the right,
As, in complete obedience
To the light's laconic outcry, next
As a sheet, near as a wall,

Out there as a mountain's poise of stone,
The world is present, about,
And I know that I am, here, not alone
But with a world and rejoice
Unvexed.[15]

But this would have to wait until he had augmented his Barthian/
Kierkegaardian model of the existential subject, comprised of pure
interiority, with a theology of the inarticulate human body that lives
in History, yes, but also, in ways that we neglect, in Nature. Once the
adrenaline rush of war had faded, and its consequent anxiety dealt with
somehow, it was finally, for Auden, time to think about the body that
shares its constitution with "birds who chirp, / Not for effect but because chirping // Is the thing to do," the body that each "escapes . . . to
join / Plants in their chaster peace which is more / To its real taste."[16]

* * *

In the last two years of the war, the energy that Eliot had devoted
to plans for social and educational renewal—plans that had been
a central focus of his thinking between the writing of *The Idea of
a Christian Society* in 1938 and the drafting in 1943 of the essays
that became *Notes toward the Definition of Culture*—began to wane.
It is hard to be sure why this had happened. He was of course aware
that schemes were being developed, at the highest levels of the
ruling classes, for a postwar world, and that those schemes openly
repudiated the ideas and hopes he treasured; how he felt about that
may be discerned from the uncharacteristically bitter tone of the
passages on education in *Notes*. But perhaps an even more important factor in his changing emphasis was the awareness that he was
growing old. He had had that awareness for a comically long time: in
"Ash Wednesday," a poem published when he was forty-two, he had

plaintively asked, "Why should the agéd eagle stretch its wings?"[17] (In letters, Auden sometimes referred to Eliot as The Agéd Eagle.) But by the time he wrote "Little Gidding," he had reached his mid-fifties, and the severe lessons offered him by the "familiar compound ghost [of] some dead master" in that poem had to be much on his mind: "Let me disclose the gifts reserved for age / To set a crown upon your lifetime's effort." Among those gifts are "the cold friction of expiring sense / Without enchantment"; "the conscious impotence of rage / At human folly"; "the rending pain of re-enactment / Of all that you have done, and been.[18] The words are a laceration and a challenge, and in light of them, it is perhaps unsurprising that Eliot began to narrow his sociological scope and chasten his political hopes.

Among the many lectures that Eliot gave during the war years, three in particular indicate the changing direction of his thought. One is "The Social Function of Poetry"; a second is "What Is a Classic?"; a third is "The Man of Letters and the Future of Europe."[19]

Eliot begins "The Social Function of Poetry" with a detailed and fastidious accounting of all the subjects he is not going to talk about. (This habit seems to have become compulsive for him during the war years.) When he finally settles down to his task, he approaches it from two directions: the point of view of the genuinely creative and imaginative poet, and then that of his or her readership, whom Eliot like Milton conceives of as "fit audience though few."

The social function for the poet, for Eliot, is primarily this: the preservation, and then the extension and improvement, of his native language in ways that allow for the accurate and vivid registering of new feelings and emotions—new sensibilities. All this is consistent with what Eliot says elsewhere, and had been saying for many years: for instance, in "Little Gidding," where the dead master declares that "our concern was to purify the dialect of the tribe" (a

line taken from Valéry); or in the famous essay on the metaphysical poets where he says that those poets possessed "a mechanism
of sensibility that could devour any kind of experience."[20] What is
distinctive about the articulation of those ideas in this new lecture
is the emphasis not just on the public dimensions of these powers
but also, and even more strongly, on their possible contribution to
national identity. It is with reference to and in strong support of the
spirit of *nationalism* that Eliot speaks.

In *Notes toward the Definition of Culture*, Eliot had written, he
said, as a sociologist, which suggests that he did not think that sociology was the sort of thing one needed formal training or professional status to pursue. Without succumbing to a cult of narrowly
defined "expertise," one might reasonably question whether this is
true. It may be that Eliot's years of meetings on matters of cultural
and political concern—in the Moot and the Chandos Group and
the St. Anne's Group, among others—gave him, if not a false sense
of authority, at least an unsustainably expansive picture of his own
intellectual scope. "The Social Function of Poetry" marks, not a retreat *from* social concern, but a retreat *to* the arena in which Eliot can
clearly claim authoritative knowledge: poetic language.

"The duty of the poet, as poet, is only indirectly to his people,"
Eliot says, and the notion of indirectness is essential to the argument he makes in this essay: "his direct duty is to his language, first
to preserve, and second to extend and improve."[21] The duty to "extend and improve" is central for Eliot, and in this context we should
remember that, for all his cultural traditionalism, he was not only innovative in his own verse but also a promoter of innovation by other
poets. (For instance, he championed Auden, and became his editor,
at a time when few editors of equal stature could see the young
poet's potential, and consistently defended Auden against attacks.[22])
Innovation in poetry is necessary, he argues, because "our sensibility

is constantly changing, as the world about us changes," and "this is the reason why we cannot afford to *stop* writing poetry." Poetry must continue to strive to come to terms (quite literally) with an ever-changing environment of experiences and ideas; it must seek verbal formulations adequate to the challenges of the moment. To adopt language from other writings of Eliot's already noted, it must strive for, even if it cannot fully succeed "under conditions / That seem unpropitious," the creation of "a mechanism of sensibility that could devour any kind of experience." Because if a people cannot "go on producing great authors, and especially great poets, their culture will deteriorate and perhaps be absorbed in a stronger one."[23]

So then the question arises: What must be done in order to ensure that a given society "go on producing great authors"? Eliot's answer is that "there should always be a small vanguard of people, appreciative of poetry, who are independent and somewhat in advance of their time or ready to assimilate novelty more quickly." In short, it is necessary for there to be a critical and readerly *elite*: "The changes and developments of sensibility which appear first in a few will work themselves into the language gradually, through their influence on other and more readily popular authors; and by the time they have become well established, a new advance will be called for."[24] And so the cycle moves on.

This argument sits oddly in relation to the ones made about education in *Notes*, for there Eliot had argued in highly traditionalist terms, and his emphasis had been on absorption of "the highest achievements of the past"; here, by contrast, he envisions a kind of Mandarin avant-garde precisely attuned to the power of the new.[25] There is no reason to think that Eliot thought the one more necessary than the other; but it does seem that he came to understand that he was more likely to shape this poetic elite than to influence the content of a governmental Education Act.

The argument of "The Social Function of Poetry" also sits oddly, but interestingly, in relation to "What Is a Classic?" That lecture to the Virgil Society is in some respects Eliot's prose at its worst; and that means that it is very bad prose indeed. What makes it so distinctively bad is the way it joins an insistence upon the most peculiarly minute distinctions with an inclination toward the most impenetrable abstractions. Early in the lecture Eliot writes, "If there is one word on which we can fix, which will suggest the maximum of what I mean by the term 'a classic,' it is the word *maturity*."[26] There follow many paragraphs devoted to exploring various venues in which maturity may be manifested—in mind, in manner, and in language (with some indication that maturity in poetic language may not always be coeval with mature prose)—and the various authors of various periods from various nations who may be said to embody one or another of these kinds of maturity. But never at any point does Eliot even hint at what he means by "maturity."

But two remarkable passages arise from the morass. Though Eliot insists that "our classic, the classic of all Europe, is Virgil," he does not quote a single word written by that poet, and only refers specifically to one passage. But that passage is, in the context of the historical moment, a telling one. "I have always thought the meeting of Aeneas with the shade of Dido, in book 7, not only one of the most poignant, but one of the most civilized passages in poetry."[27] Eliot does not define "civilized" any more than he defines "maturity," but what he means by it emerges clearly in his description of the scene. When Aeneas sees Dido among the dead—she who took her own life in grief after he left her—he pleads with her to understand that

> I was
> unwilling when I had to leave your shores.
> But those same orders of the gods that now

urge on my journey through the shadows, through
abandoned, thorny lands and deepest night,
drove me by their decrees. And I could not
believe that with my going I should bring
so a great a grief as this.

But Dido refuses to speak with him, "no more moved by his speech
than if she stood / as stubborn as flint."

Nevertheless, Aeneas, stunned by her
unkindly fate, still follows at a distance
with tears and pity for her as she goes.[28]

For Eliot, "what matters most" in this scene is not that Dido ignores
Aeneas—even if it is "perhaps the most telling snub in all poetry"—
but rather that "Aeneas does not forgive himself." Though he does
protest that he acted not according to his own will but in *pietas*, de-
votion to the "orders of the gods," his primary feeling here, indeed
the only one Virgil describes, is that he pities her (*miseratur*) for the
"unkindly fate" (*iniquo casu*) inflicted upon her by those very gods.
It is this pity that Eliot sees as the mark of civilization. Dido flees
from Aeneas in hostility (*inimica*), but he refuses to respond in the
same spirit; rather, he reaches out to her in compassion—he is genuinely stricken (*concussus*) by what she has suffered. Now, if condescension in victory were all that Eliot cared about here, he would
have done better to cite the famous speech of Anchises elsewhere in
book 6, in which Aeneas is told,

these, Roman, will be your arts:
to teach the ways of peace to those you conquer,
spare defeated peoples, tame the proud.[29]

But such behavior, admirable though it may be, is not what Eliot wants to commend. "What matters most" for him, what marks this passage as intensely civilized, is not what Aeneas *does* but how he *feels*—and, we may recall, to shape and promote the proper feelings, the "sensibility" adequate our experiences, is for Eliot "the social function of poetry."

So we have returned once more to Lewis and Maritain and Weil and before all of them Augustine: the necessity of seeking the *ordo amoris*, of training the emotional responses before training the rational ones. But for Eliot this is vital not just for the young, but for all ages; and the instrument distinctively suited to such training is poetry.

Yet, if we look at these two essays in tandem with each other, it seems there is a twofold restriction on the scope of this instrument's power. The first is simply that the cultivation and recognition of that power will be possible only for an elite: just as in *Notes* he had said that a general "respect for learning" was preferable to universal education, so in this context he insists that the poet's audience should be small.[30] But perhaps this is nothing to worry about, since, as we have noted, the truly innovative poets shape society *indirectly*, "through their influence on other and more readily popular authors."

The second restriction remains implicit and is only visible if you set the essays side by side: as deeply as Eliot loves Virgil, and as passionately as he believes that the *Aeneid* is the very embodiment of the notion of a "classic" work, he clearly does not imagine that a poem with anything like the power and influence of the *Aeneid* can be produced in his own time, because there is no longer a single language that dominates Europe—no lingua franca for the Republic of Letters. In practice, for Eliot, this means that while ideas can be shared across the boundaries that separate countries, the vital shaping of *sensibility* must go on at the national rather than the international level: "feeling and emotion are particular, whereas thought is general. It is easier to think in a foreign language than to feel in it. Therefore no art is more stubbornly national than poetry."[31] This realization "perhaps unexpectedly" raises political questions that Eliot does not especially want to raise. He understands, in light of recent history, that this poetic nationalism could be problematic: "I do not wish to leave the impression that the function of poetry is to divide people from people, for I do not believe that the cultures of the several [nations] of Europe can flourish in isolation from each other."[32] And yet he does not quite regret it either, for he feels a strong bias toward the local in preference to the universal that suits him both as a social conservative and as a poet. And indeed, though he does not say so explicitly, his argument implies that one of the most important social functions of poetry is to bring the local and immediate to our attention and attract to it our love.

But Eliot knows that the development of postwar society will not work to sustain and nourish the local things he loves. The unifying and universalizing power of Latin is gone, and it is being replaced by the very different universalizing power of science and technocracy. This is one of the chief themes of "The Man of Letters and the Future of Europe." Eliot's concern here is that the "engineering mind" cannot understand the value of local cultures, or how a series of local cultures may be independent of one another and yet intimately related: "Neither in a complete and universal uniformity, nor in an isolated self-sufficiency, can culture flourish"; rather, "a local and a general culture are so far from being in conflict, that they are truly necessary to each other." The "engineering mind" can easily grasp the binary opposition between "universal uniformity" and "complete autarchy," but "the union of local cultures in a general culture is more difficult to conceive, and more difficult to realize." And the chief social role of the "man of letters"—rather different than that of the poet or the Mandarin appreciator of poetry—is to testify to this subtle union, because "the man of letters should know that uniformity means the obliteration of culture, and that self-sufficiency means its death by starvation."[33]

That the man of letters might be unable to achieve this, that the poet and the Mandarin critic might be unsuccessful in sustaining a language that conserves but also innovates and extends, is what Eliot most fears. He concludes "The Social Function of Poetry" by saying, "What I am apprehensive of is death"—the death of genuine poetry, the death of genuine culture. It is possible, he admits, "that the feeling for poetry, and the feelings which are the material of poetry, may disappear everywhere." And if that happens, it may well "facilitate that unification of the world"—the elimination of local culture by a universalizing "engineering mind," by technocracy—"which some people consider desirable for its own sake."[34]

And thus, in "The Man of Letters and the Future of Europe," he sums up his fears in a lapidary passage that so concisely encapsulates the concerns of this whole book that I have chosen it as one of my epigraphs:

> I have suggested that the cultural health of Europe, including the cultural health of its component parts, is incompatible with extreme forms of both nationalism and internationalism. But the cause of that disease, which destroys the very soil in which culture has its roots, is not so much extreme ideas, and the fanaticism which they stimulate, as the relentless pressure of modern industrialism, setting the problems which the extreme ideas attempt to solve. Not least of the effects of industrialism is that we become mechanized in mind, and consequently attempt to provide solutions in terms of *engineering*, for problems which are essentially problems of *life*.[35]

* * *

The story this book tells overlaps with others that have been recently told. One, as already noted, involves the "nature of man" debate—the "discourse of man"—as described by Mark Greif in his *Age of the Crisis of Man*. Another is the story of the emergence of a different but closely related discourse, that of human rights. The second story has recently been told with great clarity and authority by Samuel Moyn, in his 2015 book *Christian Human Rights*. What follows is a summary of Moyn's argument, or at least the elements of it most relevant to our concerns here.

Though "human rights" may be a concept deeply embedded in the intellectual and moral history of the West, Moyn contends that the proximate cause of its emergence was the felt need, especially by the Popes Pius XI and XII, to articulate an account of the position within the social order of the individual human being that avoided the errors of the communist model, the fascist model, and the model of romantic individualism. The primary instrument employed to shape this account was the philosophical/theological concept of *personalism*, as articulated primarily by Emanuel Mounier and then by Jacques Maritain, before being appropriated for papal pronouncements.

The problems that personalism was meant to address are ones that we have seen throughout our own story. Maritain's *Integral Humanism* is a personalist manifesto; we are facing *The Twilight of Civilization* because our culture has neglected or overridden the truths of personalism. Lewis's Inner Rings trample the human person; the alternative model he articulates in *That Hideous Strength* is personalist, through and through. The *enracinement* that Weil wishes to promote is necessary for personalist reasons. The approaches to education favored by all these authors are meant to educate young people in ways that foster rather than inhibit the formation of genuine persons. (When Pink Floyd has a choir of children sing, "We don't need no

And throughout the second half of the war, Maritain strove always to think strategically about how to implement his personalist convictions in laws and institutions. There is an enormous amount of repetition in Maritain's writing during this period—the dozen books he published during the war could easily be reduced to one largish one—but the rather small set of ideas starts to get deployed in somewhat different ways. This new strategy of deployment marks a vocational transformation for Maritain, from a philosopher and theologian who spoke primarily to academic audiences to a more broadly public figure. One thinks of Yeats's description of himself, when he was a member of the Irish Senate, as "a sixty-year-old smiling public man"—though Maritain had access to a larger stage and to sources of political power, access that Eliot and the other figures of the Moot could but have dreamed of.

Maritain's changing place in the world is a useful reminder of the need to reflect on the institutional situation, the social embodiment, of ideas. Weil worked for the French Resistance in London, but almost all of the writing for which she has become famous was done in near-absolute privacy: notebooks preserved by friends, letters that a priest kept in a drawer. Auden's social thought was expressed most directly to his students, perhaps, though it came out indirectly in poems and reviews. Eliot worked through various informal groups, none of which had the kind of influence in the corridors of power that they hoped for (which may have led to his retreat from the role of political sociologist to that of the "mere" poet and critic). Thanks to his broadcast talks for the BBC, Lewis became what Bernard Nightingale in Tom Stoppard's play *Arcadia* calls a "media don"—a figure of significant public presence, though not of political influence. Maritain came to occupy a curious place well outside the boundaries of this rather scholarly continuum when, in 1944, Charles de Gaulle named him the ambassador to the Vatican of newly liberated France.

The transformation was not instantaneous, and indeed began rather before the midpoint of the war. One of the key documents, a long essay or little book called *Christianity and Democracy*, was written in mid-1942, before he had given or even composed his Terry Lectures on education. So to some extent my treatment of Maritain's at this stage of my narrative is a violation of strict chronology. But these concerns did loom larger and larger in his mind as the war went on, and, as Samuel Moyn explains, led to his period of greatest public influence, in the years immediately following the war. It seems to me right that they be dealt with here.

One of Maritain's chief tasks in these midwar writings is to insist that a seriously Christian political theology does not contradict a commitment to democracy but rather is perfectly consistent with it—indeed, makes secular democracy possible. (We may recall here Maritain's insistence to Louis Finkelstein that his Conference needed to feature only thinkers who held substantive religious beliefs because without those beliefs to undergird it, democracy would collapse of its own weight.) This is why he writes of the ways that the "evangelical inspiration" of Christianity does not echo but rather *produces* the "secular conscience" that in its turn writes the constitutions and laws of democratic societies. If people are widely beginning to understand the tragic rule of what Weil called force, the Christian Gospel is to be credited, even when it goes unacknowledged and perhaps rejected:

> [U]nder the inspiration of the Gospel at work in history, the secular conscience has understood that in the misfortunes and suffering of our existence, crushed by the iron laws of biological necessity and by the weight of the pride, injustice and wickedness

of men, a single principle of liberation, a single principle of hope,
a single principle of peace can stir up the mass of servitude and
iniquity and triumph over it, because this principle comes down
to us from the creative source of the world, stronger than the
world: that brotherly love whose law was promulgated by the
Gospel to the scandal of the mighty, and which is, as the Christian
well knows, God's own charity diffused into the hearts of men.[37]

Even those who disbelieve in the Christian God are beneficiaries of this
"diffused" charity, this common grace. Therefore "these ideas and these
aspirations remained and will always remain essentially linked to the
Christian message and to the action of hidden stimulation which this
message exercises in the depths of the secular conscience of the world."[38]

For Maritain, Christianity and democracy are mutually
interanimating and mutually sustaining. He quotes a speech by
Roosevelt's vice president, Henry Wallace: "The idea of freedom . . . is
derived from the Bible with its extraordinary emphasis on the dignity
of the individual. Democracy is the only true political expression of
Christianity."[39] And Christianity is the only genuine source and sus-
tainer of democracy—a state of affairs that remains the case even
when democracy does not know it. Early in this book, I cited Auden's
question for Niebuhr: "Does he believe that the contemplative life
is the highest and most exhausting of vocations, that the church is
saved by the saints, or doesn't he?" Maritain does, and believes that
that salvation is effectual even when hidden—though it is of course
more effectual, *more* powerful, when acknowledged and embraced.

In the last words of *Christianity and Democracy*, Maritain offers
up a peroration that summarizes his hopes:

It is necessary for the sense of the tragic in life and the sense of
the great human adventure to meet and mingle, for the spirit of

Europe and the spirit of America to work together in common good will. We don't believe paradise is set for tomorrow. But the task to which we are summoned, the task we have to pursue with all the more courage and hope because at each moment it will be betrayed by human weakness, this task will have to have for its objective, if we want civilization to survive, a world of free men imbued in its secular substance by a genuine and living Christianity, a world in which the inspiration of the Gospel will orient common life toward an heroic humanism.[40]

Maritain has reached a far more generous and hopeful position than he had articulated at the beginning of the war, when he told Finkelstein that only religious believers could participate usefully in the Conference. But there may be some wishful thinking in this re-orientation, in Maritain's notion that an unacknowledged and even rejected Christianity can nevertheless retain a sustaining power over a body of Western democracies flush with a belief in technocratic empowerment. The coming decade would see, with its increasing emphasis on the scientist as the shaper of human destiny, and the decline in influence of Christian intellectuals such as the ones described in this book, that the postwar world sought and believed in heroism—but not a heroic *humanism*.[41]

* * *

Near the outset of the war, Auden had asked of Reinhold Niebuhr, is the church, and therefore the world, saved by the saints? After the war, Eliot returned to the writing of verse drama, and in *The Cocktail Party* addressed that question. In it, a frivolous woman, Celia Coplestone, becomes—offstage, out of our sight—a Christian and then a missionary nurse. In the course of her work, she is martyred. During the eponymous cocktail party, when a man whose mistress she had been hopes that "she did not suffer as ordinary people suffer," another man who knows how her life changed says, in words that echo Weil on what force does to the human body,

> I'd say that she suffered all that we should suffer
> In fear and pain and loathing—all these together—
> And reluctance of the body to become a *thing*.
> I'd say she suffered more, because more conscious
> Than the rest of us. She paid the highest price
> In suffering.

And this reflection causes the man who had hoped Celia did not suffer to say, "But if this was right—if this was right for Celia— / There must be something else that is terribly wrong, / And the rest of us are somehow involved in the wrong."[42]

*　　*　　*

"Ares at last has quit the field"—so Auden declaimed in the first words of the poem he read to Harvard's chapter of Phi Beta Kappa in the spring of 1946.[43] One year earlier he had been investigating, for the Strategic Bombing Survey, the ruins of German cities.

Harry Levin, a member of the English faculty, was delighted by the epigrammatic wit of the poem, though disappointed by both the setting and the audience: the poem should have been read, he thought, at "an intimate evening meeting, where it might well have framed the appropriate climax to a sequence of after-dinner speeches and frequent toasts. Instead, the epigrams bypassed the superannuated alumni and thudded against the hollow rafters of Sanders Theatre during the cold sobriety of ten o'clock in the morning."[44] Levin is surely correct about the poem's wittiness, but he fails to note that in Auden's poem, humor is the surest sign of deep seriousness. "Under Which Lyre: A Reactionary Tract for the Times" is Auden's most thorough account of how best to live as a poet in a technocratic world.

It is at least possible, as Edward Mendelson has suggested, that the substance of this poem, if not its light-hearted tone, was shaped by an event in the poetic world, not at all world-historical, or not apparently so, that had occurred earlier in 1946. Bennett Cerf, Auden's publisher at Random House, had announced that he would excise from a forthcoming anthology of American poetry all poems by Ezra Pound, on the grounds that Pound, who had made radio broadcasts from Italy during the war in support of Mussolini's government, was a traitor. Auden wrote on January 29 to tell Cerf that in light of this decision he saw "no alternative for me but to sever my connection with your firm." He made a point of insisting that he made this protest not because he admired Pound's poems: "I do not care for them myself particularly," but for a very different reason: "Begin by banning his poems not because you object to them but because you object to him, and you will end, as the Nazis did, by slaughtering his wife and children." And Auden truly did not believe he was exaggerating. He continued,

> As you say, the war is not over. This incident is only one sign— there are other and far graver ones—that there was more truth than one would like to believe in Huey Long's cynical observation that if fascism came to America it would be called Antifascism. Needless to say, I am not suggesting that you desire any such thing—but I think your very natural abhorrence of Pound's conduct has led you to take the first step which, if not protested now, will be followed by others which would horrify you.[45]

Cerf tried to talk Auden into staying with Random House, but Auden was implacable, and eventually Cerf gave in and restored

Pound's poems to the anthology. The importance of this event for Auden's immediately postwar thinking will soon be clear.

Now that Ares has indeed "quit the field," what arrives in his place is not peace, but rather "that other war," that "a-historic / Antipathy" that "forever gripes / All ages and somatic types." This is the war between Hermes and Apollo, or rather between the rival followers of these gods, and though it is but "dialectic strife," "fought with smiles and Christian names," it is "just as mean" as actual warfare—"and more fanatic."

More fanatic because the temperamental difference between "the sons of Hermes" and "Apollo's children" is absolute: "Related by antithesis, / A compromise between us is / Impossible." Apollo is the god of reason and order, manifested in our time through administrative bureaucracy, claiming the authority of "common-sense." Auden knows of course that Nietzsche had contrasted the Dionysian to the Apollonian, but chooses instead as his opposition figure Hermes, "our god of dreams," of communication and interpretation. "The sons of Hermes" are the ones who forego power and control to pursue the intricacies of reflection: they are, therefore, and necessarily, "we, the unpolitical."

One might easily imagine a world in which the Apollonians and Hermetics live in peaceable neglect of one another, each group to its own natural realm; but this is not, Auden thinks, the world we live in. In his view, "Apollo's welcome to the throne" of the political sphere; but Apollo wants more:

> But jealous of our god of dreams,
> His common-sense in secret schemes
>   To rule the heart;
> Unable to invent the lyre,
> Creates with simulated fire
>   Official art.

The character of Apollonianism in our time, then, is, not to put too fine a point on it, totalitarian. Emboldened by its wartime success, the Apollonian technocracy is determined to enfold the realm of Hermes in its rough embrace and put Hermetic powers to serious work. Thus the Hermetics must dread "his threat / To organize us."

It is the intrusion of the endlessly disenchanting Apollonian regulatory regime into the realm of dreams, of "the self," that Auden most vocally laments: "when he occupies a college, / Truth is replaced by Useful Knowledge";

> His radio Homers all day long
> In over-Whitmanated song
> That does not scan,
> With adjectives laid end to end,
> Extol the doughnut and commend
> The Common Man.

Auden counsels defiance of this invasion, and imagines some glorious day when "we may behold at length / Routed Apollo's / Battalions melt away like fog," and he conjures up a Hermetic Decalogue for the faithful to memorize, recite, and obey: "Thou shalt not do as the dean pleases . . . . Thou shalt not worship projects nor / Shalt thou or thine bow down before / Administration . . . . Thou shalt not be on friendly terms / With guys in advertising firms." It's all very funny, and in its oddball way inspiring. But the descriptions of Apollo's onslaught are far more convincing than its prophecies of Hermetic victory. For there is no question that "To-day his arms, we must confess / From Right to Left have met success." For technocracy preaches a Gospel that liberals and conservatives alike are drawn to.

It is telling that Auden read this poem at Harvard. One of the dominant figures of American culture at that time was James Bryant Conant, a former professor of chemistry who had become Harvard's president in 1933. He participated enthusiastically in the techno-utopian mood of the mid-1940s and played a significant role in Washington: he was a member of the secret Interim Committee that had advised President Truman to drop atomic bombs on Japanese cities, and Auden suspected that Conant's vote to bomb had been decisive. When back in Cambridge, Conant was striving to transform Harvard from a finishing school for cultured gentlemen into a frankly Apollonian research powerhouse focused on science and technology. In so doing, he dramatically de-emphasized the humanities, believing them to have little to contribute to the postwar *pax Americana*. Some months after his visit to Harvard, Auden told Alan Ansen, "When I was delivering my Phi Beta Kappa poem in Cambridge, I met Conant for about five minutes." In the poem, he had characterized the Hermes-Apollo dichotomy as "Falstaff the fool confronts forever / The prig Prince Hal," and he said of Conant, "he is the real Prince Hal and gives the notion of sheer naked power." Auden was polite to Conant, but: " 'This is the real enemy,' I thought to myself. And I'm sure he had the same impression about me."[46]

Afterword

Stunde Null

In 1940, Jacques Ellul was a young professor of Roman law at the University of Strasbourg who took the bold step of openly renouncing Nazism and Marshal Petain's government at Vichy. Ellul had been from an early age a close and passionate reader of Marx, but had also undergone in early adulthood a dramatic conversion to Christianity—surprising his family, who had raised him in functional unbelief (he described his father as a Voltairean), and also himself. The two halves of his intellectual inheritance joined in repudiating the Nazis and their servants, but there was a price to be paid for his public stance: the Petain government declared that since his father had been born in English-ruled Malta, Ellul was a potential traitor and therefore ineligible to teach. He was forced to retire with his wife to the countryside and try to live off the land.

During those years of exile, in the countryside of southwestern France, Ellul worked steadily for the Resistance. His home became a safe place for other members of the Resistance, escaped prisoners of war, refugees from Spain, and French Jews. On several occasions, Ellul and his family hid Jews, helped them to acquire forged papers, and in some cases escorted them to safety. In 2001, seven years after his death, Jacques Ellul was recognized by Vad Yashem as one of the Righteous among the Nations.

During this time, Ellul also—demonstrating a level of energy comparable to that of Simone Weil—studied for his *agrégation* (an examination-based award for French university professors, granted to him in 1943, though he was forbidden to teach), pastored a small Protestant church, and studied theology. When France was liberated, he became deputy mayor of Bordeaux and began to speak widely to Christian groups.

In 1989, Ellul recalled the circumstances in which his first book had been written: *Presence in the Modern World*, or, in its original French, *Presence au monde moderne: Problèmes de la civilization post-chretienne.*[1] The question Ellul faced in writing that book, in the immediate aftermath of the war, was this: in what way or mode or form are Christians to be "present" in the *post-chretienne monde moderne* in which they live? He recalled that this question had been forced upon him and his fellow Christians first by the war and then by the postwar challenges of rebuilding France and indeed all of Europe.

After all, everyone was in a sense starting over. This was felt with particular intensity in Germany, of course, given the horrific destruction that had been visited on that country and the need for its government to be reconstituted from scratch. The moment that the Nazi government capitulated to the Allies came to be known in Germany as *Stunde Null*—zero hour—the moment that all the clocks got reset. So began the *Nachkriegszeit*, the time after the war. But throughout Western Europe, in France and England almost as much as in Germany, there was a similar sense of having to begin anew. And Ellul's book asks the question: what does faithful presence look like at the moment the clocks are all reset? What do Christians say, and do, at *Stunde Null*?[2]

Ellul suggests that during the war the question of the proper Christian role had been more complex for Catholics than for Protestants such as himself. After all, "Marshal Petain was a great Catholic who privileged the Catholic Church, and the 'values' that he proposed for France's motto, 'Work, Family, Homeland,' corresponded well to Catholic values." This formulation may seem rather condescending toward French Catholics, but Ellul (a great student of propaganda, about which he wrote one of his most interesting books) was surely correct in perceiving that Vichy France had certain propagandist strategies available to them when trying to win over those who assumed that France was a Catholic nation that would not have influenced those Protestants who had always known themselves to be dissenters from that dominant national self-understanding. It was simply easier for French Protestants, habituated for centuries to outsider status, to see that Hitlerism and all its appurtenances had to be resisted altogether and extirpated root and branch.

But *after* the war's end, all French Christians, Catholic and Protestant alike, found themselves in the same boat. Upon the Liberation, "On the one side were those for whom the important thing was to return to theology and building up the church. On the other were those who had a passion for politics and no longer thought about anything else (even in their pastoral ministry)."[3] For Ellul, neither of these options was valid. "Christians and the church could not hold themselves aloof from human beings, but neither could they become assimilated into one of the political currents"— most likely, in the circles Ellul knew, communism. The problem then had to be reformulated and reconsidered, and in 1945 Ellul began to put together his ideas, which he then articulated for an audience at the Ecumenical Institute at Bossey, Switzerland in 1946. Those lectures, revised, would become *Presence in the Modern World.*[4]

Already, in 1945 and 1946, Ellul discerned that Christians, though rightly committed to the reconstruction and preservation of society, were going astray—were not being fully and authentically present in the way appointed for them: "When the problem of reconstruction has arisen, many Christians, even the best ones, . . . urge people along the path that the world has chosen. They say that the United Nations is an admirable institution and the way of the future, that what matters most is producing material goods, and that prefabricated housing is the solution for everything." For Ellul there is certainly nothing wrong with the United Nations, and prefabricated housing can be very useful indeed. But the world does not need Christians to say so. "Christians participate truly in the world's preservation not by acting like others and laboring at the world's technical tasks but by fulfilling their specific role."[5] And what is that role?

Ellul thinks that this question was not widely asked during the war years. (Perhaps, had he known about Finkelstein's Conference and Oldham's Moot, he would have seen the right issues being asked among those people.) Had the right question been asked, he says, then Christians would have realized that, while summoning armies to fight against Hitler was certainly necessary, the first and most vital task of Christians in time of war was *prayer*. But Christians, while they certainly did pray, failed to give prayer the priority and centrality they were required to give it. Had they done so, then "perhaps the result would not have been this horrifying triumph of the Hitlerian spirit that we now see throughout the world."

Here at *Nachkriegszeit*, Ellul is saying what we heard others say when war first arrived. As these figures had feared, so Ellul believed it had come to pass that the Western democracies had won the war but were some considerable way along the path to losing the peace. "Materially triumphant, we are spiritually vanquished"—"And today we are witnessing the same error with reconstruction." The root cause of the failure may be identified and explained with reference to a phrase, quoted above: "the world's technical tasks."

Ellul of course does not believe that Christians should eschew "technical tasks" altogether, confining themselves to prayer.

> This does not mean that technical work should not be done, or that it is useless. No, the point is that everyone does this kind of work, and it has no meaning if it is not guided, accompanied, and sustained by another work, one that Christians alone can do and yet often do not. For the world must be preserved by the ways of God and not by the technique of human beings (although technique can enter into the ways of God if we take care to hold it under judgment and submission).

But Christians often fail to keep technique under such judgment and submission. And technique, Ellul argues, has, in part as a result of the war, entered into and come to dominate not only the material realm but thought itself. Indeed, "Technique has overtaken the realm of intellect just as it has every other realm of activity . . . . It could be said in fact that technique is today the sole route that intellect uses to truly express itself."[6] This can be seen most obviously in the sciences: "an entomologist will no longer proceed like Fabre"— that is, Jean-Henri Fabre, the great autodidact who produced, from the 1870s to the first decade of the twentieth century, a vividly written and immensely popular series of *Souvenirs entomologiques*. But Ellul discerns the same tendency in the arts, for instance in the way that "modern painting . . . is conditioned by its obsession to stake out ground and differentiate itself from photography." In *le monde moderne, la civilization post-chretienne*, "intellect is tied to its technical expression and intellectuals tend to become technicians"; the result is that even as "technical possibilities seem to increase," intellectuals' "scope of action becomes singularly restricted." The very success of technique leads to a diminished ability to imagine nontechnical action and thought.[7]

But what precisely does Ellul mean by "technique"? Soon after completing *Presence in the Modern World*, he would write the longest and most ambitious of his many books, and the only one still widely read today: *The Technological Society*. Here again the original French title is illuminating: *La technique, ou, l'enjeu du siècle*. Here the key word is *l'enjeu*, which can mean "stake" or "challenge," but also "outlook" or "worldview"—something like the German *Weltbild*. Technique then is not technology or the employment of technology: it "does not mean machines, technology, or this or that procedure for attaining an end." It is, rather, the characteristic mode of thought of the twentieth century but also what that century staked its future on, its challenge to the world—and therefore to us. And Ellul believes that this outlook, this *Weltbild*, depends on two essential commitments: to *efficiency*, and to *objectivity*. Technique is "the totality of methods rationally arrived at and having absolute efficiency in every field of human activity"; "[t]echnique is a means of apprehending reality, of acting on the world, which allows us to neglect all individual differences, all subjectivity. Technique alone is rigorously objective."[8] If a person cares about values other than efficiency and objectivity, and therefore fails to flourish under the sovereignty of technique—as happens to many people—then the regime has means of dealing with her: technical means, of course. Thus the rise of what Ellul calls *psychotechnique*: "Technique, in the form of psychotechnique, aspires to take over the individual, that is, to transform the qualitative into the quantitative. It knows only two possible solutions: the transformation or annihilation of the qualitative."[9] And it effects such transformation or annihilation through the mediation of psychotechnicians, who are the regime's instruments.

All human beings under technique are instruments of something—are technicians—and Ellul argues that the primary function of education within this regime is to use psychotechnique to create those technicians: "Education no longer has a humanist end or any value in itself; it has only one goal, to create technicians." And the educational system is vital to the sustenance and extension of technique: "It is the findings of thousands of educators which cease-lessly nourish the improvement of technique." The people whom Eliot called "educationists" are very proud of the efficiency and ob-jectivity of their system; but for Ellul, "What looks like the apex of humanism is in fact the pinnacle of human submission: children are educated to become precisely what society expects of them."[10] As Maritain would put it, technique is intrinsically *antipersonalist*.

In short, Ellul sees, in the years immediately following the war, the complete victory of what Auden called "the children of Apollo" over "the sons of Hermes." It is, then, easy to see why *The Technological Society* is seen as such a profoundly pessimistic book, and has been so influential on so many later techno-pessimists, most notably Neil Postman.[11] But Ellul did not mean for the book to be read in isolation from his other works, and writing a foreword to an American edition of the book strongly denied that he was a pessi-mist. Rather, he claimed, he was in *The Technological Society* under-taking a "sociological analysis," and a sociological analysis—being to some degree implicated itself in the regime of technique—rules out certain possibilities, among them the intervention of God in human affairs.[12] Those who had read Ellul's other books would have been aware that he possessed a specifically *theological* hope based on his belief that God loves Creation and is therefore active in his-tory—though not in ways that can be accounted for by technique.

Such hope forbids pessimism, but Ellul strongly implies, nonethe-less, that his Christian elders—a category that, taken literally, would include all of the writers studied here: Ellul was three years younger than Weil—had failed to discern the rise of the regime of technique and had not addressed it constructively until it was already secure on its throne. His emphasis on the possibility of a dramatic divine intervention—"God may work a miracle"[13]—suggests that he doubts the power of Christianity to oppose technique by its usual habits and practices. Christians had failed to be truly present in *le monde moderne*, and the whole of that world was now paying the price.

At the end of his traversal of biblical narrative in *For the Time Being*, Auden's narrator returns to "the moderate Aristotelian city / Of darning and the Eight-Fifteen, where Euclid's geometry / And Newton's mechanics would account for our experience," and finds that world—*le monde moderne*, the regime of technique—smaller and drabber than he had remembered. "To those who have seen the Child . . . / The Time Being is, in a sense, the most trying time of all."[14] But its challenge must be faced. For every Christian there remains "the Time Being to redeem / From insignificance."[15]

Auden borrows the notion of redeeming the time from the apostle Paul, who twice, in Ephesians 5:15 and Colossians 4:5, commands Christians to redeem the time. Most modern translations render this as "make the most of every opportunity" or something similar, but the Greek reads *kairon eksagorázōmenoi*, with *eksagorázōmenoi* being the same word Paul uses to describe Christ's work of redemption. It literally means to buy back, or buy out of bondage, including the bondage of slavery. Also, the word for time here, *kairon*, means not clock time—that would be *chromos*—but rather the opportune or decisive moment. We might further add that Simone Weil would surely have noted that the whole of Colossians 4:5 reads, "Walk in wisdom towards those who are outside, redeeming the time."

Jacques Ellul knew all this, which is why, perhaps, his critique of Christians for failing to be truly present in the world is succeeded by this very command. "It seems to me," he writes, that a genuine Christian "participation" in the world, "which is both real and specific for the world's preservation, can lead to the idea of redeeming the time." "To redeem the time is both a work of preservation . . . and a work of salvation . . . . The situation of Christians in the world appears then as singularly charged with meaning, if we consider that it is on their behavior and preaching (or simply on their witness) that the redemption of time depends."[16]

A genuine Christian presence is what calls the world toward the achievement of meaning—in much the way that Maritain had argued for the secret inspiration of the Gospel raising up a secular commitment to human rights—and therefore is the very means by which the time is to be redeemed, not just for Christians but for "those outside." But it must be said that there is something belated about this recognition, wise though it may well be.

When, in "Little Gidding," Eliot meets "some dead master" and receives from him the stern account of "the gifts reserved for age," the encounter ends thus: "In the disfigured street / He left me, with a kind of valediction, / And faded on the blowing of the horn"— the horn being the all-clear signal. From a numinous nighttime encounter with something eternal Eliot is returned to the workaday world, which continues to make its quotidian demands even in the midst of war. Similarly, in the last book Lewis wrote during the war, *The Great Divorce*, a long encounter with Lewis's own "dead master," George MacDonald, ends thus:

> "The morning! The morning!" I cried, "I am caught by the morning and I am a ghost." But it was too late. The light, like solid blocks, intolerable of edge and weight, came thundering on my head. Next moment the folds of my Teacher's garment were only the folds of the old ink-stained cloth on my study table which I had pulled down

with me as I fell from my chair. The blocks of light were only the books which I had pulled off with it, falling about my head. I awoke in a cold room, hunched on the floor beside a black and empty grate, the clock striking three, and the siren howling overhead.[17]

Even when the sirens fell permanently silent, because the screaming was no longer coming across the sky, and the world was no longer as cold and disfigured, but was merely the "moderate Aristotelian city," the awakening from dreams saturated with meaning and coherence was a painful one. And it was painful largely because the circumstances of the war, and the events leading up to the war, had generated a body of reflection that—while genuinely deep and rich, as I think has been seen throughout this book—came about too late to have any of the social effects that its authors hoped and prayed for. "The owl of Minerva flies only at night," as we are told (with perhaps pardonable inaccuracy) Hegel said, and it flew for these thinkers, for Maritain and Eliot and Lewis and Auden and Weil, when the wisdom it brought could no longer find its best use. It is then no wonder that after having spent the years of the war narrating, dramatizing, and arguing for a richly humane model of personal and cultural formation, they all—save Weil, lying in her grave in Kent—turned to other matters: Maritain to his human-rights work and then to aesthetics, Eliot to the theater, Lewis to the children's books that would win him his greatest and most lasting fame, Auden to his theology of the inarticulate human body and his hopes of becoming "a minor Atlantic Goethe."[18] In some ways the opportune time, the *kairos* moment for Christian cultural renewal, had passed. When the clocks were reset to *Stunde Null*, it was technique that proved adequate to that challenge.

This state of affairs can be seen especially clearly in the work of Ellul, which is why I chose to end this account by introducing this younger thinker. The book by which he is known today, *The Technological Society*, could only have been written after *Presence in the Modern World*, because it was only in light of the failures of Christendom that disfigured modernity—and that were especially evident in the wars of the twentieth century—that the functional absence of Christians from *le monde moderne* could be clearly seen, and its causes diagnosed. *The Technological Society* is not quite a post-mortem of Christian society, but it very nearly is: the patient is on his deathbed, which is why Ellul can but hope for a special divine intervention, a miracle.

Each of the writers I have studied here worked with astonishing energy to rescue their world for a deeply thoughtful, culturally rich Christianity, and to rescue that Christianity for their world. They put forth every effort to redeem the time. But on the sounding of the war's last siren, they awoke and found that the problem they all had to face was "what to make of a diminished thing."[19] Their diagnostic powers were great indeed: they saw with uncanny clarity and exposed with incisive intelligence the means by which technocracy had arisen and the damage it had inflicted, and would continue to inflict, on human persons. Few subsequent critiques of "the technological society" rival theirs in imagination or moral seriousness. But their prescriptions were never implemented, and could never have been: they came perhaps a century too late, after the reign of technocracy had become so complete that none can foresee the end of it while this world lasts. Ellul was more realistic to choose the simple hope for miraculous deliverance. If ever again there arises a body of thinkers eager to renew Christian humanism, they should take great pains to learn from those we have studied here: both what they agreed upon and what divided them. But may those future thinkers also be quickly alert to the signs of the times.

ACKNOWLEDGMENTS

I have had much help in the writing of this book. Several friends and colleagues read partial or complete drafts, or allowed me to quiz them in conversation. For all such assistance I am grateful to Philip Jenkins, Tim Larsen, Adam Roberts, Francis Spufford, and Dan Treier. In all the work I have done on Auden, Edward Mendelson has been ready with encouragement, advice, assistance in using libraries and archives, and, when necessary, firm correction of errors; I don't know how I would have managed without him, not just in the writing of this book but also in several others.

When I was making final revisions to the text, I had the inestimable blessing of several days of peaceful, focused retreat at Laity Lodge, in the beautiful Texas Hill Country. I am indebted to all the staff there, but especially to Gate Davis, my host and guide.

My wife Teri and my son Wesley have, as always, cheered me up when I was in the dumps and distracted me with funny jokes when I was uncheerupable. This would have been a far more onerous task without their assistance.

My employer, Baylor University, generously gave me a research leave when I was beginning to wonder if I would ever finish this project. Few gifts are more meaningful than the gift of time.

I want to register my thanks to my agent, Christy Fletcher, my editor, Cynthia Read, and all the staff at Oxford University Press. Many hands and minds make a book.

Finally, I wish to dedicate this book to my dear friend Gail Kienitz, who has been my advocate and encourager for a very long time now—since, in the early years of my career, I wondered whether I would ever write anything. She believed I had something to say before I did; and for those timely good words I will always be in her debt.

NOTES

Preface

1. Beevor, *The Second World War*, p. 438.
2. Churchill is quoted, for instance, in John Keegan, *The Second World War*, p. 310.
3. James Boswell, *The Life of Samuel Johnson*, p. 748.
4. The "Six Pillars of Peace" were announced in the May 31, 1943 issue of *Christianity and Crisis* and were further articulated in subsequent issues.
5. Warren, *Theologians of a New World Order*, p. 102.
6. Fitzgerald, *Human Voices*, p. 58.
7. Eliot, *Christianity and Culture*, p. 85.
8. "The abolition of educational privilege by disposing of culture at bargain prices does not admit the masses to the preserves from which they were formerly excluded but, under the existing social conditions, contributes to the decay of education and the progress of barbaric incoherence." Horkheimer and Adorno, *Dialectic of Enlightenment*, p. 130. But then Hayek: "Socialists, the cultivated parents of the barbarous offspring they have produced, traditionally hope to solve this problem by education. But what does education mean in this respect? Surely we have learned that knowledge cannot create new ethical values, that no amount of learning will lead people to hold the same views on the moral issues which a conscious ordering of all social relations raises. It is not rational conviction but the acceptance of a creed which is required to justify a particular plan. And, indeed, socialists everywhere were the first to recognize that the task they had set themselves required the general acceptance of a common *Weltanschauung*, of a definite set of values. It was in these

efforts to produce a mass movement supported by such a single world view that the socialists first created most of the instruments of indoctrination of which Nazis and Fascists have made such effective use." Hayek, "The Road to Serfdom," *Collected Works of F. A. Hayek*, vol. 2, p. 142.

9. Kynaston, *Austerity Britain*, p. 27.
10. Orwell, "The Lion and the Unicorn: Socialism and the English Genius," *Essays*, p. 291.

Dramatis Personae: September 1, 1939

1. McInerny, *The Very Rich Hours of Jacques Maritain*, p. 135.
2. Eliot, *Christianity and Culture*, p. 51.
3. Ackroyd, *T. S. Eliot: A Life*, p. 253.
4. Lewis, *Collected Letters of C. S. Lewis*, vol. 2, *Books, Broadcasts, and the War 1931–1949*, pp. 271, 234.
5. Davenport-Hines, *Auden*, p. 198.
6. Auden, "September 1, 1939," *Selected Poems*, p. 95.
7. Quoted in Pétrement, *Simone Weil*, p. 353.

Chapter 1

1. Merton, *The Secular Journal*, p. 130. Auden described his experience in an interview with Alan Levy, "On Audenstrasse: In the Autumn of the Age of Anxiety," *New York Times Magazine*, August 8, 1971, p. 10+. I have written in more detail about Auden's cinematic experience in the Appendix to my book *What Became of Wystan.*
2. From Golo Mann's contribution to *W. H. Auden: A Tribute*, ed. Stephen Spender, p. 102.
3. Auden, "Law Like Love," *Collected Poems*, pp. 260–62.
4. Rorty, "Trotsky and the Wild Orchids," *Philosophy and Social Hope*, pp. 3–22.
5. Keynes, *The Economic Consequences of the Peace*, p. 33. By the phrase "the rules of the game," I mean to refer to Jean Renoir's peerless film of that name.
6. Eliot, *Christianity and Culture*, p. 11.
7. Auden, "September 1, 1939," *Selected Poems*, pp. 95–97.
8. Lewis, *Collected Letters*, vol. 2, *Books, Broadcasts, and the War 1931–1949*, p. 272.
9. Lewis, *Collected Letters*, vol. 2, *Books, Broadcasts, and the War 1931–1949*, p. 278, where the full text of Cranmer's prayer is also cited. Lewis probably knew it from *The Remains of Thomas Cranmer, Collected and Arranged by H. Jenkyns* (Oxford: Oxford University Press, 1833), p. 186.
10. Lewis, *Collected Letters*, vol. 2, *Books, Broadcasts, and the War 1931–1949*, p. 251.

11. Lewis, "Learning in War-Time," *The Weight of Glory*, p. 52.

12. I have relied heavily in what follows on James Gilbert's *Redeeming Culture*, especially chap. 4, "A World without John Dewey."

13. Edward Purcell, in the first chapter of his superb study *The Crisis of Democratic Theory*, gives a thorough account not only of the Hutchins/Adler program but also the resistance it spawned among faculty at Chicago. In the spring of 1934, there were great debates on campus in which Adler's influence was deplored by a scientist named Anton Carlson. Three years later, Carlson had been elected President of the American Association of University Professors and delivered a presidential address attacking "neophyte administrators" who try to make universities in their own image—an obvious reference to his university's thirty-five-year-old president. Hutchins at the same time made equally oblique and yet obvious references to Carlson: in a 1934 essay called "The Issue in the Higher Learning," he wrote, "The gadgeteers and the data collectors, masquerading as scientists, have threatened to become the supreme chieftains of the scholarly world . . . . Our bewilderment has resulted from our notion that salvation depends on information." Hutchins, "The Issue in the Higher Learning," p. 178. Thus a bold (and therefore oversimplified) distinction between technological data and humane wisdom was being drawn at the University of Chicago several years before the war made it a topic of much wider interest.

14. Hutchins, "What Shall We Defend? We Are Losing Our Moral Principles."

15. Dewey, "President Hutchins' Proposals to Remake Higher Education." Hutchins denied that he was seeking so definitively to impose, which led to this sardonic reply by Dewey: "The tone and substance of President Hutchins' reply would lead one to suppose that after all he was not raising or meaning to raise any fundamental issue. I must ask his forgiveness if I took his book too seriously." Dewey, "Was President Hutchins Serious?"

16. Gilbert, *Redeeming Culture*, pp. 75, 79.

17. It is interesting to see how rarely any of the parties to this debate, and indeed any of the figures who feature in this book, reflect seriously and openly on the fact that a nondemocratic regime, Stalin's Soviet Union, was an indispensable ally to the democratic West in its struggle against the Axis powers. It is as though there were an unspoken agreement to maintain a discreet silence on the matter. In one of the few public comments made by one of my protagonists, Eliot wrote, "A considerable time must elapse before we can draw any illustration from Russia. Russia is a rude and vigorous country; it is also a very big country; and it will need a long period of peace and internal development. Three things may happen. Russia may show us how a stable government and a flourishing culture can be transmitted only through élites; it may lapse into oriental lethargy; or the governing élite may follow the course of other governing élites and become a governing class" (*Christianity and Culture*,

p. 118). Eliot also, notoriously, wrote to George Orwell, on behalf of his fellow directors of Faber and Faber, to decline to publish *Animal Farm*: "we have no conviction . . . that this is the right point of view from which to criticise the political situation at the present time." See a facsimile image of the complete letter here: Flood, " 'It Needs More Public-Spirited Pigs.' "

18. Hook, *Out of Step*, p. 337.

19. Hook, "The New Failure of Nerve." This essay is immediately followed by another making virtually the same argument in different terms: Dewey, "Anti-Naturalism In Extremis."

20. Buchman, *Remaking the World*, p. 46. For a detailed and insightful treatment of Buchman's career, see Boobyer, *The Spiritual Vision of Frank Buchman*.

21. Vidler, *Scenes from a Clerical Life*, p. 119.

22. Clements, *The Moot Papers*, p. 23.

23. Clements, *The Moot Papers*, p. 343.

24. Eliot, *Christianity and Culture*, p. 83.

25. Clements, *The Moot Papers*, p. 538.

26. Clements, *The Moot Papers*, p. 41.

27. Buller, *Darkness Over Germany*, pp. 2, 193, 190.

28. Clements, *The Moot Papers*, p. 141.

29. Clements, *The Moot Papers*, p. 439.

30. Clements, *The Moot Papers*, pp. 358, 141. It can be seen from the title of a paper that Mannheim delivered to the Moot, "Planning for Freedom: Some Remarks on the Necessity for Creating a Body Which Could Coordinate Theory and Practice in Our Future Policy," that he associated such planning with the creation of the Order. In his magisterial history *Postwar*, Tony Judt comments that at war's end the one thing everyone agreed on was that the future needed to be planned (pp. 67–70); but all of this seems foreign to Eliot in his *Idea of a Christian Society*; he does not seem to have considered how his ideas should or might be implemented.

31. Clements, *The Moot Papers*, p. 602.

32. Manent, *The City of Man*, p. 48. Perhaps this is a good point at which to note that the twentieth century produced a very wide range of critiques of modernity—and reassertions of the legitimacy of modernity. The reassessments of modernity from the Christian perspectives treated in this book are but a tiny subset of that larger body of assessments. For a useful overview of these critiques and countercritiques, see Gillespie, *The Theological Origins of Modernity*, especially the section of chap. 1 called "The Crisis of Modernity."

33. The chief weakness of Greif's book is his limited understanding of Christian thought. It is therefore useful to read, in conjunction with Greif and as a kind of corrective to his work, Samuel Moyn's *Christian Human Rights*. The current book was well under way when Moyn's extraordinarily penetrating work appeared, so I was both pleased and disconcerted to discover that, as I begin my story in January 1943, Moyn begins his in December 1942, with a declaration

by Pope Pius XII on the dignity of the human person. "Amplifying the importance of human rights before a vast public, Pius's statement . . . recrafted the meaning of the principles it merely claimed to recall to importance. It made what had been secular and liberal into a set of values that were now religious and conservative. And it provided an inkling of how Christians would come to defend the postwar democracies they later founded in Western Europe, which were religious and conservative in nature."

34. Lewis, *Mere Christianity*, pp. 28–29.
35. Bonhoeffer, *Letters and Papers from Prison*, p. 7.

Chapter 2

1. For an excellent survey of the history of these terms, see Nicholas Mann, "The Origins of Humanism."
2. Kristeller, *Renaissance Thought*, p. 10.
3. Creeds of Christendom, with a History and Critical notes. Volume II. The History of Creeds. See the full text here: http://www.ccel.org/ccel/schaff/creeds2.v.ii.i.html. The key passage:

   And not only can faith and reason never be opposed to one another, but they are of mutual aid one to the other; for right reason demonstrates the foundations of faith, and, enlightened by its light cultivates the science of things divine; while faith frees and guards reason from errors, and furnishes it with manifold knowledge. So far, therefore, is the Church from opposing the cultivation of human arts and sciences, that it in many ways helps and promotes it. For the Church neither ignores nor despises the benefits of human life which result from the arts and sciences, but confesses that, as they came from God, the Lord of all science, so, if they be rightly used, they lead to God by the help of his grace.

4. *Aeterni Patris*, "On the Restoration of Christian Philosophy." See the full text here: http://w2.vatican.va/content/leo-xiii/en/encyclicals/documents/hf_l-xiii_enc_04081879_aeterni-patris.html. The key passage:

   While, therefore, We hold that every word of wisdom, every useful thing by whomsoever discovered or planned, ought to be received with a willing and grateful mind, We exhort you, venerable brethren, in all earnestness to restore the golden wisdom of St. Thomas, and to spread it far and wide for the defense and beauty of the Catholic faith, for the good of society, and for the advantage of all the sciences. The wisdom of St. Thomas, We say; for if anything is taken up with too great subtlety by the Scholastic doctors, or too carelessly stated—if there be anything that ill agrees with the discoveries of a later age, or, in a word, improbable in whatever way—it does not enter Our mind to propose that for imitation to Our age. Let carefully selected teachers endeavor to implant the doctrine of Thomas Aquinas in the minds of students, and set forth clearly his solidity and excellence over others. Let the universities already founded or to be founded by you illustrate and defend this doctrine, and use it for the refutation of prevailing errors. But, lest the false for the true or the corrupt for the pure be drunk in, be ye watchful that the doctrine of Thomas be drawn from his own fountains, or at least from those rivulets which, derived from the very fount, have thus far flowed, according to the established agreement of learned men, pure and clear; be careful to guard the minds of youth from those which are said to flow thence, but in reality are gathered from strange and unwholesome streams.

5. Maritain, *Art and Scholasticism*, p. 22. This brief book—really no more than a pamphlet—was essentially the founding document, the rule of life, for Eric Gill's great but, thanks to his own wickedness, deeply flawed experiment in community and art-making at Ditchling in East Sussex. One of the first books published by Gill's St. Dominic's Press (in 1923) was a beautifully designed and lovingly made edition of Maritain's little treatise. For the details of this influence, see Fiona McCarthy's *Eric Gill*. It is also noteworthy that Gill's last book, which appeared in the year of his death, was published in a series called Christian News-Letter Books, another project of J. H. Oldham's and a kind of offshoot of the Moot. Eric Vidler edited the series; Oldham's own book *The Resurrection of Christendom* was the first in the series, and Middleton Murry's *Europe in Travail* was the second. Gill's contribution is called *Christianity and the Machine Age* (1940). It is not a very good book—its claim that "from a Christian point of view . . . the idea of the Machine Age [is] not only absurd, but damned" (p. 66) is perhaps its entire message—but that Gill should choose this topic, and that Oldham and Vidler should believe it important for a series "designed to assist thought upon the relation of the Christian faith to present problems," are telling points.

6. Gilson's career oddly paralleled Maritain's: they would consistently pursue very similar ideas, though they rarely acknowledged each other and were often at odds. Maritain was born in 1882, Gilson in 1884; Maritain died in 1973, Gilson in 1978. Each was a Catholic layman, each devotedly married. They now seem almost two halves of one whole, though Maritain was a far more public figure, while Gilson was known primarily to scholars.

7. Maritain, *Collected Works of Jacques Maritain*, vol. 2, *Integral Humanism, Freedom in the Modern World, and A Letter on Independence*, p. 45.

8. Maritain, *The Twilight of Civilization*, p. 4. The book is an English version of lectures that Maritain gave in Paris just before the outbreak of war, in February 1939. The first chapter, from which I have quoted, is called "The Crisis of Modern Humanism," which suggests the extent to which the book participates in what Mark Greif has called the "discourse of man." (See note earlier on Greif's *Age of the Crisis of Man*.)

9. Maritain, *The Collected Works of Jacques Maritain*, vol. 2, pp. 161, 167, 170.

10. "Three masters, seemingly mutually exclusive, dominate the school of suspicion: Marx, Nietzche, and Freud . . . . All three clear the horizon for a more authentic word, for a new reign of Truth, not only by means of a 'destructive' critique, but by the invention of an art of interpreting . . . . [All three] represent three convergent procedures of demystification." Paul Ricoeur, *Freud and Philosophy*, p. 34.
11. Maritain, *The Collected Works of Jacques Maritain*, vol. 2, p. 173.
12. Maritain, *The Collected Works of Jacques Maritain*, vol. 2, p. 196. It is questionable whether this is a fair and accurate rendering of Barth's position; in recent years, a number of theologians have seen Barth as a kind of Christian humanist, though a rather different kind than Maritain. One of Barth's most incisive and provocative statements in this matter is his essay "The Christian Message and the New Humanism," where Barth claims that the core of any Christian humanism is a doctrine of the "humanity of God." For a fuller treatment of these issues, see John Webster's characteristically incisive essay "Rescuing the Subject: Barth and Postmodern Anthropology."
13. Maritain, *The Collected Works of Jacques Maritain*, vol. 2, p. 197.
14. Maritain, *The Twilight of Civilization*, p. viii.
15. These biographical details are taken from Voderholzer's *Meet Henri de Lubac*, especially the chapter entitled "World War II and Intellectual Resistance."
16. de Lubac, *The Drama of Atheist Humanism*, p. 24.
17. Claude Levi-Strauss, *Tristes Tropiques*, p. 53. Examination results for the *agrégation* may be found at the Ressources numériques en histoire de l'éducation website: http://rhe.ish-lyon.cnrs.fr/?q=agregsecondaire_laureats
18. Auden, "Second Thoughts on Kierkegaard," *Complete Works of W. H. Auden: Prose*, p. 362; Sontag, "Simone Weil."
19. Pétrement, *Simone Weil*, p. 534.
20. Weil, *Waiting for God*, p. 27.
21. Weil, *Gravity and Grace*, pp. 115, 163. The debts we owe to "the human being as such" are the subject of *The Need for Roots*, which we will consider later.
22. Auden, "New Year Letter," *Collected Poems*, p. 214.
23. For Eliot, see "The Humanism of Irving Babbitt" (1927) and "Second Thoughts about Humanism (1928), in *Selected Essays*; for Lewis, see *English Literature in the Sixteenth Century, Excluding Drama*, pp. 18–32. Lewis also wrote in a letter to Douglas Bush of Harvard, "I take a less favourable view of the Humanists than you. I've never quite forgiven them for killing live Latin and erecting the mausoleum of Ciceronianism over its corpse." *The Collected Letters of C. S. Lewis*, vol. 2, p. 475.

Chapter 3

1. Niebuhr, *Christianity and Power Politics*, p. 52.
2. Niebuhr, "Thomism and Mysticism."

3. Schlesinger, "Reinhold Niebuhr's Long Shadow."
4. In *Remembering Reinhold Niebuhr: Letters of Reinhold and Ursula M. Niebuhr*, p. 284.
5. Auden, "Tract for the Times," *The Complete Works of W. H. Auden: Prose*, vol. 2, *1939–1948*, pp. 108–9. A few months later, Auden would review Niebuhr's massive *The Nature and Destiny of Man* for *The New Republic*, and that work he praised straightforwardly: "*The Nature and Destiny of Man* is the most lucid and balanced statement of orthodox Protestantism that we are likely to see for a long time" (p. 134).
6. Lewis, "First and Second Things," *God in the Dock*, p. 281.
7. Lewis, "The Weight of Glory," *The Weight of Glory and Other Addresses*, p. 46.
8. Weil, *Waiting for God*, p. 67.
9. Lewis, "The Weight of Glory," *The Weight of Glory and Other Addresses*, p. 50.
10. Lewis, "The Weight of Glory," *The Weight of Glory and Other Addresses*, pp. 51, 56.
11. Lewis, "Christianity and Culture," *Christian Reflections*, pp. 13, 28, 36.
12. Lewis, *The Screwtape Letters*, pp. 22–23.
13. See my discussion of the origins of the Narnia stories in that first year of the war in *The Narnian*, pp. 233–35.
14. Lewis, "Learning in War-Time," *The Weight of Glory*, pp. 58–59.
15. Davenport-Hines, *Auden*, p. 220.
16. Auden, untitled essay in *Modern Canterbury Pilgrims*, p. 41.
17. Quoted in Richard Davenport-Hines, *Auden*, p. 188.
18. Davenport-Hines, *Auden*, p. 188 (on Chester) and 201 (on Richards).
19. Davenport-Hines, *Auden*, p. 192.
20. Auden, "New Year Letter," *Collected Poems*, pp. 229–30.
21. Auden, "New Year Letter," *Collected Poems*, p. 198.
22. Auden, "New Year Letter," *Collected Poems*, pp. 232–33.
23. Auden, "New Year Letter," *Collected Poems*, p. 236.
24. T. S. Eliot, "Tradition and the Individual Talent," *Selected Essays*, p. 4.
25. Auden, "New Year Letter," *Collected Poems*, p. 236.
26. Auden, "New Year Letter," *Collected Poems*, p. 238.
27. Auden, "New Year Letter," *Collected Poems*, p. 240. Williams explores the Augustinian phrase in *Descent of the Dove*, p. 66.
28. Auden, "Jacob and the Angel," *The Complete Works of W. H. Auden: Prose*, vol. 2, *1939–1948*, p. 38.
29. Auden, "James Joyce and Richard Wagner," *The Complete Works of W. H. Auden: Prose*, vol. 2, *1939–1948*, p. 118.

Chapter 4

1. Auden, "In Memory of Sigmund Freud," *Collected Poems*, pp. 271–74.
2. Auden, "In Tine of War" XII, *Selected Poems*, p. 78.

3. Auden, "Lecture Notes," *The Complete Works of W. H. Auden: Prose*, vol. 2, *1939–1948*, p. 162. This is one of a series of collections of *pensées* Auden wrote for *Commonweal* magazine under the name "Didymus." The apostle Thomas, familiarly known as "Doubting Thomas," was known as Didymus, the twin.

4. Davenport-Hines, *Auden*, p. 214.

5. Williams, *Descent of the Dove*, p. 107. "Messias" is Williams's characteristically idiosyncratic name for Jesus.

6. Eliot, introduction to Williams, *All Hallows Eve*, pp. xiii–xiv.

7. Clements, *The Moot Papers*, pp. 55, 114.

8. Lewis, "The Inner Ring," *The Weight of Glory*, p.143.

9. Lewis, *Perelandra*, p. 14.

10. Lewis, *Mere Christianity*, p. 46.

11. Lewis's preface to *George MacDonald: An Anthology*, p. xxviii; *The Screwtape Letters*, p. 1.

12. Maritain, *The Prince of This World*, p. 7. Only three hundred copies of the pamphlet were printed. I was able to see one—inscribed to Etienne Gilson—at the Institute of Mediaeval Studies in Toronto, and took down the quotation from it.

13. Weil, *Gravity and Grace*, p. 54.

14. Lewis, *The Weight of Glory*, in the book of that name, p. 31; Auden, "The Poet of the Encirclement," *The Complete Works of W. H. Auden: Prose*, vol. 2, *1939–1948*, p. 198.

15. Auden, *For the Time Being*, p. 18.

16. Auden, *For the Time Being*, p. 21.

17. Auden, "Augustus to Augustine," *The Complete Works of W. H. Auden: Prose*, vol. 2, *1939–1948*, p. 231. Auden himself was an enthusiastic user of Benzedrine at this time.

18. Auden, *For the Time Being*, pp. 30–33.

19. Auden, *For the Time Being*, p. 53.

20. I owe this insight to Edward Mendelson, who also pointed out that this masking of the serious with the broadly comic is characteristic of Thomas Pynchon as well.

21. Auden, *For the Time Being*, p. 54.

22. Auden, *For the Time Being*, pp. 57–58.

23. Lewis, *Perelandra*, p. 70.

24. Lewis, *The Collected Letters of C. S. Lewis*, vol. 2, *Books, Broadcasts, and the War 1931–1949*, pp. 593–94.

25. Clarke, *Childhood's End*, p. 154.

26. Clarke, *Childhood's End*, p. 72.

27. Clarke, *Childhood's End*, p 198.

28. Lewis, *The Collected Letters of C. S. Lewis*, vol. 3, *Narnia, Cambridge and Joy 1950–1963*, p. 392.

29. Spufford, *Backroom Boys*, p. 9.

30. Lewis, *A Preface to Paradise Lost*, p. 99.

Chapter 5

1. Maritain, *We Have Been Friends together*, p. 75. The conclusion Jacques and Raïssa reached about the "pseudo-intelligence" of the human mind in a naturalistic cosmos is developed at greater length by C. S. Lewis in "The Cardinal Difficulty of Naturalism," the third chapter of his 1947 book *Miracles*. (This is the chapter that, famously, underwent a severe critique by the philosopher Elizabeth Anscombe and was revised for the second edition of the book, published in 1960.)
2. McInerny, *The Very Rich Hours of Jacques Maritain*, p. 151.
3. Quoted in McInerny, *The Very Rich Hours of Jacques Maritain*, p. 151.
4. See Soulez and Worms, *Bergson*, chapter 11.
5. Weil, "The *Iliad*: or the Poem of Force," 5.
6. Weil, "The *Iliad*: or the Poem of Force," p. 27.
7. Weil, "The *Iliad*: or the Poem of Force," p. 18.
8. Weil, "The *Iliad*: or the Poem of Force," p. 30.
9. Weil, "The Romanesque Renaissance," *Selected Essays*, p. 44.
10. Lewis, "On the Reading of Old Books," *God in the Dock*, p. 202.
11. Weil, "The Romanesque Renaissance," *Selected Essays*, p. 45.
12. Weil, "The Romanesque Renaissance," *Selected Essays*, p. 47.
13. Weil, "The Romanesque Renaissance," *Selected Essays*, p. 48.
14. Williams, "The Imposition of Belief," chap. 5 in *Descent of the Dove*.
15. Weil, "The Romanesque Renaissance," *Selected Essays*, p. 48.
16. Weil, "The Romanesque Renaissance," *Selected Essays*, p. 53.
17. Weil, "The Romanesque Renaissance," *Selected Essays*, p. 47.
18. Weil, "The Romanesque Renaissance," *Selected Essays*, p. 48.
19. Weil, "The Romanesque Renaissance," *Selected Essays*, p. 51.
20. Weil, "The *Iliad*: or the Poem of Force," p. 30.
21. Calder, *The People's War*, pp. 108–9.
22. *The Poems of T. S. Eliot*, pp. 213–14.
23. Quoted by Lyndall Gordon, *Eliot's New Life*, p. 110. Eliot's claim of Englishness was accompanied by his constant awareness that the claim was not necessarily reciprocated. Donald Hall, in his *Remembering Poets*, mentions visiting Eliot at Faber, probably around 1960, and having a uniformed employee comment that "Eliot was an extremely pleasant gentleman, and did I know, that he was actually an American gentleman?" (p. 87) It was as "the American gentleman" that he was always known. It is typical of Eliot's comfort with ambiguities that, when he wrote a letter to the *Christian NewsLetter* in 1945 and signed it "Metoikos"—resident alien—he could have been referring either to his place in English society or to his status as a Christian, since a version of that word is used to describe Abraham, the traveler and sojourner, in Acts 7:4.

24. Gardner, *The Composition of* Four Quartets, p. 17. The poem was originally published as part of a special supplement of the *New English Weekly*, but it proved so popular that in September Faber and Faber published the poem as a one-shilling pamphlet. Gardner also quotes a letter to Anne Ridler (March 10, 1941) in which Eliot comments, "The success of that poem is a little disconcerting: I find it hard to believe that a poem of mine which sells nearly 12,000 copies can be really good" (p. 109).

25. Churchill, *Blood, Toil, Tears and Sweat*, pp. 177–78.

26. Eliot, "East Coker," *The Poems of T. S. Eliot*, p. 190.

27. Lewis, "Learning in War-Time," *The Weight of Glory*, p. 49.

28. Eliot, "The Dry Salvages," *The Poems of T. S. Eliot*, p. 198. One of the prayers to be used at sea reads, in part,

> O ETERNAL Lord God, who alone spreadest out the heavens, and rulest the raging of the sea; who hast compassed the waters with bounds until day and night come to an end: Be pleased to receive into thy Almighty and most gracious protection the persons of us thy servants, and the Fleet in which we serve. Preserve us from the dangers of the sea, and from the violence of the enemy; ... that the inhabitants of our Island may in peace and quietness serve thee our God; and that we may return in safety to enjoy the blessings of the land, with the fruits of our labours, and with a thankful remembrance of thy mercies to praise and glorify thy holy Name; through Jesus Christ our Lord. Amen.

Eliot would also surely have known the "Naval Hymn" written in 1860 by William Whiting:

> Eternal Father, strong to save,
> Whose arm hath bound the restless wave,
> Who bidd'st the mighty ocean deep
> Its own appointed limits keep;
> Oh, hear us when we cry to Thee,
> For those in peril on the sea!

29. Eliot, *The Poems of T. S. Eliot*, p. 1048.

30. I was somewhat comforted to discover, when reading Douglas Murray's *Aldous Huxley: A Biography*, that Huxley had some years earlier noted, in a letter, the same tendency in Eliot's prose: "I never knew a writer who spent so much time explaining what he didn't mean to say and then at last saying so little" (p. 277).

31. Eliot, *Christianity and Culture*, pp. 4, 6, 13, 18, 38, 40, 56, 59.

32. "Towards a Christian Britain," p. 166.

33. Eliot, "The Dry Salvages," *The Poems of T. S. Eliot*, p. 199.

34. Eliot, *The Poems of T. S. Eliot* (commentary), p. 892.

35. Ackroyd, *T. S. Eliot*, p. 258.

36. Ackroyd, *T. S. Eliot*, p. 261.

37. Gordon, *Eliot's New Life*, p. 97. Cf. Edward Mendelson in *Early Auden*, p. 172:

> In romantic thought, repetition is the enemy of freedom, the greatest force of repression both in the mind and in the state. Outside romanticism, repetition has a very different import: it is the sustaining and renewing power of nature, the basis for all art and understanding . . . . Repetition lost its moral value only with the spread of the industrial machine and the swelling of the romantic chorus of praise for personal originality. Until two hundred years ago virtually no one associated repetition with boredom or constraint. Ennui is ancient; its link to repetition is not. The damned in Dante's Hell never complain that their suffering is repetitive, only that it is eternal, which is not the same thing.

38. Eliot, "East Coker," *The Poems of T. S. Eliot*, p. 188.

39. Weil, *Waiting for God*, p. 50. In almost every letter to Father Perrin, Weil professes her dislike of self-examination, but then examines herself further.

40. Weil, *Waiting for God*, pp. 46, 44.

41. Weil, *Waiting for God*, p. 64. It must be said that André did little to ease his sister's sense of inferiority. For instance, in the spring of 1940, when he was in a French military prison—in consequence of "a disagreement with the French authorities on the subject of my military 'obligations' "—he wrote a letter to his sister: "Some thoughts I have had of late, concerning my arithmetic-algebraic work, might pass for a response to one of your letters, where you asked me what is of interest to me in my work. So, I decided to write them down, even if for the most part they are incomprehensible to you." Near the end of the letter he writes, "When I invented (I say invented, and not discovered) uniform spaces, I did not have the impression of working with resistant material, but rather the impression that a professional sculptor must have when he plays by making a snowman." Letter translated by Martin Krieger in *Doing Mathematics*, Appendix D.

42. Weil, *Waiting for God*, p. 64.

43. Weil, *Waiting for God*, pp. 105–16.

44. Weil, *Waiting for God*, pp. 48, 54.

45. Weil, *Waiting for God*, pp. 52–53.

46. Weil, "The Romanesque Renaissance," *Selected Essays*, pp. 52–53.

47. Weil, *Waiting for God*, p. 75.

48. Pétrement, *Simone Weil*, p. 481.

49. Weil, *Waiting for God*, p. 54.

50. Pétrement, *Simone Weil*, pp. 474–76. The fact that Weil returned to the church in Harlem repeatedly may suggest that it had some real impact on her. In this light, it may be useful to remember that when Dietrich Bonhoeffer first visited New York in 1930, his experiences at a church in Harlem were transformative

for his understanding of Christian worship. See Marsh, *Strange Glory*, p. 115–18.

51. Davenport-Hines, *Auden*, p. 186.

52. Davenport-Hines, *Auden*, p. 206.

53. Lewis, *Collected Letters*, vol. 2, *Books, Broadcasts, and the War 1931–1949*, p. 425.

Interlude

1. Day, "Day after Day—January 1943," pp. 4, 6.

2. https://www.koinoniafarm.org/brief-history/.

3. Bonhoeffer, "After Ten Years" *Letters and Papers from Prison*, p. 5; Marsh, *Strange Glory*, pp. 340–44.

4. Sherry, *The Life of Graham Greene*, p. 154.

5. Greene, *Three Entertainments*, p. 460.

6. Gilkey, *Shantung Compound*, p. 192.

Chapter 6

1. Maritain, *The Twilight of Civilization*, p. viii.

2. Maritain, *Education at the Crossroads*, p. 4.

3. Maritain, *Education at the Crossroads*, pp. 5–6.

4. John Keegan, *The First World War*, p. 6; Auden, "The Unknown Citizen," *Collected Poems*, pp. 250–51.

5. Maritain, *Education at the Crossroads*, p. 8.

6. Lewis, "Membership," *The Weight of Glory*, p. 164. On the pervasiveness in Auden's thought of his distinction between nature and history, see Mendelson, *Later Auden*, pp. 310–14. Though there may be distinctively Christian reasons for critiquing the material and numerical notion of the "individual" in favor of some deeper and richer model, others made very similar arguments: for instance, Dwight Macdonald in "A Theory of Popular Culture," which appeared in *Politics* in February 1944 and later was revised and expanded into his famous "Masscult and Midcult."

7. Maritain, *Education at the Crossroads*, pp. 9, 10.

8. Maritain, *Education at the Crossroads*, p. 15.

9. Maritain, *Education at the Crossroads*, p. 30.

10. Maritain, *Education at the Crossroads*, pp. 34, 39. Here we might recall the disagreement between Lewis and Arthur C. Clarke about what counts as genuine liberation.

11. Maritain, *Education at the Crossroads*, p. 35.

12. Maritain, *Education at the Crossroads*, p. 91.

13. Maritain, *Education at the Crossroads*, pp. 100, 102, 113, 115.
14. Lewis, *The Abolition of Man*, p. 75.
15. In a long letter written probably in late 1951, Tolkien described his whole personal mythology or legendarium as "mainly concerned with Fall, Mortality, and the Machine." The fallen person "will rebel against the laws of the Creator—especially against mortality," which

   > will lead to the desire for Power, for making the will more quickly effective,—and so to the Machine (or Magic). By the last I intend all use of external plans or devices (apparatus) instead of development of the inherent inner powers or talents—or even the use of these talents with the corrupted motive of dominating: bulldozing the real world, or coercing other wills. The Machine is our more obvious modern form though more closely related to Magic than is usually recognized. (*The Letters of J. R. R. Tolkien*, pp. 145–46)

   The resemblance of this account to Lewis's views on magic and science will be immediately evident. In *The Lord of the Rings*, the chief personification of the lure of the Machine is the wizard Saruman, of whom Treebeard the Ent says, "He is plotting to become a Power. He has a mind of metal and wheels; and he does not care for growing things, except as far as they serve him for the moment" (p. 473). By Tolkien's own account (p. xxiii), he wrote this part of his novel in 1942, that is, at about the time that Lewis was thinking seriously about science, technology, magic, and power. It seems certain that the two of them, along with the other Inklings, talked much of these matters in the war years. It might also be recalled that Auden used the term "the Machine" in "New Year Letter."

16. Lewis's *English Literature in the Sixteenth Century, Excluding Drama* is a volume in the Oxford History of English Literature series, which is why in his many complaints about it he always referred to it as his OHELL book. It was later retitled *Poetry and Prose in the Sixteenth Century*.
17. Lewis, *English Literature in the Sixteenth Century Excluding Drama*, pp. 13–14.
18. In both of his key essays, "Nature on the Rack" and "Wrestling with Proteus," Pesic quotes and extensively interprets the passages from Bacon and Leibniz I have cited here.
19. Lewis, *The Abolition of Man*, pp. 53–54.
20. Lewis, *The Abolition of Man*, p. 73.
21. Lewis, *The Abolition of Man*, p. 74. This argument should be compared with the one made by Robert Maynard Hutchins and Mortimer Adler, and so strenuously objected to by Sidney Hook, that the Western democracies are more threatened by their professors than by Hitler.
22. Lewis, *The Abolition of Man*, pp. 2–3.
23. Lewis, *The Abolition of Man*, p. 15.
24. Lewis, *The Abolition of Man*, p. 16.

25. Lewis, *That Hideous Strength*, p. 127.
26. Lewis, *That Hideous Strength*, p. 175.
27. Lewis, *That Hideous Strength*, pp. 182–83.
28. Marie Lloyd, Eliot wrote when she died in 1922, "is the expressive figure of the lower classes." In her music and comedy, working people "find the expression and dignity of their own lives." Such a gift is not available to either the aristocracy, who "are subordinate to the middle class, which is gradually absorbing and destroying them," or to the middle classes themselves, who "have no such idol" as Marie Lloyd because they are "morally corrupt." And even the lower classes, who have tragically just lost this "expressive figure," may not last much longer, since their representative dramatic form is being replaced by the "cheap and rapid-breeding cinema," which threatens to reduce the lower classes to "the same state of protoplasm as the bourgeoisie." Eliot, *Selected Essays*, p. 407.
29. Lewis, *That Hideous Strength*, p. 36.
30. Lewis, *The Screwtape Letters*, pp. 31–32.
31. For these and other details of Auden's time at Swarthmore, see Nicholas Jenkins's "Introduction" to Auden's lecture on "Vocation and Society," pp. 1–14. He made his comment about the jukebox in Alan Ansen, *The Table Talk of W. H. Auden*, p. 40.
32. For details about the character and purposes of *The Sea and the Mirror*, especially its exploration of the relationship between Christianity and art, see Arthur Kirsch's introduction to his critical edition of the poem.
33. Eliot, "Little Gidding," *The Poems of T. S. Eliot*, p. 204; Ackroyd, *T. S. Eliot*, p. 279.
34. Auden, *The Sea and the Mirror*, p. 6.
35. Heaney, *The Government of the Tongue*, p. 126.
36. Auden, "La Trahison d'un Clerc," *The Complete Works of W. H. Auden: Prose*, vol. 2, *1939–1948*, p. 148.
37. Auden, "Vocation and Society," *The Complete Works of W. H. Auden: Prose*, vol. 2, *1939–1948*, p. 176.
38. Auden, "Vocation and Society," *The Complete Works of W. H. Auden: Prose*, vol. 2, *1939–1948*, p. 177. Auden borrowed the term "subjective requiredness" from one of his Swarthmore colleagues, a Gestalt psychologist and German refugee named Wolfgang Köhler.
39. Auden, "Vocation and Society," *The Complete Works of W. H. Auden: Prose*, vol. 2, *1939–1948*, pp. 178–79.
40. Auden, "Vocation and Society," *The Complete Works of W. H. Auden: Prose*, vol. 2, *1939–1948*, p. 182.
41. Eliot, "Little Gidding," *The Poems of T. S. Eliot*, p. 209.
42. Auden, "Vocation and Society," *The Complete Works of W. H. Auden: Prose*, vol. 2, *1939–1948*, p. 182. However inconsistent Auden may have been in assessing the quality of Eliot's poetry, there was no one he admired more unreservedly. One of the talks given to Finkelstein's Conference on Science, Philosophy and Religion

in Their Relation to the Democratic Way of Life was one on "Primary Literature and Coterie Literature" by Van Wyck Brooks, which was highly critical of Eliot. Auden commented, "As for Mr Van Wyck Brooks, if I ever meet him, I shall slap his face for his remarks" (quoted in Jenkins, "Introduction," p. 8). In a letter to Louise Bogan in April 1945, Auden said of Eliot, "I shall never be as great and good a man if I live to be a hundred." Carpenter, *W. H. Auden*, p. 413.

43. Ackroyd, *T. S. Eliot*, p. 223.

44. Eliot, *Christianity and Culture*, p. 85.

45. Eliot, *Christianity and Culture*, p. 100.

46. Though he does not say so, and may not be aware of it, the complications he explores here are dramatized brilliantly in the debate about Ivan's article on church-state relations in *The Brothers Karamazov*, part 1, book 2, chapter 5.

47. Eliot, *Christianity and Culture*, p. 102.

48. Eliot, *Christianity and Culture*, p. 105. He had written on the previous page:

> the reader must remind himself, as the author has constantly to do, of how much is here embraced by the term *culture*. It includes all the characteristic activities and interests of a people: Derby Day, Henley Regatta, Cowes, the twelfth of August, a cup final, the dog races, the pin table, the dart board, Wensleydale cheese, boiled cabbage cut into sections, beetroot in vinegar, nineteenth-century Gothic churches and the music of Elgar.

49. Eliot, *Christianity and Culture*, p. 103.

50. Eliot, *Christianity and Culture*, p. 103.

51. Eliot, *Christianity and Culture*, p. 106.

52. He does not of course use that word, which was not coined until 1958, by Michael Young in his dystopian satire *The Rise of the Meritocracy*. As many have commented before, there are multiple and perhaps savage ironies involved in using that term seriously, given its origin, but it fulfills a function no other word quite manages to fulfill.

53. Eliot, *Christianity and Culture*, p. 171.

54. Eliot, *Christianity and Culture*, p. 120.

55. Eliot, *Christianity and Culture*, p. 120.

56. Dent's story is told briefly and crisply in his obituary in the *Independent*, February 12, 1995, http://www.independent.co.uk/news/people/harold-dent-1572842.html.

57. Eliot, *Christianity and Culture*, p. 177.

58. Eliot, *Christianity and Culture*, p. 179.

59. Eliot, *Christianity and Culture*, p. 185.

60. Eliot, *Christianity and Culture*, p. 185.

61. Eliot, preface to Weil's *The Need for Roots*, pp. vii–ix.

62. Weil, *Waiting for God*, pp. 117, 119.

63. "Thou shalt love the Lord thy God with all thy heart, and with all thy soul, and with all thy mind. This is the first and great commandment. And the second is like unto it, Thou shalt love thy neighbour as thyself. On these two commandments hang all the law and the prophets" (Matthew 22:37–40).
64. Auden, "Squares and Oblongs," *The Complete Works of W. H. Auden: Prose*, vol. 2, *1939–1948*, p. 346.
65. Weil, *Waiting for God*, p. 120.
66. Pétrement, *Simone Weil*, p. 460.
67. Weil, "A War of Religions," *Selected Essays*, p. 218.
68. Eliot's introduction to *The Need for Roots*, p. xiv.
69. Eliot's introduction to *The Need for Roots*, p. x.
70. Pétrement, *Simone Weil*, pp. 443, 478.
71. Weil, *Gravity and Grace*, pp. 161, 162.
72. Weil, *Waiting for God*, p. 77.
73. O'Brien, "The Anti-Politics of Simone Weil."
74. Weil, *Gravity and Grace*, pp. 164–67.
75. Weil, *The Need for Roots*, p. 126.
76. Eliot's introduction to Weil, *The Need for Roots*, p. ix.
77. Weil, *The Need for Roots*, p. 42.
78. Weil, *The Need for Roots*, p. 185.
79. Lewis, *The Abolition of Man*, p. 26.
80. Weil, *The Need for Roots*, p. 186.
81. Weil, *The Need for Roots*, p. 99.
82. Weil, *The Need for Roots*, pp. 200–201.
83. Weil, *The Need for Roots*, p. 213.
84. Weil, *The Need for Roots*, p. 258.
85. Weil, *The Need for Roots*, p. 294.
86. Weil, *The Need for Roots*, p. 274.
87. Weil, *The Need for Roots*, p. 295.

Chapter 7

1. Auden, *The Complete Works of W. H. Auden: Prose*, vol. 2, *1939–1948*, p. 184.
2. Arendt, *Between Past and Future*, p. 4.
3. Auden, *The Age of Anxiety*, p. 3.
4. Letter to Elizabeth Mayer, May 9, 1945 (cited in Mendelson, *Later Auden*, p. 284).
5. Auden, *For the Time Being*, pp. 10–11.
6. On the status of this poem as a "Dream Quest," see the introduction to *The Age of Anxiety*, pp. xxix–xxx.
7. Auden, *The Age of Anxiety*, p. 83.
8. Auden, *The Age of Anxiety*, p. 84.
9. Auden, *The Age of Anxiety*, p. 85.

10. Auden, *The Age of Anxiety*, p. 93.
11. Auden, *The Age of Anxiety*, p. 100.
12. Auden, *The Age of Anxiety*, p. 102. This is Deuteronomy 6:4: "Hear, O Israel: The Lord our God is one Lord." Edward Mendelson makes the illuminating point that—for good or ill or both—Auden does not think of Rosetta's Judaism in ethnic or even sociological terms, but rather as a body of belief:

    > The poem does not mention Rosetta's faith until she names it in her final speech, just as Malin says nothing about his Christianity until he returns to the solitude and silence that prompt his credo. The moral point of not identifying her earlier as a Jew is that the poem does not categorize her by ethnicity or race: her Judaism is a creed, and the poem takes no interest in it until she does. (*Later Auden*, p. 256)

13. Auden, *The Age of Anxiety*, p. 108.
14. Auden, *For the Time Being*, p. 64.
15. Auden, "Prime," *Collected Poems*, p. 625.
16. Auden, "Homage to Clio" and "Compline," *Collected Poems*, pp. 608, 638. On Auden's "theology of the inarticulate human body," see Mendelson, chap. X, "The Murmurs of the Body," *Later Auden*.
17. Eliot, "Ash Wednesday," *The Poems of T. S. Eliot*, p. 87.
18. Eliot, "Little Gidding," *The Poems of T. S. Eliot*, p. 205.
19. "The Social Function of Poetry" began life as a lecture given in Norway in 1943. "What Is a Classic?" was spoken to the Virgil Society, of which Eliot was then president, in 1944. Both talks were revised and published as essays in 1945, and they are collected in *On Poetry and Poets*. The third essay stands alone.
20. Eliot, "The Metaphysical Poets," *Selected Essays*, p. 247.
21. Eliot, "The Social Function of Poetry," *On Poetry and Poets*, p. 9.
22. Harry Levin, later to become a very eminent critic, was a senior at Harvard in 1932–33 when Eliot was the Charles Eliot Norton Professor of Poetry, and he later recalled that "his predictions for Auden's future virtually constituted a laying on of hands." *Memories of the Moderns*, p. 151.
23. Eliot, "The Social Function of Poetry," *On Poetry and Poets*, p. 10.
24. Eliot, "The Social Function of Poetry," *On Poetry and Poets*, p. 11.
25. I have used the term "Mandarin" here because Eliot's proposal rhymes with the argument put forth by the coiner of that term, Cyril Connolly, in *Enemies of Promise*, part 1, especially chapters 2 and 7. But Eliot does not quote Connolly.
26. Eliot, "What Is a Classic?," *On Poetry and Poets*, p. 54. I cannot guess what work the phrase "the maximum of" is doing in that sentence, but apparently Eliot thought it was doing something.
27. Eliot, "What Is a Classic?," *On Poetry and Poets*, p. 63.
28. Virgil, *Aeneid*, book 6, lines 605–12, 624–26.
29. Virgil, *Aeneid*, book 6, lines 1135–37.

30. "If a poet gets a large audience very quickly, that is a rather suspicious circum-stance." Eliot, "The Social Function of Poetry," *On Poetry and Poets*, p. 11.

31. Eliot, "The Social Function of Poetry," *On Poetry and Poets*, p. 8. One element noticeably missing from Eliot's analysis: the rather obvious fact that the same language may be spoken in multiple countries.

32. Eliot, "The Social Function of Poetry," *On Poetry and Poets*, pp. 14, 13.

33. Eliot, "The Man of Letters and the Future of Europe," p. 384.

34. Eliot, "The Social Function of Poetry," *On Poetry and Poets*, p. 16.

35. Eliot, "The Man of Letters and the Future of Europe," p. 386.

36. Weil, *The Need for Roots*, p. 3.

37. Maritain, *Christianity and Democracy*, p. 33.

38. Maritain, *Christianity and Democracy*, p. 35.

39. Quoted by Maritain in *Christianity and Democracy*, p. 36.

40. Maritain, *Christianity and Democracy*, pp. 61–62.

41. See my account of this decline in "The Watchmen." A similar diminishment of the role of theologians and other Christian thinkers in bioethics debates is traced by John H. Evans in *Playing God?*

42. Eliot, *The Cocktail Party*, pp. 184, 185.

43. Auden, "Under Which Lyre," *Collected Poems*, pp. 333–38.

44. Levin, *Memories of the Moderns*, p. 152.

45. Quoted by Mendelson in *Later Auden*, p. 262.

46. Ansen, *The Table Talk of W. H. Auden*, p. 11. As Adam Kirsch notes in "A Poet's Warning," an essay about Auden's delivery of the poem at Harvard,

> Twenty-six thousand Harvard alumni had served in uniform during the war, and 649 of them had perished. The University itself had been integrated into the war effort at the highest level: President James Bryant Conant had been one of those consulted when President Truman decided to drop the atomic bomb on Japan. William Langer, a professor of history, had recruited many faculty members into the newly formed Office of Strategic Services, the precursor to the CIA. Now that the Cold War was under way, the partnership between the University and the federal government was destined to grow even closer.
>
> As if to symbolize that intimacy, the 1946 Commencement saw honorary degrees awarded to the chiefs of the U.S. Army, Navy, Marines, and Air Force. More questionable was the choice of that year's Phi Beta Kappa orator: Byron Price, who had served as di-rector of the federal Office of Censorship, in charge of monitoring press coverage of the war. Price used the occasion to deliver a rather ominous exhortation to "the man of letters," whom he accused, 10 months after the war ended, of still not doing enough for national morale. "How often," he asked, "shall the seeker find between these

myriad covers an ounce of literary beauty, or a thimbleful of spiritual elevation? We are served a fare of dissoluteness and destruction. We are asked to sneer at man and regard him as no better than the worm. We are invited to improve our minds by studying the endless sagas of criminals and harlots, moving in sordid surroundings, and worshiping only the flesh."

Afterword

1. This book was first published in English under the title *The Presence of the Kingdom* (New York: Seabury Press, 1967), and under that title it remains best known. But it has recently been retranslated by Lisa Richmond with the more accurate title *Presence in the Modern World*, and that is the translation I will use here.

2. Ian Buruma, in his fine book *Year Zero: A History of 1945*, writes,

   The desire to retrieve a sense of normality is one very human response to catastrophe; human and fanciful. For the idea that the world as it was before the war could simply be restored, as though a murderous decade, which began well before 1939, could be cast aside like a bad memory, was surely an illusion.

   It was, however, an illusion held by governments as much as by individual people. The French and Dutch governments thought that their colonies could be repossessed and life would resume, just as it had been before the Japanese invaded Southeast Asia. But it was only that, an illusion. For the world could not possibly be the same. Too much had happened, too much had changed, too many people, even entire societies, had been uprooted. Nor did many people, including some governments, want the world to go back to what it had been. (pp. 7–8)

3. Ellul, *Presence in the Modern World*, pp. xvi–xvii.

4. From this Ecumenical Institute arose, in 1948, the World Council of Churches, one of whose leading voices, in its early days, was J. H. Oldham. The WCC effectively replaced the Moot at the center of Oldham's activities in the years immediately preceding his retirement.

5. Ellul, *Presence in the Modern World*, pp. 12–13.

6. Ellul, *Presence in the Modern World*, p. 72.

7. Ellul, *Presence in the Modern World*, p. 73.

8. Ellul, *The Technological Society*, pp. xxv, 131.

9. Ellul, *The Technological Society*, pp. 286–87.

10. Ellul, *The Technological Society*, pp. 248, 86, 348.
11. A useful survey of Ellul's influence, and shifting reputation, may be found in Samuel Matlack's "Confronting the Technological Society."
12. Ellul, *The Technological Society*, pp. xxvii, xxx.
13. Ellul, *The Technological Society*, p. xxxi.
14. Auden, *For the Time Being*, p. 64.
15. Auden, *For the Time Being*, p. 65.
16. Ellul, *Presence in the Modern World*, pp. 13, 14.
17. Lewis, *The Great Divorce*, pp. 145–46.
18. Maritain's last major book, *Creative Intuition in Art and Poetry*, was published in 1953. Auden's hope to become "a minor Atlantic Goethe" is registered in "The Cave of Making," *Collected Poems*, p. 693.
19. Robert Frost, "The Oven Bird," *The Poetry of Robert Frost*: "The question that he frames in all but words / Is what to make of a diminished thing," p. 120.

BIBLIOGRAPHY

Ackroyd, Peter. *T. S. Eliot: A Life*. New York: Simon and Schuster, 1984.

Ansen, Alan. *The Table Talk of W. H. Auden*. Edited by Nicholas Jenkins. London: Faber, 1990.

Arendt, Hannah. *Between Past and Future: Eight Exercises in Political Thought*. Enlarged ed. Harmondsworth: Penguin, 1977. First published 1961.

Auden, W. H. *The Age of Anxiety: A Baroque Eclogue*. Edited by Alan Jacobs. Princeton, NJ: Princeton University Press, 2011.

Auden, W. H. *Collected Poems*. Edited by Edward Mendelson. New York: Modern Library, 2007.

Auden, W. H. *The Complete Works of W. H. Auden: Prose*. Vol. 2, *1939–1948*. Edited by Edward Mendelson. Princeton, NJ: Princeton University Press, 2002.

Auden, W. H. *The Complete Works of W. H. Auden: Prose*. Vol. 5, *1963–1968*. Edited by Edward Mendelson. Princeton, NJ: Princeton University Press, 2015.

Auden, W. H. *For the Time Being: A Christmas Oratorio*. Edited by Alan Jacobs. Princeton, NJ: Princeton University Press, 2013.

Auden, W. H. *The Sea and the Mirror: A Commentary on Shakespeare's* The Tempest. Edited by Arthur Kirsch. Princeton, NJ: Princeton University Press, 2003.

Auden, W. H. *Selected Poems*. Second expanded edition. Edited by Edward Mendelson. New York: Vintage, 2007.

Auden, W. H. Untitled essay. *Modern Canterbury Pilgrims*. Edited by James A. Pike. London: Mowbray, 1956.

Barth, Karl. "The Christian Message and the New Humanism." In *Against the Stream: Shorter Post-War Writings, 1946–52*, pp. 181–91. New York: Philosophical Library, 1954.

Beevor, Antony. *The Second World War*. New York: Little, Brown and Company, 2012.

Bonhoeffer, Dietrich. *Letters and Papers from Prison.* Enlarged ed. Translated by Reginald Fuller, Frank Clark, et al. New York: Touchstone, 1997. First published 1953.

Boobyer, Philip. *The Spiritual Vision of Frank Buchman.* University Park, PA: Penn State University Press, 2013.

Boswell, James. *The Life of Samuel Johnson.* New York: Everyman's Library, 1992. First published 1791.

Buchman, Frank. *Remaking the World: Selections from the Speeches of Dr. Frank N. D. Buchman.* London: Heinemann, 1941.

Buller, E. Amy. *Darkness over Germany.* London: Longmans, Green, 1943.

Buruma, Ian. *Year Zero: A History of 1945.* New York: Penguin, 2013.

Calder, Angus. *The People's War: Britain, 1939–1945.* New York: Pantheon, 1969.

Carpenter, Humphrey. *W. H. Auden: A Biography.* Boston: Houghton Mifflin, 1981.

Churchill, Winston. *Blood, Toil, Tears and Sweat: The Great Speeches.* Edited by David Cannnadine. London: Penguin, 2007.

Clarke, Arthur C. *Childhood's End.* New York: Del Rey Impact, 2001. First published 1953.

Clements, Keith, ed. *The Moot Papers: Faith, Freedom and Society 1938–1944.* London: Bloomsbury, 2015.

Cochrane, Charles Norris. *Christianity and Classical Culture: A Study of Thought and Action from Augustus to Augustine.* Indianapolis: Liberty Fund, 2003. First published 1940.

Connolly, Cyril. *Enemies of Promise.* New York: Persea, 1983. First published 1938.

Davenport-Hines, Richard. *Auden.* New York: Pantheon, 1995.

Dawson, Christopher. *The Judgment of the Nations.* London: Sheed & Ward, 1942.

Day, Dorothy. "Day after Day—January 1943." *Catholic Worker,* January 1943. http://www.catholicworker.org/dorothyday/articles/221.html.

Dewey, John. "Anti-Naturalism in Extremis." The Partisan Review (January 1943): 24–39.

Dewey, John. "President Hutchins' Proposals to Remake Higher Education." *The Social Frontier* 3, no. 22 (January 1937): 103–104.

Dewey, John. "Was President Hutchins Serious?" *The Social Frontier* 3, no. 24 (March 1937): 167–69.

Eliot, T. S. *Christianity and Culture: The Idea of a Christian Society and Notes towards the Definition of Culture.* New York: Harcourt Brace Jovanovich, 1949.

Eliot, T. S. *The Cocktail Party.* New York: Harcourt, Brace & World, 1950.

Eliot, T. S. "The Man of Letters and the Future of Europe." *Horizon,* December 1944, pp. 382–89.

Eliot, T. S. *On Poetry and Poets.* New York: Farrar, 1957.

Eliot, T. S. *The Poems of T. S. Eliot, Volume I: Collected and Uncollected Poems.* Edited by Christopher Ricks and Jim McCue. Baltimore: John Hopkins University Press, 2015.

Eliot, T. S. "Towards a Christian Britain." In *The Complete Prose of T. S. Eliot: The Critical Edition: The War Years, 1940–1946,* edited by David E. Chinitz and Ronald Schuchard, 162–68. Baltimore: Johns Hopkins University Press, 2017.

Eliot, T. S. *Selected Essays*. New York: Harcourt, Brace & World, 1950.

Ellul, Jacques. *Presence in the Modern World*. Translated by Lisa Richmond. Eugene, OR: Cascade Books, 2016. First published 1948.

Ellul, Jacques. *The Technological Society*. Translated by John Wilkinson. New York: Vintage, 1964. First published 1954.

Evans, John H. *Playing God? Human Genetic Engineering and the Rationalization of Public Bioethical Debate*. Chicago: University of Chicago Press, 2001.

Fessard, Gaston. "France, prends garde de perdre ton âme!" *Cahiers du témoignage chrétien*, November 1, 1941.

Fitzgerald, Penelope. *Human Voices*. New York: Mariner Books, 1999. First published 1980.

Flood, Alison. "'It Needs More Public-Spirited Pigs': TS Eliot's Rejection of Orwell's Animal Farm." *Guardian*, May 26, 2016. https://www.theguardian.com/books/2016/may/26/ts-eliot-rejection-george-orwell-animal-farm-british-library-online.

Frost, Robert. *The Poetry of Robert Frost: The Collected Poems, Complete and Unabridged*. Edited by Edward Connery Lathem. New York: Macmillan, 2002.

Gardner, Helen. *The Composition of* Four Quartets. London: Faber, 1978.

General Education in a Free Society: Report of the Harvard Committee. Introduction by James Bryant Conant. Cambridge, MA: Harvard University Press, 1950. First published 1945.

Gilbert, James. *Redeeming Culture: American Religion in an Age of Science*. Chicago: University of Chicago Press, 1997.

Gilkey, Langdon. *Shantung Compound*. San Francisco: HarperSanFrancisco, 1975. First published 1966.

Gill, Eric. *Christianity and the Machine Age*. London: Sheldon Press, 1940.

Gillespie, Michael Allen. *The Theological Origins of Modernity*. Chicago: University of Chicago Press, 2008.

Gilson, Etienne. *Le thomisme: Introduction au système de saint Thomas d'Aquin*. Paris: Librairie philosophique J. Vrin, 1922.

Gilson, Etienne. *Reason and Revelation in the Middle Ages*. New York: Charles Scribner's Sons, 1938.

Gordon, Lyndall. *Eliot's New Life*. New York: Farrar, Straus, Giroux, 1988.

Greene, Graham. *Three Entertainments: A Gun for Sale, the Confidential Agent, Ministry of Fear*. London: Penguin, 1992.

Gregory, Brad. *The Unintended Reformation: How a Religious Revolution Secularized Society*. Cambridge, MA: Harvard University Press, 2012.

Greif, Mark. *The Age of the Crisis of Man: Thought and Fiction in America, 1933–1973*. Princeton, NJ: Princeton University Press, 2015.

Hall, Donald. *Remembering Poets: Reminiscences and Opinions: Dylan Thomas, Robert Frost, T. S. Eliot, Ezra Pound*. New York: Harper & Row, 1978.

Hayek, F. A. *The Collected Works of F. A. Hayek*. Vol. 2, *The Road to Serfdom: Text and Documents: The Definitive Edition*. Edited by Bruce Caldwell. Chicago: University of Chicago Press, 2007. First published 1944.

Heaney, Seamus. *The Government of the Tongue*. London: Faber, 1988.

Hook, Sidney. "The New Failure of Nerve." *Partisan Review* 10, no. 1 (January–February 1943): 2–23.

Hook, Sidney. *Out of Step: An Unquiet Life in the 20th Century*. New York: Harper & Row, 1987.

Horkheimer, Max, and Theodor W. Adorno. *Dialectic of Enlightenment: Philosophical Fragments*. Translated by Edmund Jephcott. Stanford, CA: Stanford University Press, 2002. First published 1947.

Hutchins, Robert Maynard. "The Issue in the Higher Learning." *International Journal of Ethics* 44, no. 2 (January 1934): 175–84.

Hutchins, Robert Maynard. "What Shall We Defend? We Are Losing Our Moral Principles." Reprinted in *Vital Speeches of the Day*. Vol. 6, 547–49. http://www.ibiblio.org/pha/policy/1940/1940-06-11a.html.

Jacobs, Alan. *The Narnian: The Life and Imagination of C. S. Lewis*. San Francisco: HarperOne, 2005.

Jacobs, Alan. "The Watchmen: What Became of the Christian Intellectuals?" *Harper's Magazine*, September 2016, pp. 54–60.

Jacobs, Alan. *What Became of Wystan: Change and Continuity in Auden's Poetry*. Fayetteville: University of Arkansas Press, 1998.

Jenkins, Nicholas. "Introduction to 'Vocation and Society.'" In *'In Solitude, for Company': W. H. Auden after 1940: Unpublished Prose and Recent Criticism*, edited by Katherine Bucknell and Nicholas Jenkins, 15–30. Auden Studies 3. Oxford: Clarendon, 1995.

Judt, Tony. *Postwar: A History of Europe since 1945*. London: Penguin, 2005.

Keegan, John. *The First World War*. New York: Vintage, 2000.

Keegan, John. *The Second World War*. New York: Penguin, 1989.

Kermode, Frank. *The Genesis of Secrecy: On the Interpretation of Narrative*. Cambridge, MA: Harvard University Press, 1979.

Keynes, John Maynard. *The Economic Consequences of the Peace*. New York: Harcourt, Brace and Howe, 1920.

Kirsch, Adam. "A Poet's Warning." *Harvard Magazine*, November–December 2007. http://harvardmagazine.com/2007/11/a-poets-warning.html.

Krieger, Martin. *Doing Mathematics: Convention, Subject, Calculation, Analogy*. Singapore: World Scientific Publishing, 2003.

Kristeller, Paul Oskar. *Renaissance Thought: The Classic, Scholastic, and Humanist Strains*. New York: Harper and Row, 1961.

Kynaston, David. *Austerity Britain: 1945–51*. London: Bloomsbury, 2007.

Leavis, F. R. *Education and the University: A Sketch for an "English School."* London: Chatto & Windus, 1943.

Levin, Harry. *Memories of the Moderns*. New York: New Directions, 1982.

Levi-Strauss, Claude. *Tristes Tropiques*. Translated by John and Doreen Weightman. London: Penguin, 1973. First published 1955.

Lewis, C. S. *The Abolition of Man: or, Reflections on Education with Special Reference to the Teaching of English in the Upper Forms of Schools.* San Francisco: Harper SanFrancisco, 2001. First published 1944.

Lewis, C. S. *Christian Reflections.* Edited by Walter Hooper. Grand Rapids, MI: Eerdmans, 1967.

Lewis, C. S. *The Collected Letters of C. S. Lewis.* Vol. 1, *Family Letters 1905–1931.* Edited by Walter Hooper. San Francisco: Harper SanFrancisco, 2004.

Lewis, C. S. *The Collected Letters of C. S. Lewis.* Vol. 2, *Books, Broadcasts, and the War 1931–1949.* Edited by Walter Hooper. San Francisco: Harper SanFrancisco, 2004.

Lewis, C. S. *The Collected Letters of C. S. Lewis.* Vol. 3, *Narnia, Cambridge and Joy 1950–1963.* Edited by Walter Hooper. San Francisco: Harper SanFrancisco, 2007.

Lewis, C. S. *English Literature in the Sixteenth Century, Excluding Drama.* Oxford: Oxford University Press, 1953.

Lewis, C. S. *God in the Dock: Essays on Theology and Ethics.* Grand Rapids, MI: Eerdmans, 1970.

Lewis, C. S. *The Great Divorce.* San Francisco: Harper SanFrancisco, 2001. First published 1946.

Lewis, C. S. *Mere Christianity.* San Francisco: Harper SanFrancisco, 2001. First published 1952.

Lewis, C. S. *Miracles.* San Francisco: Harper SanFrancisco, 2001. First published 1947, 1960.

Lewis, C. S. *Out of the Silent Planet.* New York: Macmillan, 1965. First published 1938.

Lewis, C. S. *Perelandra.* New York: Macmillan, 1965. First published 1944.

Lewis, C. S. *A Preface to* Paradise Lost. Oxford: Oxford University Press, 1979. First published 1942.

Lewis, C. S. *The Problem of Pain.* San Francisco: Harper SanFrancisco, 2001. First published 1940.

Lewis, C. S. *The Screwtape Letters.* San Francisco: Harper SanFrancisco, 2001. First published 1942.

Lewis, C. S. *That Hideous Strength.* New York: Macmillan, 1965. First published 1946.

Lewis, C. S. *The Weight of Glory and Other Addresses.* San Francisco: Harper SanFrancisco, 2001.

Lewis, C. S., ed. *George MacDonald: An Anthology.* New York: HarperCollins, 2001. First published 1946.

Lindsay, D. Michael. *Faith in the Halls of Power: How Evangelicals Joined the American Elite.* New York: Oxford University Press, 2007.

Lubac, Henri de. *The Drama of Atheist Humanism.* Translated by Edith M. Riley, Anne Englund Nash, and Mark Sebanc. San Francisco: Ignatius Press, 1995. First published 1949.

MacDonald, Dwight. "A Theory of Popular Culture." *Politics* 1, no. 1 (February 1944): 20–23.

Manent, Pierre. *The City of Man*. Translated by Marc A. LePain. Princeton, NJ: Princeton University Press, 1998. First published 1994.

Mann, Nicholas. "The Origins of Humanism." In *The Cambridge Companion to Renaissance Humanism*, edited by Jill Kraye, pp. 1–19. Cambridge: Cambridge University Press, 1996.

Maritain, Jacques. *Art and Scholasticism and the Frontiers of Poetry*. Translated by Joseph W. Evans (from the third French edition, 1935). New York: Scribner, 1962.

Maritain, Jacques. *Christianity and Democracy and the Rights of Man and Natural Law*. San Francisco: Ignatius Press, 2011. First published 1944.

Maritain, Jacques. *The Collected Works of Jacques Maritain*. Vol. 2, *Integral Humanism, Freedom in the Modern World, and A Letter on Independence*. Edited by Otto Bird, translated by Otto Bird, Joseph Evans, and Richard O'Sullivan, K.C. Notre Dame, IN: University of Notre Dame Press, 1996.

Maritain, Jacques. *Creative Intuition in Art and Poetry*. Bollingen Series 35:1. New York: Pantheon, 1953.

Maritain, Jacques. *Education at the Crossroads*. New Haven, CT: Yale University Press, 1943.

Maritain, Jacques. *The Twilight of Civilization*. Translated by Lionel Landry. New York: Sheed and Ward, 1943.

Maritain, Raïssa. *The Prince of this World*. Translated by Gerald B. Phelan. Ditchling: St. Dominic's Press, 1936.

Maritain, Raïssa. *We Have Been Friends together*. New York: Longman, Green, 1945.

Marsh, Charles. *Strange Glory: A Life of Dietrich Bonhoeffer*. New York: Knopf, 2013.

Matlack, Samuel. "Confronting the Technological Society." *New Atlantis*, Summer/Fall 2014, pp. 45–64.

McCarthy, Fiona. *Eric Gill: A Lover's Quest for Art and God*. New York: Dutton, 1989.

McInerny, Ralph. *The Very Rich Hours of Jacques Maritain: A Spiritual Life*. Notre Dame, IN: University of Notre Dame Press, 2003.

Mendelson, Edward. *Early Auden*. Cambridge, MA: Harvard University Press, 1983. First published 1981.

Mendelson, Edward. *Later Auden*. New York: Farrar, Straus and Giroux, 1999.

Merton, Thomas. *The Secular Journal*. New York: Farrar Straus & Giroux, 1977.

Moberley, Walter. *The Crisis in the University*. London: SCM Press, 1949.

Moyn, Samuel. *Christian Human Rights*. Philadelphia: University of Pennsylvania Press, 2015.

Mumford, Lewis. *Faith for Living*. New York: Harcourt, Brace and Company, 1940.

Mumford, Lewis. *Values for Survival: Essays, Addresses, and Letters on Politics and Education*. New York: Harcourt, Brace and Company, 1946.

Murray, Nicholas. *Aldous Huxley: A Biography*. New York: St. Martin's Press, 2002.

Niebuhr, Reinhold. *Christianity and Power Politics*. New York: Charles Scribner's Sons, 1940.

Niebuhr, Reinhold. "Thomism and Mysticism." *Saturday Review*, August 8, 1936, p. 16.

Niebuhr, Ursula, ed. *Remembering Reinhold Niebuhr: Letters of Reinhold and Ursula M. Niebuhr.* San Francisco: HarperSanFrancisco, 1991.

O'Brien, Conor Cruise. "The Anti-Politics of Simone Weil." *New York Review of Books,* May 12, 1977. http://www.nybooks.com/articles/1977/05/12/the-anti-politics-of-simone-weil/.

Orwell, George. *Essays.* Edited by John Carey. New York: Everyman's Library, 2002.

Pesic, Peter. "Nature on the Rack: Leibniz's Attitude towards Judicial Torture and the 'Torture' of Nature." *Studia Leibnitiana* Bd. 29, H. 2 (1997): 189–97.

Pesic, Peter. "Wrestling with Proteus: Francis Bacon and the 'Torture' of Nature." *Isis* 90, no. 1 (March 1999): 81–94.

Pétrement, Simone. *Simone Weil: A Life.* Translated by Raymond Rosenthal. New York: Pantheon, 1976.

Pfau, Thomas. *Minding the Modern: Human Agency, Intellectual Traditions, and Responsible Knowledge.* Notre Dame, IN: University of Notre Dame Press, 2013.

Purcell, Edward A., Jr. *The Crisis of Democratic Theory: Scientific Naturalism and the Problem of Value.* Lexington: University Press of Kentucky, 1973.

Ricoeur, Paul. *Freud and Philosophy.* Translated by Denis Savage. New Haven, CT: Yale University Press, 1970.

Rorty, Richard. *Philosophy and Social Hope.* New York: Penguin, 1999.

Sayers, Dorothy. *Begin Here: A War-Time Essay.* London: Gollancz, 1940.

Schlesinger, Arthur Jr. "Reinhold Niebuhr's Long Shadow." *New York Times,* June 22, 1992. http://www.nytimes.com/1992/06/22/opinion/reinhold-niebuhr-s-long-shadow.html.

Sherry, Norman. *The Life of Graham Greene: Vol. 2, 1939–1955.* New York: Penguin, 2004.

Sontag, Susan. "Simone Weil." *New York Review of Books,* February 1, 1963. http://www.nybooks.com/articles/1963/02/01/simone-weil/.

Soulez, Philippe, and Frédéric Worms. *Bergson.* Paris: Presses universitaires de France, 2002.

Spender, Stephen, ed. *W. H. Auden: A Tribute.* New York: Macmillan, 1975.

Spufford, Francis. *Backroom Boys: The Secret Return of the British Boffin.* London: Faber & Faber, 2003.

Tolkien, J. R. R. *The Letters of J. R. R. Tolkien.* Edited by Humphrey Carpenter, with the assistance of Christopher Tolkien. Boston: Houghton Mifflin, 2000.

Tolkien, J. R. R. *The Lord of the Rings.* 50th anniv. ed. Boston: Houghton Mifflin, 2004.

Vidler, Alec. *Scenes from a Clerical Life.* London: Collins, 1977.

Virgil. *The Aeneid of Virgil: A Verse Translation.* Translated by Allen Mandelbaum. Berkeley: University of California Press, 1982.

Voderholzer, Rudolf. *Meet Henri de Lubac.* Translated by Michael J. Miller. San Francisco: Ignatius Press, 2008. First published 1999.

Warren, Heather A. *Theologians of a New World Order: Reinhold Niebuhr and the Christian Realists, 1920–1948.* New York: Oxford University Press, 1997.

Weaver, Richard. *Ideas Have Consequences.* Chicago: University of Chicago Press, 1948.

Webster, John. "Rescuing the Subject: Barth and Postmodern Anthropology." In *Karl Barth: A Future for Postmodern Theology?*, edited by Geoff Thompson and Christiaan Moster, pp. 49–69. Adelaide: ATF Press, 2000.

Weil, Simone. *Gravity and Grace*. Translated by Emma Crawford and Mario Von Der Ruhr. London: Routledge, 2002.

Weil, Simone. "The *Iliad*: or the Poem of Force." *Chicago Review* 18, no. 2 (1965): 5–30. Originally published in English in the November 1945 issue of *Politics*.

Weil, Simone. *The Need for Roots: Prelude to the Declaration of Duties towards Mankind*. Translated by Arthur Wills. London: Routledge, 2002. First published in French 1949; first English edition 1952.

Weil, Simone. *Selected Essays 1934–1943*. Translated by Richard Rees. Oxford: Oxford University Press, 1962.

Weil, Simone. *Waiting for God*. Translated by Emma Craufurd. New York: Harper & Row, 1973. First published 1951.

Williams, Charles. *All Hallows Eve*. Vancouver: Regent College, 2003. First published 1945.

Williams, Charles. *The Descent of the Dove: A Short History of the Holy Spirit in the Church*. Grand Rapids, MI: Eerdmans, 1939.

INDEX

Abolition of Man, The (Lewis), xii, 132,
134–35, 138, 164
Adler, Mortimer
and Conference on Science, Philosophy
and Religion, 13, 19–21
on democracy, need for philosophical
justification of, 15–18, 21
on education, 14, 17–18, 19, 51
on hierarchy of disciplines, 19
Hook's critique of, 20–24
and morality, need for foundation for,
7, 13–18
"On the Fundamental Position," 19–20
philosophy of, as Aristotelian-Thomist,
14, 18, 41
rejection of relativism of pragmatism and
positivism, 14, 16–19, 20
resistance to theories of, at University of
Chicago, 211n13
on threat posed by professors, 13, 17, 20
Adorno, Theodor, xiv, 209n8
Aeneid (Virgil), 180–82
Aeterni Patris (1879 papal encyclical), and neo-
Thomist doctrine, 39–40, 49, 213–14n4
"After Ten Years" (Bonhoeffer), 120
Age of Anxiety, The (Auden)
anxiety of postwar reconciliation as
theme of, 171, 173

characters in, as embodied Four
Faculties, 171
confusions of characters in, 171
on humanity's wait for His World, 174–75
on Jews' postwar relation to God, 173–74
"Lament for a Lawgiver" dirge in, 172–73
plot of, 172, 173
and postwar return to freedom, anxiety of,
172–73, 176
on psychological consequences of
war, 170
Rosetta's Judaism in, 173–73, 226n12
writing of, 145
Age of the Crisis of Man, The (Greif), 34,
185, 212n33
Albigensian heresy, Weil on, 97–98
All Hallows' Eve (Williams), 73
Allies
confidence of, in 1943, ix–x
demand for unconditional surrender, x
view of war as moral contest, 15
Weil on relative weakness of, 4
See also moral values, Allied
"And the age ended" (Auden), 72, 142
Animal Farm (Orwell), 124, 136
Ansen, Alan, 195
Apollonian totalitarianism, Auden on
ongoing postwar battle with, 192–95